EXPLORING OLD DUDDINGSTON AND PORTOBELLO

EXPLORING OLD DUDDINGSTON and PORTOBELLO

Tracing the development of the lands of the old Barony of Duddingston

DENNIS B. WHITE

MAINSTREAM PUBLISHING

First published in Great Britain 1990 by
MAINSTREAM PUBLISHING COMPANY (EDINBURGH) LTD
7 Albany Street
Edinburgh EH1 3UG

British Library Cataloguing in Publication Data
White, Dennis B.
Exploring Old Duddingston and Portobello.
1. Edinburgh. Social life, history
I. Title
941.34

ISBN 1-85158-299-1

The publishers gratefully acknowledge the assistance of The Scottish Life Assurance Company.

The publishers also gratefully acknowledge Mr Brian P. Scott of Scott Vehicle Services for his contribution, and Tennents Taverns for sponsorship of the promotion of this book.

Typeset in Aster by Blackpool Typesetting Services Ltd, Blackpool.
Printed in Great Britain by Martin's of Berwick, Berwick-Upon-Tweed.

FOR MY FAMILY

CONTENTS

ILLUSTRATIONS AND MAPS

CHAPTER 1

CHAPTER 2

CHAPTER 3

CHAPTER 4

CHAPTER 5

CHAPTER 6

CHAPTER 7

CHAPTER 8

CHAPTER 9

FOREWORD

During the last two decades or so there has been a distinct upsurge in the appearance of articles and books on local history in Scotland and this is all to the good. It has, of course, long been the case that most places have had a book devoted to them, one which could be turned to in order to find out a particular piece of information. But these vary greatly in the amount, and authenticity, of the details they contain. Some districts have what amounts to mere outline sketches while others are fortunate to have a work of considerable scholarship. Such is the case with the old villages of Portobello and Duddingston, namely William Baird's *Annals* published in 1900 and running to over 500 pages.

However, no single book no matter how comprehensive, can do justice to every aspect of a community's history and there are many facets capable either of expansion or of being looked at in a different light. New sources provide fresh material and more modern outlooks call for new interpretations. There is also a demand for more extensive detail, e.g. about what has happened to buildings, water courses, open spaces, as well as about former inhabitants.

One inhabitant of Portobello during the third quarter of the 19th century was David Laing. In 1898 Baird had this to say of him: "Portobello may well be proud to own him as a citizen. He has been styled 'the Prince of Scottish Literary Antiquarians of this Century'. . . . A literary life such as his, extending to over fully sixty-four years is a circumstance almost unparalleled in the present day". (p.476)

Laing was the Librarian of the Signet Library from 1837–78 and it is therefore appropriate that many of the sources used by Mr White were discovered in that Library. In particular, the collection of Session Papers - old law documents covering the 18th and early 19th centuries - has proved to be a mine of information. Mr White has also unearthed many other sources, of varying degrees of obscurity, and linked selected extracts using the development of the area as his theme with the result that much of the information he cites, and the arguments he puts forward, are new. He has thus, with good justification, greatly expanded a facet only briefly touched on in previous works on Duddingston.

I am sure that his research will prove to be of considerable value to both present and future residents of Duddingston and Portobello, especially as this is the first in-depth publication on the Barony of Duddingston for almost a hundred years.

G. H. Ballantyne
Librarian, Signet Library
Edinburgh
February 1989

PREFACE

To many, the name "Duddingston" may mean a loch, a golf course, a crossroads, an old village or a new housing development which is actually situated in the lands of Niddry. To confuse matters further, there is another Old Duddingston, in the parish of Abercorn and west of South Queensferry. The name appears in England also. Historically, the "Edinburgh" Barony of Duddingston was much larger than the combined Old and New Towns of Edinburgh and there is a need, I think, to know how such a large part of today's Edinburgh typically developed.

This book has been written for the person who is not only interested in the history of the early development of the Duddingston and Portobello area, but also in the relationships between "what is" and "what was". It attempts to bring together rich ingredients of historic Duddingston and Figgate from as many different sources as possible; to reveal how the development of the area, in terms of roads, buildings and spaces, has progressed from the days of the footroads, the runrig system of farming and the defined "touns" of Easter and Wester Duddingston. Indeed, what it purports to do, is to show the reader where these footroads were, the positions and names of the fields (and what was grown in them) and the earlier layouts of the old "touns".

No local area, however, is isolated. There are always aspects which are of a wider interest, such as language, development of roads, mills, coal mines and farming. Duddingston's heritage is rich in such information.

The sketch maps in this book may not tell the indigenous reader exactly what was "happening" on the site of his or her house about 200 years ago, but they will be as close as it is possible to demonstrate. Much of the information in this book has come from archive material which is relatively obscure - by that I mean either in book form but not easy to find, or not on the bookshop or lending library shelves at all. It is the result of a search of, and beyond, the more "common" history books on the Edinburgh area - and certainly beyond their occasional references to Duddingston at the end of their own stories.

I acknowledge, however, the immense and valuable work in the shape of William Baird's *Annals of Portobello and Duddingston* (1900) and also two "parish" booklets; *Duddingston Kirk and Village* by the late Bill Cruikshank and *St Phillips, Joppa* by the late W. A. Maclean.

I hope that any omissions and mistakes will be generously overlooked in what is an attempt to consolidate data on the development of Duddingston from as many different sources as possible.

Above all, I hope that this work will enable the reader to be able to come to terms, to a greater extent, with today's busy, suburban environment in the old Barony of Duddingston and the lands of Figgate; to be able to understand, and relate more closely to, the area.

My net proceeds from the sale of this book will be donated to St Columba's Hospice and to Portobello District Local History Society.

Finally, I should be delighted to receive any constructive information on Duddingston concerning what has been both included and excluded from this book.

Dennis B. White Edinburgh October 1989

ACKNOWLEDGMENTS

I would like to extend my sincere thanks to the following:

Mainstream Publishing (Edinburgh) Ltd, for helping to establish this record of the Barony of Duddingston, and all the staff and appointed representatives for their parts in the various stages of production.

In particular, Peter MacKenzie, Judy Moir, Dorothy Mitchell Smith and Claire Watts.

George Ballantyne for his assistance with the Signet Library archives and for kindly agreeing to write the Foreword.

The various parties who have kindly agreed to sponsor this book. Their role in promulgating local history is particularly appreciated: Scottish Life Assurance Company, 19 St Andrew Square, Edinburgh; Scott Vehicle Services, Milton Road East, Edinburgh.

The staff of all the public, and other, archives from which information was gratefully obtained and whose names appear in Appendix IV. Their kind and efficient assistance was very much appreciated.

The various parties, mentioned within this book, who kindly allowed me to quote passages, or reproduce illustrations, from their records or publications.

The many "local" people who responded positively to my requests for information or photographs and, in particular, those whose photographs have been selected on this occasion and whose names appear in Appendix IV. One of the many pleasures in writing this book has been the way people have been so helpful; this experience has confirmed my view that most people feel, almost without realising it, that local history is important as a way of both identifying with the environment and acknowledging the "ongoing" community.

John Glass, and other staff, of Edinburgh ITEC, Abbeymount Techbase, for use of computer-aided design software and computer equipment for re-scaling map sketches.

Edward Gladstone, fellow member of Portobello District Local History Society and previous owner (and restorer) of Duddingston House, for his kind assistance during the computer phase mentioned above.

Mr Tom Cumming for re-drawing the various re-scaled map sketches.

Friends, colleagues and acquaintances for their interest and encouragement.

A special thanks to my wife, Kathleen, our daughter, Anne-Marie and our son, Brendan for their endless patience and support during both the research (missing-not-here) periods and the word-processing (present-not-here) periods over the last six years.

CHAPTER 1
DUDDINGSTON DEFINED

THE MEANING OF THE WORD

As is the case with many place-names, there are at least two theories concerning their origin and meaning, and Duddingston is no exception. The Revd Wm. Bennet, in his *Statistical Account of Scotland (Duddingston)* in 1794, mentions that it means, from the Gaelic, "on the sunny side of the hill" (which certainly applies to Wester Duddingston i.e. Duddingston Village) but William Baird, in his *Annals of Duddingston and Portobello*, states his case in favour of the name deriving from the family name of Dodin (12th century).

Although agreeing with the "Town of Dodin" theory, G.W.S. Barrow presents, in his *Old Edinburgh Club* article of 1959, a very credible case for pushing the origins back even further with the theory that the area was called, prior to the English "Dodiston" - Treverlen, this time from Welsh origins.

> Mr Barrow argues that . . . *one of the earliest recorded names for Arthur's Seat, or at least for a considerable part of it, was Craggenemarf . . . or the Crag.*
>
> *The ground on which Holyrood Abbey was founded in 1128, together with some part - no doubt the nearest part - of Arthur's Seat, was royal demense, to be seen simply as an eastern extension of the territory attached to the King's castle of Edinburgh. The rest of Arthur's Seat was already understood to belong to the village or estate of Treverlen, and from c 1090 to c 1130 was held by Uviet the White.*
>
> *Uviet granted part of Arthur's Seat to the canons of Holyrood, retaining the rest. . . . On Uviet's death his lands were acquired by the King, who then gave Treverlen and its 'crag' to the monks of Kelso. . . . It was very likely Abbot Arnold (1147-60) who feued out Treverlen to Dodin: certainly Dodin was in possession between 1153 and 1159, and we know that Abbot Arnold was feuing out some of Kelso's Clydesdale property to laymen in this period.*
>
> *It may indeed have been Dodin who built the present parish church. If this was a new church, or on a different site from the previous one, and if Dodin founded a more compact settlement beside it, that would easily account for the replacement of "Treverlen" in popular speech by the new name "Dodinestun", Duddingston. However this may be, the name Duddingston had arrived as early as 1159 and had come to stay.*

These arguments, of course, are deductions based upon dates and names which appear in old charters and other documents.

DEFINING THE AREA

The idea that Arthur's Seat was once part of the lands of Duddingston may seem strange, but it is relevant to note that, according to the *Acts of the Lords of Council in Public Affairs, 1501–1554*, there was an Action in 1544 by the Crown against tenants of Sir David Murray (of Balvard) in Wester Duddingston who, " . . . between April and June 1543, cast down 24 roods of stone

Plate 1 *Aerial view of part of Wester Duddingston – 7th December 1951* (Crown Copyright – RAF photograph)

Towards Whinny Hill from the east. Duddingston Row is under construction; the road to Niddrie used to run along the border of the Golf Course. The part of the field in the foreground is where Southfield Farm used to be, before it was "moved", in about 1825, to its latter site – seen in front of Southfield Farm House (middle right). A water cast used to run through this part of the field, carrying water from the Braid Burn, to Easter Duddingston. The east lodge at the Policy Gate can just be seen; on an estate plan of 1827, the lodges at both east and west gates were called "Porters' lodges". The army of "Nissen" huts surround the Golf Course and the "Temple" is clearly shown in the middle of what was once a field called "Carnbuck". The most striking feature is the landscape beyond Duddingston Road West – the same fields are identified on old maps in Chapter 5. Meadowfield Farm is just "above" Duddingston crossroads.

dyke 'fornent' the lands and loch of Duddingston at the 'north syde and eist end' of the dyke, depriving the Queen (Mary, Queen of Scots) of 400 acres possessed by her and her father for some 11 years prior to that for arable purposes and horse pasture and 'parkit' by the King 'within the dykes of the park . . . '".

The knocking down of about 170 yards of wall (northwards from the loch) implies that the tenants felt aggrieved that the wall had been built in the first place (by James V) and that the lands of the Park had been used previously by them. In fact, the record goes on to say that, although the King "possessed" the Park (since 1534 and until he died in 1542), Andro Murray, now of Balvard, had a "Royal Licence to his father, David, . . . to endure till repayment of a debt of 600 merks". The tenants were "assoilzied" (acquitted) of the charge, as the debt had not been repaid to Murray, but still lost the right to use the land within the Park.

The Records of the Burgh of Edinburgh, 1528-57 (and Treasurer's Accounts) report that, in 1553-4, £110 10s was spent upon the repair of gaps, 17 roods in length, in the Park Dyke. It is not clear whether this repair related to the incident in 1543, or to a further problem. Details of these, and other Dyke expenses, together with a reference to the cost of the actual building of the Park Dyke, in about 1541, are given in Appendix I.

Whether or not the tenants were aggrieved at the loss of access to the slopes of Arthur's Seat, the same Sir David Murray, the then laird of Duddingston, accepted from the Lord High Treasurer on 24th January, 1542, £400 "in recompense of his lands of Duddingstone tane into the new park beside Halyrude Hous" and, by doing so, provides us with positive proof that the lands of Duddingston once extended into Holyrood Park. The Treverlen theory comes that much closer to reality.

Putting the "Treverlen" concept aside, however, the "modern" Barony of Duddingston actually consists of two "original" Baronies - Easter and Wester Duddingston. What is known as Duddingston Village is the descendant of the "town" of Wester Duddingston and that part of Milton Road East, now containing the Queen's Bay Nursing Home and the King's Manor Hotel, represents the site of the Easter "town". Both towns had their respective Baronies attached but they were eventually merged, in the 16th century.

The Figgate (also referred to as Fegot, Fichet, Figget, Ficket, Friggatt, Freegate or the Figgat Whins) was part of the Barony of Duddingston, but was a "separate tenement", that is it was possessed by owners other than the parties who owned the rest of the Barony. It was part of the old Duddingston parish; it later extended eastwards into Easter Duddingston, towards Magdalene Pans (later "Joppa" pans), was an integral part of the rural scene (sheep and cattle grazing) and it fitted snugly between rural Duddingston and the sea and became, unexpectedly, the focal point for rapid change.

Baird, when defining the outline of the lands of Figgate, quotes from an old charter, dated 20th May, 1466 as follows (additional comments are in brackets):

> *. . . it lies in length and breadth on both sides of the King's Highway* (the old Roman Road - The Fishwives' Causeway), *between the Fegot Myrehead* (near where Hope Lane crosses the railway line) *and a certain heap of stones there deposited on the east side on the one part, and descending from the east by a certain ditch made long ago* (on the line of Christian Path), *and march stones placed therein as far as the marches of the town of Wester Dodingston* (a line roughly from Rosefield Park to Bridge Street) *westward on the other part, ana*

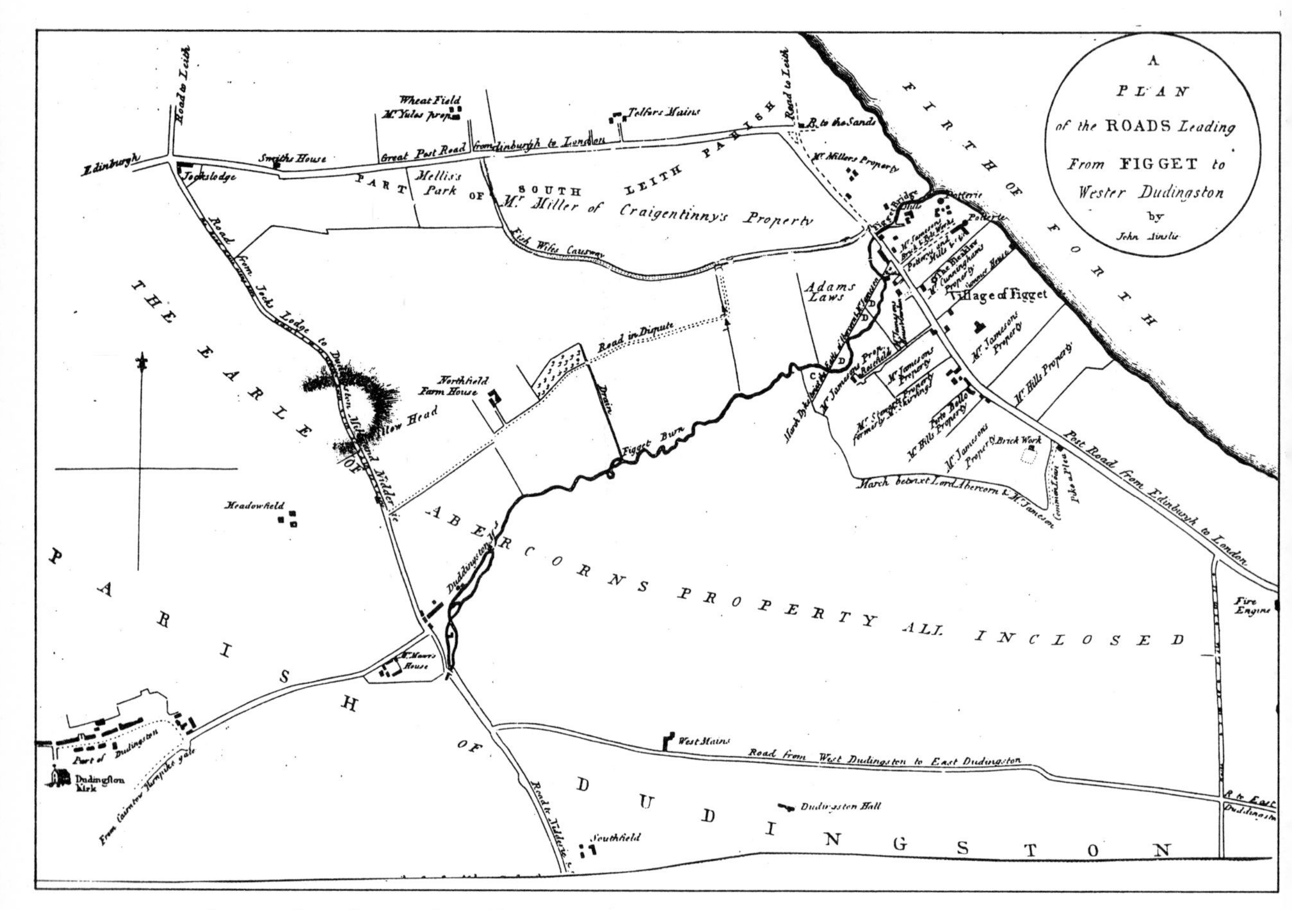

Plate 2 *Plan of part of Duddingston and Figgate – 1787* (Reproduced with permission of the Signet Library)

Although the plan was based upon a survey, the Village of Figgate was drawn on a slightly less accurate basis, but it still offers a very good picture of "Portobello" at that time. The historic outline of the lands of Figgate is shown in the text. The Fishwives' Causway, Causey or Causeway was, by then, not on its original line. It once continued to the Smith's House, at Jock's Lodge, at its west end and to somewhere near where Hope Lane is now, on the east. Northfield Farm House was only 26 years old and Meadowfield Farm had been built about 17 years earlier.

thence from the Fegot as the water runs into the sea (the point on the Promenade where the Figgate enters the sea), *and the foot of a lech on the north side* (ditch which can be traced by the high boundary wall separating the gardens on the east side of Marlborough Street from those of Bellfield), *and so from the lech by the marches boundaries and divisions ascending to the foresaid Fegot Myrehead and the foresaid heap of stones on the east side* (. . . back to the 'heap of stones' in Hope Lane).

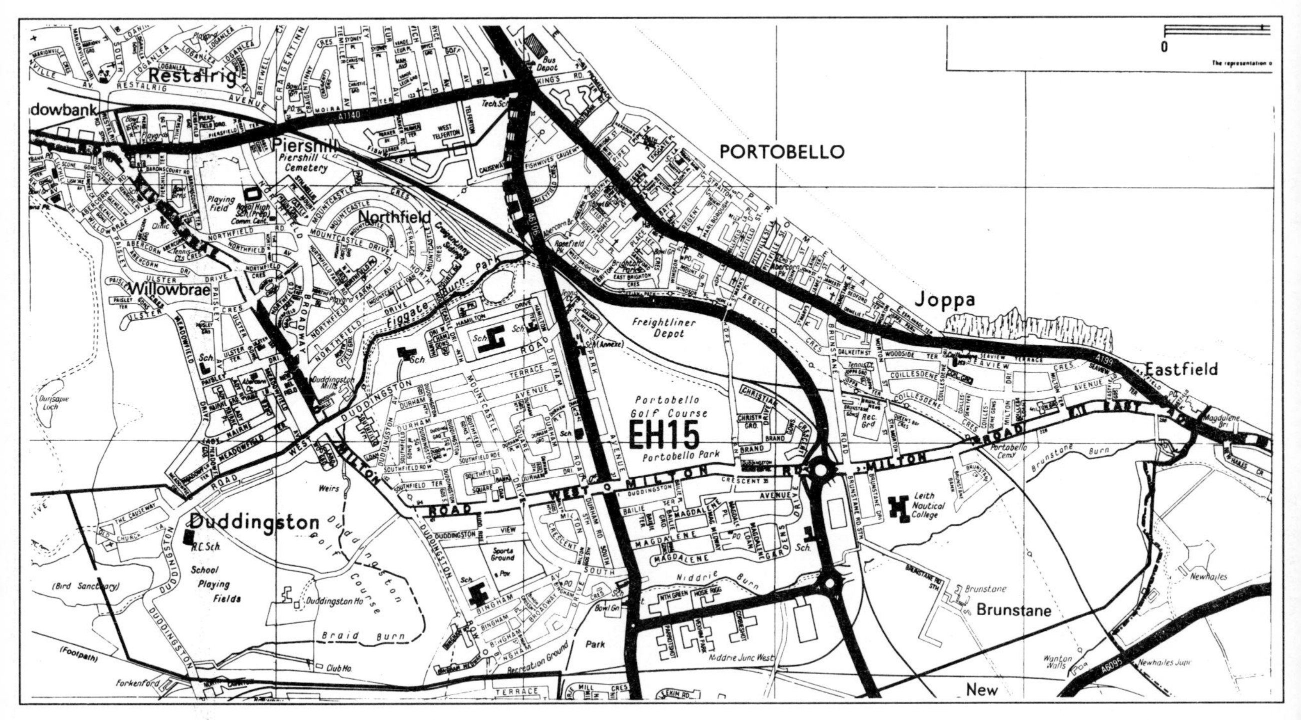

Plate 3 *The "Barony of Duddingston" in 1986* (Copyright © Geographia Limited MCMLXXXVIII. Reproduced with permission) (© Crown Copyright)

What the area covered by this book looks like today, in terms of road layout.

Although both the Figgate Whins and Portobello House were referred to as place-names in the years after the house was built and before other buildings appeared, this defined area later became known as the Village of Figgate before it was generally called Portobello.

The overall area about to be studied lies within the following modern boundaries – Jock's Lodge, Fishwives' Causeway, the Figgate Burn (north of Portobello High Street), the sea, Maitland Bridge, Brunstane Burn, (although a few acres of land north of Brunstane Burn belonged, at one stage, to Brunstane Estate), a line just south of the Bingham area and Duddingston Golf Course, Bawsinch Nature Reserve, Duddingston Village, the Park Dyke proceeding north to Willowbrae Avenue (the rear garden walls on the south side of Willowbrae Avenue form this boundary), Willowbrae Avenue to Willowbrae Road and back to Jock's Lodge.

The 1986 sketch-maps contain this area and show the current street organisation and Appendix II contains an indexed list of all the current street names, with derivations.

NEIGHBOURING ESTATES AND LANDS

The Barony is surrounded by other old family estates. Working from Jock's Lodge in the same directional order, we have, or had, Parson's Green Estate (which area was previously known as the Parson's Knowe), owned by a Mr Mitchell and then a Mr Simpson; Restalrig, owned by the Logans (the Barony of Restalrig embraced the lands of Lochend, Barbersburn, North Park, Craigentinny, Fillyside, Wheatfield, Cow Park, Piersfield, Piershill and Threesteps); the Craigentinny Estate, owned by the Nisbet and the Miller Families; (the Figgate Whins were owned, shortly before it developed into a village, by Baron Mure of Caldwell, Glasgow - he sold about 40 acres to Wm. Jamieson); Brunstane Estate, owned by the Crichtons and the Thirlestane, Lauderdale, Argyll, Fletcher and Abercorn families; the Niddrie Estate, owned by the Wauchopes; Craigmillar, owned by the Prestons and Gilmours; the lands of Cairntows (part of the Niddrie Estate); the lands of Peffermill, owned by the Prestons, one Edgar (who built "Peppermill House" in 1636), and the Gilmours; Prestonfield, owned by the Dicks; and the King's Park (currently called Holyrood Park) walled-in from about 1541 by James V and looked after by "Hereditary Keepers" - initially Sir Andrew Murray of Arngask, in 1567, and then the Hamilton Family, from 1646 until 1845.

Appendix III shows the main owners of the old lands of Figgate, Brunstane and Duddingston.

OLD PARISH BOUNDARY

Duddingston Barony once matched almost exactly the parish outline, except that the parish boundary ran, almost in a straight line, from Willowbrae Avenue to where the Fishwives' Causeway crosses Baileyfield Road, thereby missing out that area, nearest to the Portobello Road, from Jock's Lodge to the Fishwives' Causeway.

The parish boundary also included that area contained by Baileyfield Road, King's Road, Fishwives' Causeway and the sea, whereas this section was not part of the Duddingston Barony but part of Craigentinny. It should also be said that the Prestonfield Estate was part of Duddingston Parish from 1631 to 1895.

In 1884, the *Ordnance Gazatteer* described the area as; maximum length - three and five-eighth miles; maximum width - one and a quarter miles; area - 1899 acres (143 foreshore and 25 water).

LOOKING FOR PERSPECTIVE

Historians, geologists and archaeologists tell us that the Barony was, at different times, subterranean, volcanic, tropical, ice-covered, inhabited by Picts and wild animals, visited by the Romans, covered by forest, owned by the old Roman Catholic Church and by a series of wealthy land-owning families, sacked by Hertford, stalked in by Cromwell and camped on by Prince Charlie and his Highland Army.

Hugh Miller, who was born in a humble cottage in Cromarty (now in the hands of the National Trust for Scotland) and who achieved great acclaim as a stone mason, geologist and writer, lived in Portobello in his last years; in Shrub Mount, just west of the Police Station. He studied the rocks in Joppa Quarry and elsewhere, cut some of the stones of Niddrie House, and wrote about the geology of the area in his *Edinburgh and its Neighbourhood.* He described what he called the Midlothian Coal Measures as being a deep valley (about 3,000 feet deep) filled with sandstone, (rough boulder clay and) smoother brick clay, and coal seams - these three commodities have played very important roles in the development of the area, particularly Portobello.

T.C. Day and G.P. Black, in their respective books on Arthur's Seat, also demonstrate the alternating sequences of subterranean and volcanic action evidenced by sandstone layers, containing marine fossils, between lava flows. The land in the Meadowfield area not only contains a layer of sand, about a foot beneath the soil, but this fact is enshrined in the name of an old field west of Duddingston crossroads - Sandilands. This field name was also used near "Joppa" - which, on the face of it, is more understandable.

Easter Duddingston has had coal works for hundreds of years. One pit was sunk at what is now called Joppa (Morton Street/Joppa Road - previously called Mount Pleasant) and another at Brunstane Burn (upstream from where the old mill was, near Maitland Bridge). It seems strange that the tallest building (Coillesdene House) in the Joppa area was erected on, or very near, a mine shaft, for that is where another of the pits was supposed to have been, according to Baird.

Deep in the ground under "Mount Pleasant" (Joppa), there was, and probably still is, what was known as a coal level - a tunnel, seven feet high and four feet wide, for draining the mines - running from as far as Woolmet, to this place.

There is, for the world to see, much evidence of very early habitation on Arthur's Seat, in the form of cultivation terraces, wall bases (between Arthur's Seat and Crow Hill) and sites of forts (Dunsapie Hill and above Samson's Ribs). The Royal Scottish Museum has, amongst other local items, a Roman ring found in 1969 on the hill above Samson's Ribs (above the crags).

In addition to all this is the overwhelming role that agriculture has played here, as well as in most other areas. Probably since man thought it safe to come down from his ancient forts and cultivation terraces on Arthur's Seat, he has worked the soil on the lower levels here for his food. The oldest surviving Duddingston Charters (about 12th century) refer to grain and mills and, even then, we had Easter and Wester Duddingston (with its Church) delineated.

SOME NATURAL FEATURES - "ANCIENT"

EXTRACTS FROM HUGH MILLER'S *BRICK-CLAYS OF PORTOBELLO*

The following descriptive excerpts, written in the 1850s, provide us with a very meaningful picture of the likely ancient geological development of the area. The sections not in italic type, or those in brackets, are additional comments.

Plate 4 *Clay bank next to Portobello High Street*

The thick bed of clay dominates this view. The work being carried out is the extension of the Power Station in the 1920s.

What are known as the Portobello brick-clays occupy a considerable tract of comparatively level country, which intervenes between the eastern slopes of the Arthur's Seat group of hills and the sea. The covering of rich vegetable mould which forms the upper stratum of the tract – so valuable to the agriculturist – precludes any very exact survey of their limits; but we know from occasional excavations in the tract, and at least one natural section, that they extend over an area of at least a square mile.

A well, sunk a few years ago at Abercorn Place (now part of Portobello Road, just west of the north entrance to Northfield Cemetery), *one hundred and ten yards on the upper or Edinburgh side of the first milestone from Portobello, passed through a stratum of the brick-clays six feet in thickness; and several excavations made in the immediate neighbourhood, on the farm of Mr Scott of Northfield* (Farm), *laid open the continuous bed which they form at various points, fully a mile distant from the sea, where they averaged in thickness from five to seven feet. In all probability, judging from the general level, and their gradual thinning out, they terminate in this direction about the middle of the field which extends to the house of Willow Bank* (now Willowbrae House Clinic, near the south corner of Willowbrae Avenue and Willowbrae Road; the field was previously called "Water Pans" and the point referred to would be about where the Royal High Primary School now stands), *while more to the south they appear about sixty yards below the mill of Easter* (actually Wester) *Duddingston, in the section formed by the Figget Burn, whence they stretch eastwards to near Joppa Quarry* (where Quarry Park is now, east of Brunstane Road). *They aquire their greatest elevation at Stuart Street* (now Abercorn Gardens, between Northfield Cemetery and Northfield Broadway) *and its neighbourhood, where they rise about eighty feet over the high-water line; and attain to their greatest known depth in the town of Portobello, at the paperworks of the Messrs Craig, where at one point, immediately beside the burn, they were perforated several years ago, in sinking a well, to the depth of not less than a hundred feet. Their extent along the shore to the west has not been very definitely traced, but from their eastern extremity near Joppa, to where they terminate beyond the brickworks of Mr Ingram, cannot greatly exceed a mile. The boulder clay appears all round the edges of the area which they occupy, and forms, I cannot doubt, the basin in which they rest. It appears in a characteristic section a little above Duddingston Mill, charged with its grooved and polished boulders: it was cut through to a considerable depth by the excavations for the North British Railway, in the vicinity of Stuart Street and Abercorn Place, and there found underlying the brick-clays; and it appears along the shore, accompanied by some of its most striking phenomena, both to the east and west of Portobello, a little beyond the limits of the basin. In short, the Portobello brick-clays may be regarded as occupying a boulder-clay basin or valley about a mile in length and breadth, not reckoning on their unknown portion, which seems to extend outwards under the sea; and, thinning out all round the edges of the hollow, they attain, where deepest in the lower reaches of the Figget Burn, a thickness, as I have already said, of at least a hundred feet.*

Their colour is very much that, on the average, of the boulder-clay of the district: they bear a deep leaden hue; nor can I doubt that their materials were originally derived from it. But they must have been deposited at a somewhat later time, and under different conditions. They are finely laminated throughout: even their most compact beds, when exposed edgewise for a few weeks to the weather, are found to consist of hundreds of layers, thin as sheets of pasteboard; and there run throughout the deposit thin strata of silt or sand, that, unlike the arenaceous intercalations of the boulder-clay, preserve for many yards the same thickness, and maintain in many cases nearly the same level. The brick-clays in this locality must have been slowly deposited in comparatively tranquil waters, undisturbed, apparently, by the restless agencies which, during the boulder-clay period, grooved and furrowed the solid rocks of the country, and transported and left their strange marks on the great stones to which the boulder formation owes its name.

The thin beds of sand which in several places overtop the brick-clays in the Figget valley may have been either deposited by the waters of the stream during land-floods, and, of consequence, ere the upheaval of the old coast-line; or they may have been drifted by storms from the sea during unusually high tides, or wafted by the winds from the beach; and the overlying strata of moss and silt are the deposits of a still later time, when what had been previously in succession a quiet muddy arm of the sea, and next a brackish reed-bearing estuary, had probably existed alternately as swamp and lake, – a lake dammed up, it is probable, by a sand-bar or storm-beach, raised by the waves along the line of the shore.

The entire deposit, old (boulder clay) *and new* (brick clay) *furnishes us with two little bits of picture. We are first presented with a scene of islands – the hills which overlook the Scottish capital, or on which it is built – half sunk in a glacial sea.*

Plate 5 *Portobello Harbour*

This stood next to where the Open Air Pool was, until recently, and the base stones can still be seen at low tide.

> *A powerful current from the west, occasionally charged with icebergs, sweeps past them, turbid with the washings of the raw, recently-formed boulder-clays of the great flat valley which stretches between the Friths of Forth and Clyde; and in the sheltered tract of sea to the west of the islets, amid slowly revolving eddies, the sediment is cast slowly down, and, layer after layer, the brick-clays are formed along the bottom. And then, in long posterior ages, after the land has risen – all save its last formed terrace – and the subarctic rigour of its climate has softened, we mark a long withdrawing estuary running along what is now the valley of the Figget Burn. It is skirted by the aboriginal trees of the country, – oak, and birch, and alder, and the Scotch fir; and where a sluggish stream creeps through the midst, we see it thickly occupied by miniature forests of reeds and rushes.* (Miller found many traces of such flora.)

SOME NATURAL FEATURES – "MODERN"

In the last 800 years or so, over which period records of some description or other survive, dominant surface features like Arthur's Seat, Duddingston Loch, the Figgate Burn and the Firth of Forth have been present. Man has made some alterations to these natural features, however; Arthur's Seat has been walled-in since about 1541 and its flora affected substantially by grazing horses, cattle and sheep; Salisbury Crags have been quarried (some of its stone still paves London streets today, as well as forming a base for the old Edinburgh-Musselburgh Road from Clockmill to Portobello) and materially altered at the east end; two man-made lochs have appeared –

Plate 6 *Duddingston House*

This sketch shows something of the character of the Policy grounds surrounding the House – "cascades, waterfalls, canals and ponds", and cattle and sheep grazing.

Dunsapie and St Margaret's (both in the middle of the 19th century). Duddingston Loch, which is fed from the Wells o' Wearie and other springs, has had its level influenced by its owners (Dicks of Prestonfield) and by Duddingston tenants. The Figgate Burn, the life blood of the agricultural scene, has driven oat, wheat and barley mill wheels at Duddingston "Mylne Town" since "beyond the memory of man" by various systems of lades drawing water from it; in the early 1800s, it also turned a Mr Smith's white lead mill wheel at Rosefield, Portobello, and, prior to 1787, another mill-wheel (paper mill) nearer the sea, beside the harbour. Before all this, however, it had been altered to supply water to Easter Duddingston (town), the Magdalene Salt pans (later "Joppa"; but the pans on the *south* side of the road) and a water wheel ("water engine" or "water gin") which was used, from at least the 17th century, to drain the Duddingston coal pits.

The part of the burn, south of Duddingston crossroads, is called the Braid Burn and it passes through Duddingston Golf Course - previously called Duddingston Policy (the "Pleasure Gardens" of the 8th Earl of Abercorn) - on its way to the sea. During the 1760s, the Earl of Abercorn, as part of his landscaping project, employed a gardener, Robert Robinson (who may have been a pupil of Capability Brown), to landscape the grounds and alter the course of the burn. In December 1766, Robinson had 120 men working for him and the final result was a combination of magnificent canals, cascades, waterfalls, ponds and tree plantings (many of which still survive).

It would seem, from an examination of old maps, that the basic line of the burn as it enters the Barony at Forkenford (between Bawsinsh Nature Reserve and Craigmillar), and as it progresses eastwards, then turns northwest to meet the private road leading to Duddingston House from Milton Road West, has not changed a great deal. It does seem, however, that it was given better definition by the removal of many bends and the introduction of wider areas; islands and ponds were also added. Its older course, however, is open to question, as will be seen in a later chapter.

The shore at Portobello has been adorned in the past by the famous pier (1871-1917) and has had recent replenishments of sand dredged from the Forth but, unfortunately, the most important effect of man on the "Frith of Forth" is the modern problem of pollution. We can no longer eat what that famous Duddingston resident, Lady Nairne, called in her lovely song, "Caller Herrin'", the "lives o' Men" i.e. herring from the "Frith of Forth".

As has been said, agriculture was the dominant activity of man in the Duddingston area until fairly recently. Later chapters will consider the extent of this and the progression towards replacing the plough with the bulldozer; the horse with the car; and the grain with bricks and mortar.

CHAPTER 2
THE VIEW FROM THE MANSE IN 1794

It is of interest to consider the scene during the 18th century and to that end, comments from the Revd Wm. Bennet, minister at Duddingston from 1786 to 1805, which tell us much about the environment in Duddingston about 200 years ago, follow (*Statistical Account, 1794*). It is of interest to reflect that English was first taught in Edinburgh in 1750.

Before "the view from the manse" is considered, a view of inside and around the manse, and of the minister himself, provides additional information. The following picture comes from a Court of Session case of 1797, between the Tutors-at-law of ten-year-old Sir Alexander Dick of Prestonfield, who had just lost his father, and the boy's grandmother, Mrs Trotter of Mortonhall. The Tutors-at-law, upon advice of eminent council, wanted to place him under the charge of Mr Bennet, "who keeps an academy at Duddingston".

It was said by the Trotters' advisers however, that "Mr Bennet professes to keep no academy, but that he only receives into his house a small and select number of gentlemen, whom he can treat as his own children, and wishes to educate along with them; children of persons with whom he is connected, or for whom he has personal esteem. He has declined many invitations to increase the number and has only six". The Trotters preferred no one else, but as Mr Bennet already had other boys under his care, who lived in the house with him, they thought it improper to send Sir Alexander to an academy, or boarding-house, amongst other boys as he had a health problem.

Advisers were sent to investigate the suitability of Duddingston Manse and reported as follows:

> *We have examined into every circumstance with particular attention and so far as we are able to judge both the house and the adjacent grounds are free from any suspicion of dampness. The soil is light, upon a rocky bottom. The house stands upon an eminence sufficiently elevated above the surface of the lake, to place it beyond the reach of any inconvenient exhalation. Besides, on that side, the bottom of the lake is all channel* (small stones) *and there is marshy ground adjoining to the edge of the water. From these circumstances, we think that there is no reason to be afraid of insalubrity from the vicinity of the lake.*
>
> *The house is sufficiently commodious and the room which is destined for the reception of Sir Alexander, is spacious, well aired and seems to be perfectly dry. The garden declines toward the southwest and both from this exposure and from the protection of artificial fences, it is well screened from the effects of the east wind. Upon the whole, therefore, we consider the manse of Duddingston to be placed in a sufficiently eligible situation.*

This manse, which was built in 1750, stood next to where the Session House now stands and was to be replaced by the present one only eight years after this report was written. It was for the use of the Revd John Thomson.

The paragraphs in italic type are taken from Mr Bennet's Account, and each one is followed by additional comments.

SHEEP'S HEIDS

The distance of the village (Wester Duddingston) *from the city of Edinburgh is little more than a mile; and the path that leads to it through the steep acclivities and chasms of the hill, though formerly difficult to pass, has yet proved sufficiently alluring to induce many of its opulent citizens to resort thither, in the summer months, to solace themselves over one of the ancient homely dishes of Scotland, for which the place has been long celebrated; and, in winter, to attract crouds to witness or to partake of the amusements of skating upon its lake. The use of singed sheep's heads boiled or baked, so frequent in this village, is supposed to have arisen from the practice of slaughtering the sheep fed on the neighbouring hill for the market, removing the carcases to town, and leaving the head, &c. to be consumed in the place.*

The path referred to is more or less where the road from Duddingston Village to St Leonard's is now. The previous minister, also a Mr Wm. Bennet (uncle of this Wm. Bennet) reported to the Earl of Abercorn in 1752 on the state of the former path (wide enough for only one person) and asked for financial help to improve it, partly on the basis that it would encourage people to come from Edinburgh for the purposes of worshipping in Duddingston Kirk and contributing to the "poor" collection. In 1817, the Revd John Thomson (minister and famous Landscape painter), Sir Keith Dick and Guthrie Wright (factor) ventured forth in the pouring rain to decide upon the future line of the path. Two hundred men from "Burrowmuirhead" Links, with an overseer, carried out the work and the path was widened to six feet; that path later (*c* 1860) became the roadway. Sheep grazed in the Park, prior to going to the slaughterhouse at Slateford, until 1979.

POPULATION OF WESTER DUDDINGSTON

Wester Dudingston was once a large and populous village. Most of the tenants upon the Barony resided in it prior to the year 1751. Before the same period it furnished 36 horses to carry coals in sacks or creels to Edinburgh. About 40 years ago it supplied above 30 weavers' looms. These were chiefly employed in manufacturing a very course flaxen stuff, then known by the name of Dudingston hardings. But the trade has declined; and there now remain but five weavers in the village. No place could be better adapted for some such manufactory as this, from its access to water, fuel and the necessaries of life, as well as from its vicinity to Edinburgh. The houses have been suffered to drop into ruin, and those which remain are chiefly occupied by labouring people, whose wives, with some widows in the place, employ themselves in washing linen, or carry milk to the inhabitants of the neighbouring city, for which their vicinity to the Loch of Dudingston, and to many old and excellent pasture fields, affords them the most convenient opportunities. Formerly it is supposed to contain above 500 inhabitants. At present the number does not exceed 200.

The village used to be larger by about five acres – it extended south eastwards to cover the area where Holyrood School is now. When the Earl of Abercorn laid out and enclosed his Policy (in the 1760s), the village was reduced in size. At this time, carts were not too plentiful in the Lothians because

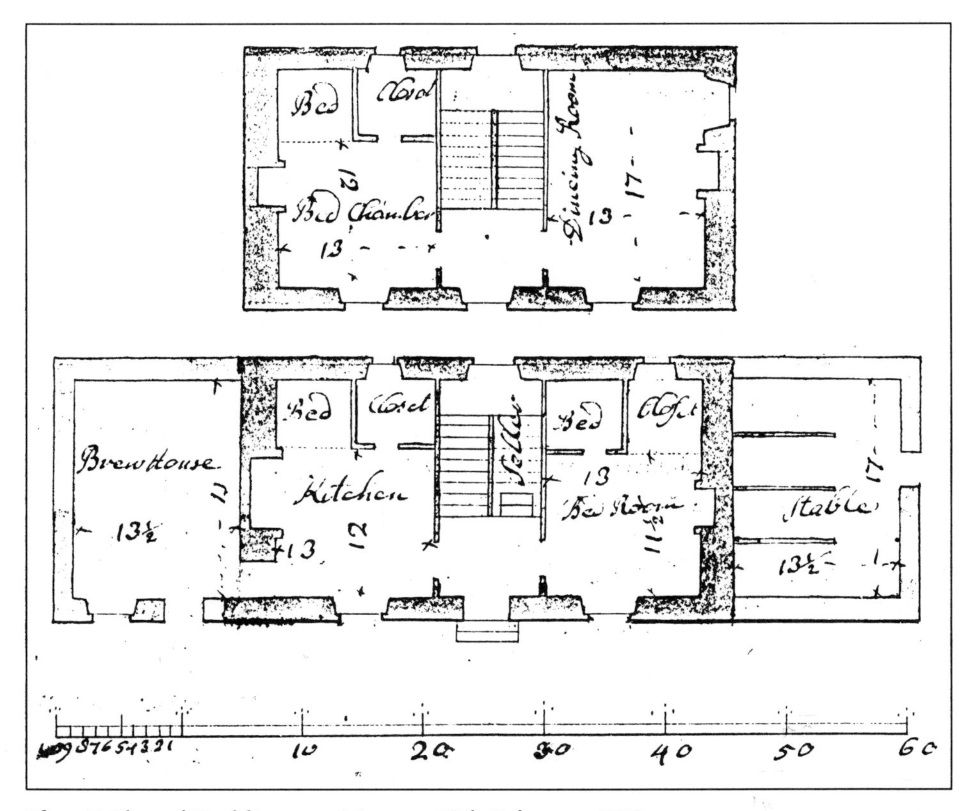

Plate 7 *Plan of Duddingston Manse – 20th February 1758* (Reproduced with permission of the Keeper of the Records of Scotland)

This was the house which was built for Revd Bennet (the first Revd Bennet) and in which both Mr Bennets lived. The boys in Mr Bennet's "Academy" lived here also, and it was here that the frail ten-year-old Sir Alexander Dick would have lived in 1797. This building stood next to the Session House at the Kirk Gate and the wall leading from the Session House, towards the present manse, is possibly a remnant of this old manse, or its outbuildings.

of the state of the roads and the cost of the tolls. The washer-women often had disputes with the Dicks of Prestonfield, who owned the Loch, over the use of the Loch water for bleaching their linen – the song "The Wells o' Wearie" reflected such disputes. The old pasture fields were the "Commons" of the touns and other field areas and are mentioned in a later chapter on fields.

> *Easter Dudingston has not varied so much in its size and population. It has lately been rebuilt in part, and the new houses according to their original destination, are for the most part occupied by colliers.*

The Easter Town was mainly that area now occupied by the King's Manor Hotel (for many years the Milton House Hotel) and the Queen's Bay Nursing

Plate 8 *The Kirk Gate area, c 1910*

The Session House (built about 1825), Jougs and Loupin' on Stane are as expected, but there is a barren appearance about the Crow Hill and this section of "Old Church Lane", which replaced the old path to Edinburgh in the 1860s.

Home. The two main tenant families which lived there (as well as in Wester Duddingston), were the Scotts (later of Northfield Farm) and the Horns.

In the grounds of the Queen's Bay Nursing Home is to be seen a collection of large stones which are covered with cup-shaped indentations. In Appendix III, reference is made to a contract of land exchange (excambion) in Duddingston/Brunstane between the Earl of Islay (later the 3rd Duke of Argyll) and Lord Milton (Andrew Fletcher). A related document, signed by "Islay" and Duncan Forbes, dated 26th July 1734 (Fletcher of Saltoun Papers, MS17477), states that . . . "the grounds (of Brunstane) should be divided . . . by pitted march stones". The cluster of "pitted stones" behind the front garden wall of the Nursing Home could well be some of the actual stones referred to in that document.

THE FIGGATE

Portobello and Brickfield, now the most populous and prosperous villages of the parish, are but of very recent origin and name. The grounds on which they are built are a part of the Figget lands, which altogether consist of about 70 acres. These continued down the year 1762 or 1763 a mere waste, covered by the most part with furze or whins, and were commonly let to one of the Dudingston tenants. In one or other of the above mentioned years, the lands of Figget were sold and the purchaser immediately began to improve his property, and in a few years parcelled it out into different feus. He soon indemnified himself for the expences of improvements with the crops he raised, and by the feu duties ensured an annual income of about 7 per cent for the original price. Portobello Hut was the first house raised in the midst of the original waste about the year 1742, and derived its title from the Spanish American city of that name, of the capture of which, the news had arrived in Britain about that period. Since the cultivation and improvements of the neighbouring soil, besides the ordinary houses

Plate 9 *Sketch of Portobello House*

This was the first house in the lands of Figgate. George Hamilton lived in it and perhaps even named it Porto Bello to commemorate a naval victory at the Central American town of Puerto Bello, but it was built about 1753, by Easter Duddingston tenant farmer, Peter Scott, for his shepherd (who may have been George Hamilton).

> *required for the brick, pottery, and tile manufactures, a number of gay or commodious dwellings have been erected by the feuers, either for their own accommodation or for bathing quarters, for which the agreeable softness of the adjacent sandy beach, the purity of the air, and the convenience of the Musselburgh or rather London post road form obvious recommendations.*

Tradition has is that Portobello Hut, or House, was built by an ex-sailor, George Hamilton, who was supposed to have taken part in the conquering of the Central American town of Puerto Bello in 1739. Baird says it appears to have been built a few years after the 1745 Rebellion "and was inhabited by one George Hamilton". Baird was correct in not stating, as others have done, that Hamilton actually built Portobello House, as Session Papers in the Signet Library contain evidence that it was built by Mr Peter Scott, of Easter Duddingston – the tenant referred to above as having rented the Figgate Whins for grazing. The same source states that Peter Scott's son, Andrew, built Northfield Farm, in 1761, from stones taken from a quarry near the Maitland Pans (Lower Joppa Quarry, between the sea and the main road). The person who bought the Figgate Whins and who let part of it for grazing, was Baron Mure of Caldwell, Glasgow. He was a Baron of the Exchequer; a friend of Andrew Fletcher (Lord Milton) and an enthusiastic agriculturist, which was perhaps just as well, given the usual description of the lands of Figgate. A significant topographical event occurred in Edinburgh at this time, when, in 1763, the Nor' Loch was drained.

Chapter 4 expands on the evidence available concerning the date of building "Portobello Hut" – the first house to be built in the lands of Figgate.

STATE OF THE ROADS

The prosecution of such (estate) *improvements, however, at any distance from the city, might have been much if not totally obstructed, from the state of the roads, which were generally ruinous, and often impassable in the winter season. It might arise partly from this circumstance, which formed another obstacle to cultivation; that it was not till after the year 1750, that carts came to be in general use; at least to the west of Edinburgh, though they had been long employed upon the east side, the conveyance of all materials having been before that period, in sacks, hurdles or creels, upon the backs of horses.*

In a legal case of the 1560s, concerning the water supply of Duddingston Mills, carts were mentioned as being in general use in this area. The state of the roads probably resulted in the users varying their route, thus altering the lines of the roads. When the Turnpike Road Acts were enforced and toll bars set up, many people used sledges instead of carts in order to avoid payment, as the tolls related to wheeled vehicles. The law was, of course, changed.

THE RUNRIG SYSTEM

The estate of Dudingston, was much later (than surrounding estates, such as Prestonfield and Restalrig) *in undergoing any effective improvement. The tenants originally possessed their lands in runridge or rundale; and in each of the villages of Wester and Easter Dudingston in which they resided, they had access to a common, upon which they pastured their sheep, horses and other cattle, which were kept by a common herd.*

Improvement meant enclosing the fields with hedges, ditches or walls; changing the field system from small runrig fields to larger fields which could be crossed-ploughed and drained and cropped more effectively. Such improvements, of course, changed the social structure as one tenant farmer worked an area previously farmed by all the tenant farmers of that village. Portobello Hut, previously referred to, was built as a herd's cottage before 1754. It stood on the south side of today's Portobello High Street, between the High Street and Lee Crescent. A later chapter deals with the field names, sizes and locations, as well as attempting to show their locations in relation to present street layouts.

NEW FARMS

About the year 1751, the proprietor, the late Earl of Abercorn, began to subdivide his estate into commodious farms, to build convenient farm-houses, and offices upon each, and to enclose them with ditches and hedges. The estate was thus reduced into a regular and progressive state of cultivation; and the country beautified and adorned with hedge-rows, clumps and plantations of various forms and extent. Though the rents comparatively have been greatly advanced, in consequence of these improvements; the tenants are all thriving, live comfortably, and perhaps are in every respect, in a better condition than their predecessors.

Plate 10 *Southfield Farm House*

One of only two of the old farm houses which still exist in the Barony.

The farms thus built were Northfield Farm in 1761 and, referred to above, Southfield Farm – the original farm was where the playing fields now are on the east side of Duddingston Row (formerly Bingham Road) – and Meadowfield Farm, off Paisley Drive (now demolished). The dates of the latter two farms were approximately 1770. The offices mentioned were the various farm buildings, such as byres, stables and brew-houses.

DUDDINGSTON HOUSE

In 1763, soon after the Earl had completed the subdividing and enclosing of his estates, he began to build his mansion house of Dudingston, upon an elegant and commodious plan, the work of the late Sir William Chalmers (Chambers). *The house and offices were finished in 1768; and continue to exhibit a beautiful specimen of Greek architecture and elegance, and of English accommodation and affluence. The noble villa was surrounded with shrubbery, pleasure grounds, canals, gardens; and in the formation of the whole, it is supposed, above £30,000 sterling, were expended. The beautiful variety of the ground, the happy position of the clumps and groves, the striking diversity of the water embellishments, canals, lakes, isles, and cascades; above all, the grandeur and beauty of the surrounding scenery and prospects, independently of the magnificent form and architecture of the house itself, must render the place singularly picturesque, elegant and attracting.*

Plate 11 *Duddingston House - 1912*

Sir William Chambers designed another building in Edinburgh - the Head Office of the Royal Bank of Scotland, St Andrew Square and similarities can be spotted in the frontal architecture.

Duddingston House does not have a basement (although the part containing the servants' quarters does), and is built of polished ashlar, lined on the inside with courses of thin, red brick. Its offices, which consisted mainly of servants' quarters and a stable block for about 30 horses, straggled in a northern direction, close to a road which used to run between Wester Duddingston and Niddrie. The house was really built as a summer residence of the 8th Earl of Abercorn, who never married, and therefore was never a family home in the normal (baronial) sense. After he died, the house was either virtually empty, but looked after, or let. Although details of the house are well documented elsewhere, it is of interest to note that, during preparation of the laying of the foundations of the pending housing scheme adjacent to the house (May 1989), workmen discovered a large, deep stone-lined well near the northern corner of the the stable block. It narrows at the neck to about four feet across, is about 30 feet deep, and has now been filled with concrete due to its proximity to the new road. Two such wells are now known here; the other is about 20 feet deep and is close to the south west wall of the "Chapel", that section topped by a recently reconstructed tower.

In 1831, the then tenant, a Mr Adam Hay, complained about the water supply to the house; it took a man two or three hours per day to pump it . . . "the only supply being from a well of hard water which is brought into the house by means of a force Pump" (probably the 20 foot well mentioned above). Mr Hay proposed that, if the Marquis of Abercorn paid for a supply to be brought in, he would pay 5 per cent per annum over and above his rent. The factor, Mr Guthrie Wright, made a survey and reported . . . "a most abundant supply of the finest and purest spring water may be obtained from Arthur's Seat, at a level of 200 or 300 feet above Duddingston House which would send it all over the premises; that the distance is about 1,300 or 1,400 yards . . . making the fountain on the hill, where the springs would be collected . . . the spot is only about 100 yards from the March between it and Lord Abercorn's property . . . it would drain about 20 acres of land which is

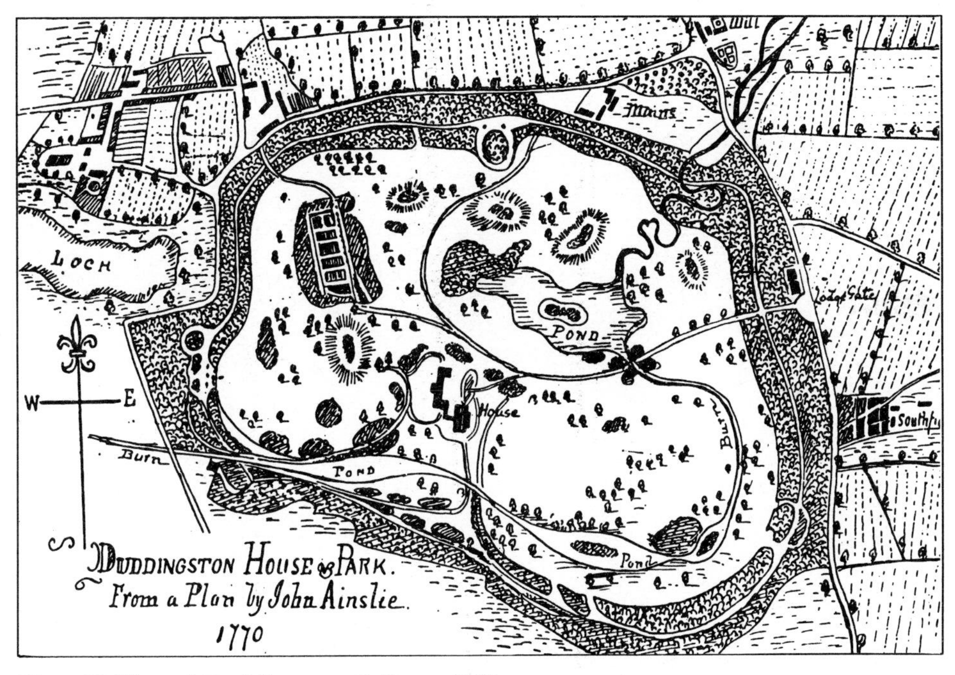

Plate 12 *Plan of Duddingston Policy - 1770*

John Ainslie shows, in this view 17 years earlier than his plan of the Figget, something of the old layout of Wester Duddingston just after Duddingston House had been built (1768). The kitchen garden, the site of which is now taken up by Holyrood School, has replaced part of the old village.

at present a mere bog (Dunsapie and surrounding area). All that would be required would be to obtain consent of the Earl of Haddington (Keeper of the Park) to drain the marsh, collect the springs, make a little Fountain or Tank and lay a pipe (one inch diameter) for carrying the water for 100 yards into the Marquis's own land (Sir Robert Dick of Prestonfield had made a similar arrangement to operate near Samson's Ribs)." The cost was about £300 (including two new water closets), the tank is referred to in the caption to Plate 25 and the water was possibly piped to the deeper well, mentioned above. The tank, which used to have an iron door, has been filled in but part of its wall can still be seen. The actual route of the pipe from the hill to the house is not known, but it is likely to have been laid in a fairly straight line.

The grounds, or policy, included what is now Duddingston Golf Course, and the area containing Holyrood R C High School and the Playing Fields to the south of the school (shared between that school and Portobello High School). The main access was via the east lodge gates (at Milton Road West, although originally, this road was further north and the drive came off the "Road to Niddery" i.e. Duddingston Row) and a secondary access to the village of Wester Duddingston (west lodge gates). That route is still in existence (recently scraped out and re-made as an access road to serve the new houses mentioned above), although the lodge houses are no longer there. There used to be an access track from the road which leads to the Duddingston Golf Club premises, to the mansion house, as well as a series of "rides" through the plantations (many trees from which still survive), which surrounded the whole complex. The largest pond (with its surviving ice-house) occupied that low area between the mansion house and the "temple"; that domed, columnar structure which occupies a prominent position on the golf course and which is the only remaining part of the once large array of stone adornments of the policy. It was re-roofed with glass fibre in recent years by pupils of Holyrood High School.

THE SOIL

The soil is naturally but poor or indifferent in the greater part of the parish, generally a brown earth, seldom exceeding 16 inches in depth, and often not attaining to so much; towards the east, inclined to and resting of a strong clay; and near the sea-coast degenerating into a light, but with culture not unproductive, sand.

A later chapter will deal with this matter in relation to the fields, which, incidentally, had some interesting old names. That chapter will also have a look at exactly what was grown in the fields in 1800–02.

The great object of ambition (agriculture), *is the multiplying of wheat crops. The fallowing, drill, pasture, and turnip husbandry, are little practised in this neighbourhood, from the deafness of the ground; and the easy though expensive aquisition of the richest manure. Crops of artificial grass and clover are frequently introduced, generally cut twice in the season, and seldom allowed to remain above two years in the ground. Potatoes are also a staple commodity, often sublet like clover. Barley, oats, pease, as usual have their place, though the last as seldom as possible; but assuredly the finest crops of each species of grain that can be seen any where, are raised here. Grounds that are kept in pasture, are seldom occupied by sheep to any extent; but are generally grazed by milk cows, and road horses from the neighbouring city.*

The advent of land enclosure and the growth of Portobello, which rose on what was by that time no more than sheep pasture, signalled a significant reduction in the numbers of sheep grazed. That valuable commodity, dung, was applied, when the potatoes were sown, at the rate of 35 cart-loads per acre. That part of Duddingston Golf Course which lies to the south of Woodlands Grove, and was called Karin Buck (Cairnbuck), was let to a Mr Mawer, the late 8th Earl of Abercorn's "overseer", or gardener, in 1790 for the purpose of grazing horses at a nightly rate.

There was an interesting Court case in 1798, between Mr Mawer and General Dugald Campbell, who had rented Duddingston House, and involving the Factor, Mr Walter Scott (senior). Mawer had been gardener to the Earl of Abercorn to oversee and erect the improvements carried on in the parks and policy of Duddingston.

Mawer had also rented the Earl's Farm (which became "Woodlands"), retained a barn-yard (120 yards long and 30 yards wide) for the accommodation of the cattle and horses admitted to the pasture and sublet the rest of the farm to Louis Cauvin (mentioned later), who allowed his brother, Joseph Cauvin, WS, to occupy the farm lodge as summer quarters. There was access from the farm to the 21.5 acres of "Kirnbuck". The problem was, however, that the horses were peeling, or "barking", the trees beyond an acceptable level, and Walter Scott was now going to erect fences round all the clumps of trees, which would have the effect of closing the access between the pasture field and the farm area. Apparently, 428 trees had been peeled in a four month period.

Mawer proposed "to employ two boys, as herds, to prevent as much as is in their power the peeling and barking of the trees". This was tried, but had no effect. Mr Scott "undertook to the charge of annointing the trees with lime water", but this did not work either; Mawer thought that Scott's mixture wasn't right. In a further attempt to avoid the enclosing of the pasture, Mawer suggested advertising the grazing with the proviso - "That no horse, known to have barked trees, is to be admitted and that such horses as may be found to have barked trees are to be turned out immediately, or on being discovered". The factor ignored this suggestion and proceeded to erect his fences.

WILLIAM JAMIESON

To the spirited and continued exertions of one patriotic gentleman, are to be ascribed the various useful works which now occupy and adorn the once desart lands of Figget, and which contribute to supply the village of Brickfield or Portobello with near 300 inhabitants. Mr William Jamieson, an eminent tradesman and architect in the city of Edinburgh, having purchased about 40 acres of the Figget lands, built upon this property, in 1767, a handsome dwelling house; and having discovered a rich and deep bed of clay under the sand, he began soon after that period, the manufacturing of bricks; which by the number of hands employed, and houses required for their accommodation, gave rise to the above mentioned rapid increase in his village. The same clay has been found equally well adapted for the fabrication of tile, brown pottery, and white stone wares, all of which are carrying on with hopes of increasing success.

Baird describes Jamieson as the "father of Portobello", and one can see why from this passage. His house was Rosefield, which was on the east side of Rosefield Park. He bought his parts of Figgate from Baron Mure, and the name Brickfield soon appeared on the scene, for obvious reasons. A triangular field, bordered by Baileyfield Road, Fishwives' Causeway and the Figgate Burn, was called Brickfield. The name "Portobello", obviously had to compete with "Figget" (or Figgat) and "Brickfield". A lesser contender, "Bilbao", appears on a late 18th-century map also.

Plate 13 *Joppa salt pans, c 1900*

An old coal pit caved in just west of the pans in 1801, affecting the road.

SALT

> *Salt has been long prepared upon the sea-coast, in the parish. Maitland pans derive their name from, and were probably erected by, some of the Lauderdale family, at one time proprietors of the land around. Magdalene pans, and Magdalene Bridge, are supposed to have been named from a neighbouring chapel dedicated to St Magdalene, situated in the parish of Inveresk. The prosperity and produce of the salt-works, is in a considerable degree, regulated by the state of the coal. A few years ago, the number of salters with the officers employed in the work, amounted to 17. Their labours afforded employment to above 40 carriers, all women, who retailed the salt in Edinburgh, and through the neighbouring districts. The quantity of salt delivered by the six pans, regularly employed, used to be about 18,000 bushels annually.*

What he calls Maitland pans were what later became known as Joppa salt pans and the seaside location still contains some evidence of the older walls and buildings. What he calls Magdalene pans were just to the east of the Barony and parish and the Maitland Bridge, between the main road and the sea; they were later called Pinkie pans. Baird says that this was the older of the two sites, dating from prior to the Reformation and that salt was formerly made from evaporated sea water, before the method switched to using rock salt from Cheshire. The names of the two pans were often interchanged, causing confusion. Lawrie, on his map of 1763, correctly shows Joppa pans as Maitland pans, but as "Magdaline" pans on his map of 1766.

On all other old maps prior to 1800, Joppa pans are shown as "Magdalen" pans and the older pans, "Magdalen" pans, were not named at all.

Two of the old Laing Charters (No. 2076 & 2287 dated 11th February, 1631 and 24th February, 1641 respectively) indicate when the salt pans were built at what is now called Joppa. The first charter says . . . "that piece of waste land or rock, for constructing one or more salt pans, with their houses etc., lying within the bounds of Easter Duddingston, near the sea, and bounded between two great fixed rocks, lying between the sea on the north and the highway on the south, and containing fourteen falls in breadth from east to west . . . ". The second says . . . "(refers to the first)..and the six salt pans, built by David Preston, lying within the bounds of Easter Duddingston, near the sea. Sasine given on the ground by presenting the "schellis" (shells) of the said salt pans . . . ". So it is now known who really built the pans there - David Preston of Craigmillar. By 1641, there were six salt pans plus houses on this site.

The name of the coal used in the pans was the "small coal", or "panwood" and one boll of salt was produced from four and two-thirds bolls of panwood. The "hot salt" was stored in "girnalls", from which it was taken to be sold. The six pans referred to were all at these two sites, but it should be realised that, in the 18th century, there were salt pans on the south side of the Musselburgh Road - where Coillesdene House stands now - before a coal pit (according to Baird) was later sunk on the same site. The map of 1801 shows a small road, called "Bunkers Hill", running up on a slope from the Salt works on the south side of the road towards the area where Coillesdene House was (marked "Old Salt Pans" on the map). The bunkers would have been the heaps of coal destined for the salt works.

COAL

Thirteen seams of coal have been discovered and wrought upon the estate of Duddingston. These are of various qualities, and some excellent in their kinds. They crop, as indeed the strata of all minerals upon this coast preserve the same inclination, to the west; the dip or declination, is nearly at an angle of 45 degrees from the horizon to the east, a circumstance which of itself must always have rendered the working of the coal difficult. Most of the above seams have been wrought from a very remote period of time, which cannot now be ascertained, where they approach the surface, and as far as a simple free level could clear them of water. Under the Duchess of Argyll, a rude machine composed of, and named, "chain and buckets", was employed to raise the water in the mines from a great depth. When the property fell into the possession of the late Earl of Abercorn, the coal and salt works were at first let to Mr Biggar of Woolmet, an enterprising man, who opened a level from the sea, and carried it through the estates of Dudingston, Niddry, and part of Edmonston, up to Woolmet Bank, a powerful drain of above 3 miles in extent, of most essential advantage to the more elevated coal works of the neighbouring proprietors, but eventually productive of ruin to that of Dudingston, besides opening the generating source of interminable law pleas. About the year 1763, the Earl of Abercorn began to erect a steam engine of very considerable power upon the Dudingston coalliery, extending its operation to the depth of 52 fathoms. This engine was rendered useless in 1790, when on the 20th of March the whole seams of coal were overflowed and choaked from the communication of the level with the higher grounds. Before this period another engine of greater power had been erected near the southern boundary of the parish to work the coal of Brunstane which lies beyond its limits. The cylinder was 66 inches in diameter, ten strokes are made in the minute and each stroke delivers 60 gallons of water. The shaft of this engine pit reaches to the depth of 60 fathoms, and intersects three seams of coal, the first 7 feet thick, the next 9, and the last 15. The other materials through which it descends, are chiefly very deep strata of a course red free-stone, some of clay, and nearest to the coal a kind of pyrites schist, which the workmen call bands of bleas. The porous quality of the free-stone rock, the number of cutters, and above all inauspicious communication of the fatal level, admit such an influx of water, as has all along rendered this undertaking singularly laborious and expensive, and at last reduced it to a languishing condition. The number of coalliers, bearers and other workmen employed at the coalliery before 1790, used to be about 270. The number is now greatly reduced.

When the Barony belonged to the family of Argyll, prior to 1745, the coal works were let to an Easter Duddingston tenant, Andrew Horn (1738). He eventually had to cease operations, due to the inability of the "water engine" to drain the mine sufficiently - that is why the Earl of Abercorn later installed a steam engine. In 1746, John Biggar, of Woolmet, took over the lease and, without advising the Earl of Abercorn, apparently, began to cut his level from Joppa to Woolmet, via Brunstane and Edmonston. The Earl of Abercorn, when he found out, took legal action, as he maintained that the level could bring so much water from the other lands that his estate could be flooded; he also maintained that Biggar was simply doing this to be able to drain the coal fields further inland, which he had also leased, in order to mine more lucrative areas. As Mr Bennet indicates, the lawyers probably ended up the richest of all. The level mentioned, runs from Joppa (the "Mount Pleasant" site) to Woolmet, via the junction of Brunstane Road and Milton Road East and cuts through the west end of what was Brunstane estate, just east of the new Asda site. The other steam engine was near the Brunstane Burn, which is on the border with Brunstane Estate. More detail will be given later on the coal workings, but suffice to say that a further 28 coal seams were subsequently discovered.

STONE

Quarries of grit and free-stone have been opened upon the sea-shore, and of whin, or basaltic rock, near the situation of the church. Detached strata of clay have been wrought, so pure and unmixed with heterogeneous matter, that crucibles, bricks, &c. formed of it are capable of resisting a very great degree of heat. In the bed of Dudingston Burn, there is a stratum of black coloured stone, soft, smooth, and unctuous in appearance, which, as it admits of an agreeable polish, might be converted to useful architectural purposes if wrought below the crop rock, and treated with skill.

In *Building Stones of Edinburgh*, by Bunyan, Fairhurst, Mackie and McMillan, it is stated that there were three quarries at Joppa; "one was situated at the shore where sandstone was obtained; a second quarry was opened about 1780 and a third more extensive working called "The Quarry" . . . the latter two quarries exposed good seams of fireclay and before the end of the 18th century a large brickmaking works was established near the shore (making up to 18,000 bricks per week)". On the 1801 map, the name, "Joppa", appears to refer to both field and the brickwork complex. The first of these quarries was between the main road and the sea, (between Joppa Road and Esplanade Terrace, just east of the present Post Office) and the third one, "Joppa Quarry", was further south but to the east of Brunstane Road, i.e. Quarry Park. The position of the second quarry is not clear, but the first one produced the stones for the building of Northfield Farm in 1761 - according to the Session Papers in the Signet Library; "The stones (sandstone) used in erecting this farm-stead (Northfield) were brought from Abercorn's quarries upon the sea-side near the fire engine" (i.e. coal engine, at what was later called "Mount Pleasant", for raising the water out of the pit).

It has to be assumed that the quarry near the church was that rock outcrop between the lochside and the wall, south west of Duddingston church and within Holyrood Park. The part of the Duddingston (Figgate) Burn referred to, is that deep ravine between Milton Road West and Southfield Farm House, near the mill site.

In about 1822, Robert Louis Stevenson's father, who was an engineer, was asked for an opinion as to whether Joppa Quarry was capable of producing good stone for the future building of farmsteads; or could stone at the salt pans or Brunstane Burn be used instead? The report suggested that Joppa Quarry would have to be considerably extended to extract enough good stone for building, as most of the ready stone was suitable only for drains or rubble masonry. It was reported that good stone was seen in the slopes of the salt pans and at Brunstane Burn and much was made of the increasing value of stone due to the rapid expansion of Portobello.

There were two quarries at Brunstane Burn - one was north east of Brunstane House, just north of the burn, and the other was just south of the burn on the line of the present railway (near the B&Q Superstore).

THATCH

The reeds (of Duddingston Loch), which grow at the west end of the lake in great luxuriance and plenty, and cover above five acres of ground, have been employed by weavers to supply their looms; and form, besides, a most valuable thatch for any species of houses; which by the strength and hardness of the fibres, resists the attacks of sparrows, mice and the common vermin which infest and deface straw roofs; and for the same reasons, will last incomparably longer than any common thatch; while a smaller quantity will suffice for the same work, and form a light, firm, and durable roof.

At the east end of the loch, cattle were allowed to drink water; tenants frequented the waterside, and once bleached their linen there, therefore reeds did not have much opportunity to grow at that end of the loch; this is also borne out by old photographs taken a hundred years later. If this thatch

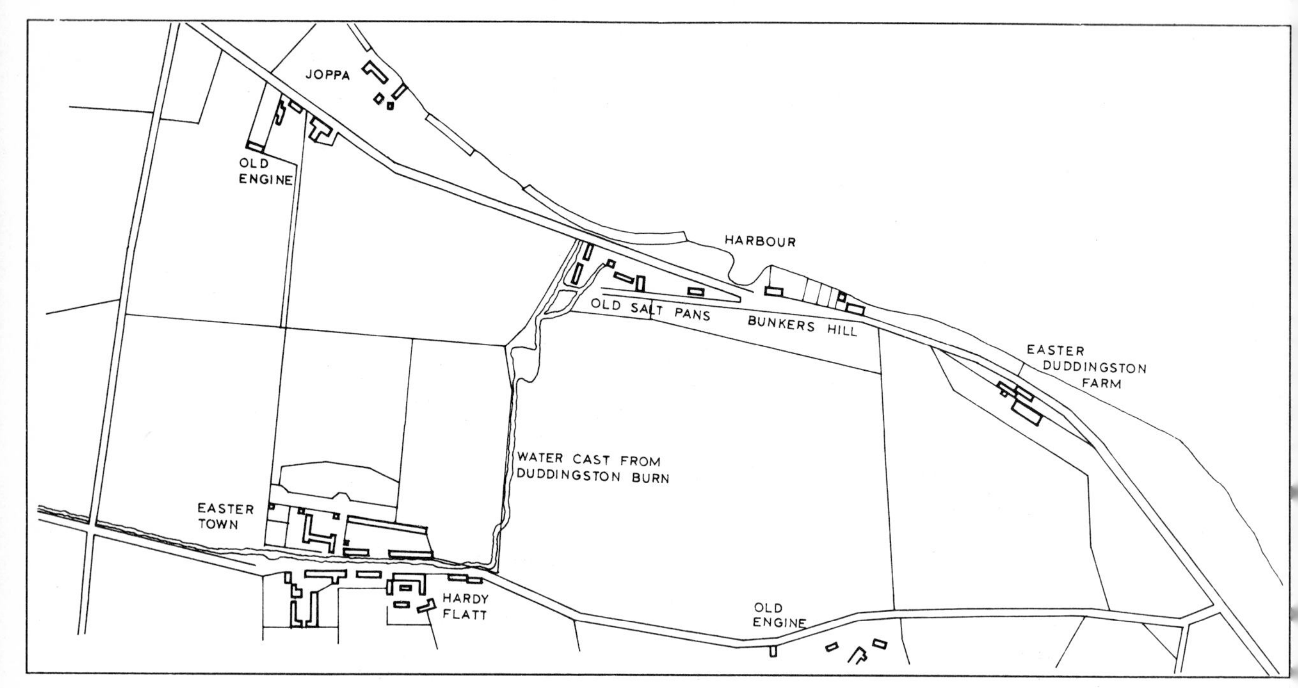

Plate 14 *Map of Joppa - 1801*

This sketch demonstrates that the name "Joppa" was first applied to a field which contained one of the early brick works. The name first appears on old maps around 1770. The harbour is mentioned in a later chapter, relative to a lease of the salt pans.

was deemed to be too hardy for sparrows and mice, one can imagine what the texture of the "Duddingston Hardings" must have been like.

According to Session Papers in the Signet Library, Sir Patrick Thomson, who owned Duddingston at the time, renounced, in about 1670, all right to Duddingston Loch in favour of Sir Robert Murray of Prestonfield. Duddingston people could "no longer use the loch for fishing, laying in of lint or to washing thereat", but they could water their horses and cattle.

As well as reeds, paddock pipes grew here. The reeds were sold to weavers in bunches and "by threaves" to those who wanted them for thatch.

PRESERVED TREES

At the mouth of Dudingston or the Figget burn, have also been observed, immersed in a deep stratum of clay, the trunks of large oak trees, which when cut or broken, have been found black as ebony to the heart.

This fits in with the other geological evidence of previous types of environment here.

FISHWIVES' CAUSEWAY

A causeway of considerable antiquity forms upon the north-east boundary of this path; and is conjectured by some, to be a remnant of one of those regular roads which the unfortunate Mary is said to have been so attentive to encourage, for the improvement of her rude kingdom. Several roads of this kind, converged to the palace of Holyrood house, and this which now bears the name of the Fish-wives' Causeway, once formed a part of the great post-road to London.

This road is thought to be of Roman origin and in *Edinburgh 1329–1929*, by Mr D. Robertson, Miss M. Wood and Mr M. Mears, it is mentioned that it did indeed come from Holyroodhouse, but went in a straight line to the east, instead of curving round towards Abbeyhill, as the road does today. The writer of that section of the book explains the rationale behind the position of our main roads to and from the city and points out that there are "certain irregularities . . . . the existing roads on the north and east of the city appear to have their origin . . . when there was as yet no settlement at Edinburgh. Thus Portobello High Street is in direct continuation of the road leading westward from the old bridge at Musselburgh and points not towards Edinburgh but to Leith and Cramond. In the same way Milton Road, which leaves the coast road at Magdalene Bridge, must originally have terminated in the very old village of Duddingston, while "Fishwives' Causeway", a traditional Roman paved way, branched off sharply at the west end of Portobello and apparently ended at Willowbrae Road south of Piershill. Willowbrae Road is part of another early route which left the southern Roman Road to Inveresk near Pathhead and passed through Restalrig towards Leith. Thus in going from Edinburgh to Musselburgh today, 1929, we have either to make a sharp turn at the west end of Portobello or to make use of the new by-pass via Willowbrae and Milton Roads (then recently widened) instead of proceeding by a direct line; in either case making use of roads which did not originally lead to the city. Connection with the old coast road to Musselburgh was probably first made either by a junction with Fishwives' Causeway, or by a direct continuation towards the west end of Portobello." This picture can now be qualified.

In General Roy's military map of Scotland, the Duddingston section of which appears to have been surveyed in the summer of 1753, (and a sketch from which is shown in Chapter 4), the Fishwives' Causeway is seen to run in a direct line from Jock's Lodge to what is now the point where Portobello High Street becomes Abercorn Terrace; *roughly where Hope Lane is.* This point, and the next, do not appear to be mentioned or indicated in other records. Re-scaled map comparisons, combined with statements made by witnesses in several Court of Session cases of the 18th century, allowed these points to emerge.

It seems that, just after this period, the bridge over the Figgate Burn was re-built in its present position and that "the Roman Road" was diverted to meet what was then *the brand new High Street.* This would have been part of the "improvements" referred to above, when the shape of the Village of Figgate, as known later, was formed and when the natural pasture land was put under the plough for the first time near the field later called Brickfield

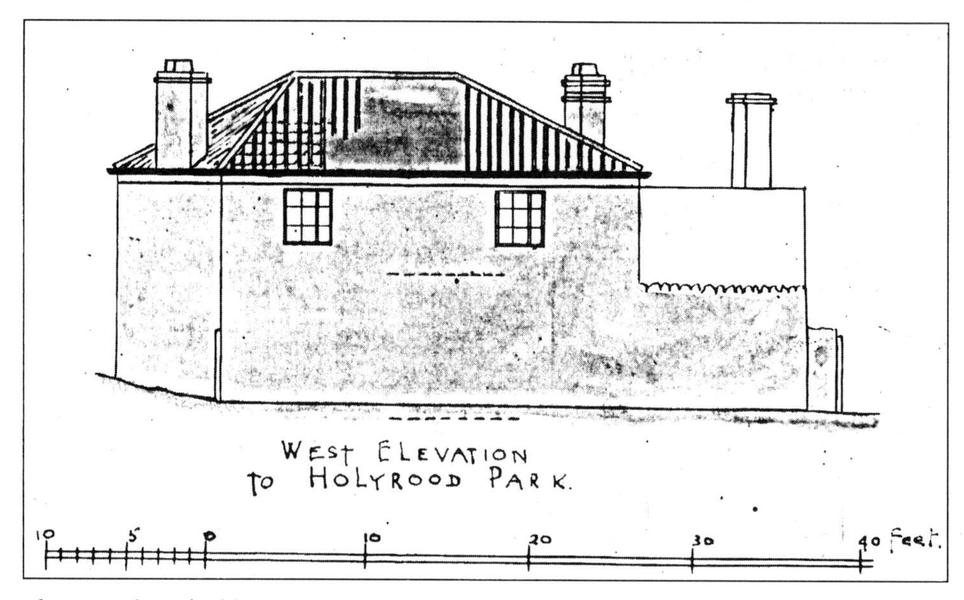

Plate 15 *Plan of Old House at Entrance to the Park at Duddingston* (Reproduced with permission of the Keeper of the Records of Scotland)

A sketch, showing the alteration to the house, in 1929. A member of the Gilchrist family (see Plate 21*) was born in this house in 1895.*

(and probably elsewhere). The line of the old road was altered and a new link within the Village of Figgate (whose eastern border was what became Hope Lane) - the later High Street - was formed.

Andrew Scott, farmer of Northfield, dug up the causey stones from this (Brickfield) section of the road and gave them to Wm. Jamieson to use in building the wall on the west side of his property. Other stones for this wall also came from a quarry at Cairntows, near Craigmillar. John Ainslie's Plan of the Village of Figgate, drawn in 1787, indicates that the Earl of Abercorn and Baron Mure exchanged pieces of land next to the Figgate Burn in order to achieve a straight border on the north west side of the Figgate lands (south of the Post Road).

In 1846, when the railway was being laid, the remaining section of the Fishwives' Causeway was moved to accommodate the tracks and what we see today is this revision - surviving only because the Railway Company had to retain an established right of way.

"WATER SPOUT"

On the 13th September, 1744, a water-spout broke upon the top of Arthur's Seat, and dividing its force, discharged one part upon the western side, and tore up a channel or chasm, which still remains a monument of its violence (the "Gutted Haddie")*; the other division took its direction towards the village of Dudingston, carried away the gable of its most westerly cottage, and flooded the loch over the adjacent meadows.*

Plate 16 *Duddingston Village from the Park*

This view depicts a quiet moment at about the turn of the century. The old house, shown in Plate 15, *has smoke coming from the chimney, confirming that it was a house. In 1853, however, it was the "Lochside Tavern", according to the Ordnance Survey map. The house is still of the original length in this view.*

Apart from the question of where the water actually came from (it has been reported that it was an extraordinary deluge, with hail stones five inches in diameter), there is an initial difficulty in appreciating how a cottage was so exposed; they were, as far as is now known, outwith the confines of the Park Dyke ("East Lodge" was built in the 1850s). If the gable was actually part of the Dyke, as is the case with an old, small building next to the Park entrance, then it is still difficult to imagine how a quantity of water, having poured down the hill from the direction of Dunsapie Loch (not yet made), could have, presumably, left the Dyke intact but not the part that happened to form the gable of the cottage. Or is it? That small building, which is now a garage and which was reduced in size in 1929, and which appears on the first Ordnance Survey map as Lochside Tavern, actually stands next to the lane (the old "road" to Edinburgh) and therefore any rush of water gushing down the hill next to the dyke would have hit the corner of any building there with extra force . . . .

POPULATION OF THE PARISH

The state of population has been for some time very variable. From the late interruptions and threatened decay of the coal works, a great body of the people employed in them have removed to scenes more favourable to the regular and durable exercise of their occupations. In one village alone, Joppa, which was solely inhabited by coalliers, above 30 houses have been deserted, or suffered to fall to ruin, within the space of the last 4 years. To counterbalance in part, this deficiency of population, several families of new manufacturers, &c. have in the same period settled in Portobello &c. A migratory colony, besides, of bathers, summer lodgers &c. upon the same coast, continue every year to increase their numbers. But these cannot with propriety be rated among the established inhabitants of the parish. In 1755, the number was 989. In the year 1794, the number of souls was found to be 910, of whom there were 428 males, and 482 females.

The name "Joppa" seems to have been introduced about 1770 as it is to be seen on Armstrong's map of 1773. It does not appear on any earlier maps. The name seems to have been introduced simply because of its biblical counterpart and a similar coastal position (similarly, Egypt Farm and the Jordan Burn appeared at Morningside at about the same time). On General Roy's map, surveyed in 1753, the only buildings on or near the coast between Magdalene Bridge and Leith were shown to be at the "Magdalen" pans (i.e. later called Joppa pans).

The population in the parish in 1703 numbered, according to the Kirk records, 689 (Wester Duddingston - 444; Easter Duddingston - 151; Magdalene pans (later "Joppa" pans) - 64; and Prestonfield - 30). The Wester Duddingston figure included 23 people from the Mill Town (Duddingston Mill area) and also residents of what Roy's surveyor called North and South Mains - i.e. what later became Duddingston Cottage (where Southfield Square is now) and Eastfield Farm (as already stated,this was north of where the new Asda Store is now). The present population level is around 40,000.

Mr Bennet's ministry was brought to a sudden and melancholy end on 15th April, 1805, on which day he was drowned in Duddingston Loch, his dead body being found in the water near to the manse.

CHAPTER 3
MADE TO MEASURE IN 1752

WHAT PRINCE CHARLIE SAW

In September, 1745, when a large contingent of men of the Highland Army, which had just taken over the city of Edinburgh, camped on the slope above Dunsapie bog and in the area which is now known as Duddingston Golf Course, Portobello had not yet been born. Portobello Hut or House was probably built about 1753. There appears to have been no buildings, apart from whatever structures the coal pit required at that time, on the coast between Magdalene salt pans and Leith.

The name, "Joppa" had not yet been "transplanted" from the Far East; the *then* mansion house of Duddingston was an older building on part of the site of the present Holyrood High School; Eastfield (farm) was in its original position - just north of the Brunstane Burn and south of Magdalene Gardens, but there was, between Magdalene salt pans and Maitland Bridge, a steading called Eastertoun Mains (or Easter Diddiston Farm), which appears to have given rise to the present name of "Eastfield".

The Highlanders, as they trooped from the King's Park and up the lane that then served as one of "the roads from Edinburgh", to the Sheep's Heid Inn and down the Causeway (simply called "The Street"), would have then, as now, turned right to the inn, the front section of which is now a restored building which is marked as having housed the Young Pretender for the night before the Battle of Prestonpans. Baird says that old residents had told him that the actual house was not the one so marked (the old Abercorn Inn), but that old house which stands round the corner from it, about 50 yards nearer to the hill.

(Incidentally, on a feuing plan of 1827, the names of the streets which comprise the present layout, were East, North, West and South Streets.)

The sight that would have met the Highlanders' eyes, however, upon looking toward what is now Holyrood High School, would have been very different from today's view. The village was much larger then and extended towards, and to the far end of, the school. In fact, it was about five acres larger in area than it is now. The public road to Niddrie was not via the "Mill Town" (Duddingston Mill), but via a road that, like the eastern end of the village itself, was "erased" when the 8th Earl of Abercorn laid out and enclosed his Policy during the 1760s. That road passed close to the "offices" of the (later) new Mansion House, possibly just touching the line of the present private road near the House, and proceeded to join what is now Duddingston Row (roughly where Bingham Way is now) after crossing the Braid Burn at its south-eastern corner.

There was a footroad, or path, from the north-east corner of the village which led up the hill and, generally following the line of the Park Dyke, curved round to what is now the Park entrance at Muschet's cairn and Meadowbank. The little lane that is still to be seen in that corner of the

Plate 17 *"Prince Charlie's House"*

The house is on the right and was the "Abercorn Inn" on the first Ordnance Survey map of 1853.

village, and which now leads to a private house (Sycamore Bank), gives access to a horse paddock (part of the minister's Glebe and let by the Church of Scotland). The village Police Station used to stand on the corner of this lane.

The then narrow, wavering road to the Mill Town followed the general line of the present Duddingston Road West after it left the village and no doubt the tartan-clad soldiers knew this road from their probable visits to the mills for food. The layout was then quite different from that of today's. There were several small mills on three main sites - the first was in the general area of the most recent mill complex, the second was near the old school and the third was further down the Figgate Burn; just up from where the footbridge crosses the burn today. All the mills were grain mills.

On a map, the main route through the Barony would appear to have been today's A1 - Willowbrae Road, Milton Road West, Milton Road and Milton Road East. As will be seen later, however, this was not the principal route, as far as the Barony was concerned. The "western part" of the road was then called the road from Leith to Niddrie, but the public road section did not pass through the Mill Town, but ran via Wester Duddingston; a lesser road went

Plate 18 *Wester Duddingston c 1870* (Reproduced with permission of Aberdeen University)

The village of Wester Duddingston around 1870. It looks familiar, but there are significant differences, e.g. the "Lochside Tavern" at the Park Gate is still of its original length; the early 20th-century villas which now guard the brae are not yet in existence; the "gerse yard" and "calf ward" are still awaiting their transformation by the Drs Neil; another building is yet to appear near the top of Old Church Lane; only crops separate the village from "Cauvin's Hospital" and cattle graze quietly in the Policy about 25 years before any golf ball was struck there. "Prince Charlie's house" ("Abercorn Tavern") is clearly seen.

along what was later called, until recently, Bingham Road, to the estate and village of Niddrie. The "eastern part" turned off to the east, as it does today, but with two major differences (four, if one considers the width and surface!). The prince and his men, on that September morning, would likely have used this road, which turned off the Niddrie road, not where the entrance to Duddingston Policy was later to be erected, but further north, on roughly the same line as Southfield Road West. This road joined the "Milton Road" line roughly where Duddingston Road South crosses Milton Road West. The modern line of "Milton Road" was not laid until about 1830.

The other difference in the road line was where this road from "Wester Duddingston to Musselburgh" went between Easter Duddingston and the coast road at Magdalene Bridge. After passing through Easter Duddingston, the Highlanders' route would have taken them further to the right, down nearer to the Brunstane Burn, before veering back toward the present line of Milton Road East, to prepare to drop down to the coast road.

Earlier mention was made of taking water from the Braid (Duddingston) Burn to supply the Easter Town; the salt pans and the water wheel, whose job it was to lift the water out of the Duddingston coal pit. The stone water cast which transported the water from the point where the road to Niddrie crossed the Braid Burn, passed under the road from the Mill Town to Niddrie (now Duddingston Row) and accompanied the road east as far as Easter Duddingston (east end), before turning north to run down to the pit area. The cast passed under the road near the top of Hope Lane (east end of Portobello Golf Course) and it is possible that this is the reason for the double bend in Milton Road West at this point. The reasoning behind the position of Easter Duddingston, whose area was as tightly packed then as its present grouping of more recent buildings suggests, is difficult to explain - possibly due to its proximity to Brunstane and its position on the hill.

Prince Charlie's army passed a crossroads more or less where the present one is at Brunstane Road; to the south lay the road to Brunstane as is the case today - there was a large dovecot on the right, just past the start of the actual track to Brunstane House, several feet above the present railway lines and adjacent to the car park of B and Q Superstore. To the north of the crossroads, there was, of course, no Morton Street or Brunstane Road and Joppa and its (upper) quarry had not yet appeared; so where did the road lead to? It travelled to where Morton Street now meets Joppa Road, i.e. it was at a greater angle than either Brunstane Road or Morton Street are today, and over what later became one of the biggest and most well-known quarries in the area. The road was made to bring the coals from the pit to Brunstane House, in the days when the Duchess of Lauderdale lived there, and was thus called the Black Road.

One of the most striking features about the scene at that time, apart from the complete absence of the metropolis of Portobello or, indeed, any of the sea of present-day buildings, was the extent and position of the "Fishwives' Causey", or Causeway. As already said, it stretched right across the Barony from Jock's Lodge (about the site of the Abercorn Inn at Piershill) close to the point where Hope Lane now meets Portobello High Street. At that point, it was on the present Joppa Road line, but whereas the old road went more

Plate 19 *Old cottages in Duddingston Village*

They used to stand in the lane which was once on a route to Edinburgh. An adjoining cottage can be seen in the old sketch in Plate 17. *The village police station was once housed here.*

or less straight toward Jock's Lodge, the line of the later High Street veered further north from about the bottom of what became Hope Lane (later to be on the eastern border of the village of Figgate/Portobello). The line of the present promenade was, interestingly, the only other main (foot) road (to Leith) here at that time; the High Street line was a later development and Portobello Hut actually stood to the north of the old road, whereas it was to the south of the "High Street". Roads and coal will be looked at again later.

THE BUILDINGS OF THE BARONY IN APRIL, 1752 (AND PROBABLY 1745)

The Earl of Abercorn, in order to decide how to plan improvements to his estate, commissioned a survey of the Barony and this was carried out by a "land measurer" by the name of Robert Johnstoun. The road layout of the area was almost the same as that described above and shown in the sketch of Roy's map, 1753. Johnstoun detailed all the buildings, as well as the fields, in both Easter and Wester Duddingston (but not the lands of Figgate or Magdalene pans). Here are the details of the buildings; the roads and fields will be documented in later chapters. This was carried out at a time when almost all the tenant farmers lived in the two "touns", but farmed all the fields together using the runrig system. The Wester town was still its "original" size, but plans were afoot to make significant changes, as indicated above.

Unfortunately, the plan which was drawn up with this data no longer exists, or at least cannot be traced, therefore the exact locations of almost all of the buildings cannot now be ascertained (good indications are given in some instances). The details are shown to give an idea of the architecture of, and a feel for, the period and the drawing (based upon Roy's map) puts the general groupings of the buildings into some perspective. Comments have been added where further information has been gained from various sources over a long period. Italic text denotes data from the report and the additional comments appear after each "block". The tenants shown are the principal ones; the remainder of the population were sub-tenants and servants.

WESTER DUDDINGSTON

(Height = Ground to outside eaves and most roofs, if not all, were thatched)

Number of Houses	*Tenants' names who occupy same*	*No. of Floors*	*Height ft*	*in*	*Length ft*	*in*	*Widness ft*	*in*
	The Kirk		*21*	*02*	*60*	*03*	*25*	*06*
	North Part of -do-		*18*	*00*	*17*	*07*	*19*	*00*
	House at the Church Yeard Gate	*1*	*6*	*10*	*14*	*09*	*10*	*06*
1	*Manse or Minister's house*	*3*	*24*	*00*	*40*	*00*	*21*	*01*
2	*An office house at the east end and another at the west end*	*1*	*4*	*11*	*16*	*00*	*21*	*01*
3	*Byre*	*1*	*6*	*10*	*17*	*01*	*14*	*01*
4	*Barn*	*1*	*6*	*06*	*27*	*03*	*16*	*02*

The house at the "Church Yeard Gate" was approximately where the road now runs on its way down to the Park Gate.

The present manse was built in 1805, replacing an older one, which was built only 55 years earlier, in 1750, for Revd William Bennet (the first Wm. Bennet). That manse stood next to where the Watchtower (now Session House) is; the old wall next to the road and adjoining the Session House, with its curious features, wall-joins, blocked-up windows and doorway, could be part of the old manse and office house complex.

In about 1744, a reporter, writing on behalf of the new minister, Mr Pollock, said of the even earlier manse, which is the one itemised in Johnstoun's Report:

> *The Manse standing with the back of it directly exposed to the west-winds was almost wholly uncovered on that side by the Storm in January 1739 and lay in that condition exposed to all weathers till about a year ago when it was patched up again. It is to be supposed that the timber of the Roof must be greatly*

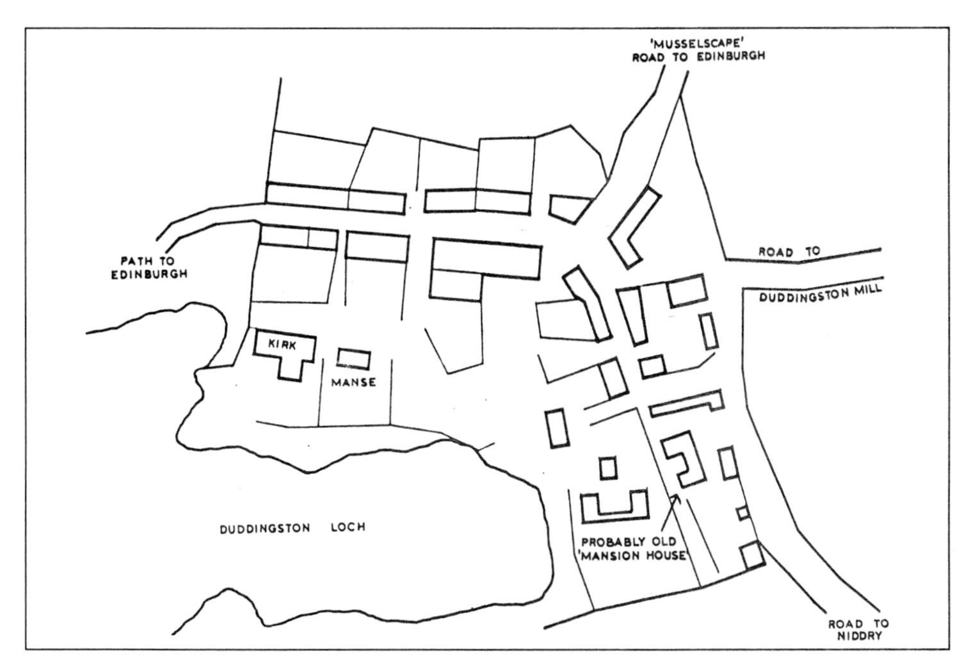

Plate 20 *Sketch of Wester Duddingston 1753*

This rough sketch, taken from Roy's map, gives a reasonable indication of the old layout of Wester Duddingston. Roy's is one of two maps which survive (the other is a Board of Ordnance map, but it is thought to be based on Roy's) to demonstrate what the "toun" looked like prior to the changes brought about by the Earl of Abercorn, in the period 1745–70. The details of Robert Johnstoun's Report, combined with this sketch plan, is the nearest it is possible to get to the "original" layout. The development of the village since then can be seen by comparing this layout with those in the 1801 and 1853 sketches.

dammaged and as the rain had free access to every room in the house the floor and even the walls must have suffered considerably. Mr Pollock lodges at present in a private Room in Duddingston till something be done to make it habitable, and is resolved to accept chearfully of whatever his Grace shall think fit to be done, without troubling his Grace with any visitation of Prebytery unless his Grace shall require it for the sake of the other Heritors. Mr Pollock in all this refers himself to the well-known Generosity of his Noble Patron in whose hands he is convinced he is entirely safe.

The writer of that passage obviously worked hard on behalf of Mr Pollock. It was to be another 6 years, in fact, before the house would be rebuilt. According to Baird, Mr Pollock accepted an appointment in the Professorship of Divinity in Marischal College, Aberdeen, and left Duddingston in 1745.

	The houses and yeards annually taken up by my Lords factor	*No. of Floors*	*Height ft in*	*Length ft in*	*Widness ft in*
1	*The Mansion House West Part*	*3*	*20 09*	*45 09*	*19 08*
	East Part	*3*	*20 09*	*58 09*	*19 09*
2	*Office Houses Belonging to -do-*	*1*	*6 04*	*48 09*	*18 09*
3	*Two Pavilions in Southmost Garden*	*2*	*13 07*	*21 01*	*21 01*
4	*A Row of Houses Sett: East End*	*1*	*6 06*	*80 03*	*18 09*
5	*To Washer Women: West End*	*1*	*6 06*	*107 03*	*18 09*

The factor at this time was Robert Brisbane, who actually lived at Brunstane. The mansion house, as already said, was in the area of Holyrood High School, on the part nearest to the Golf Course. It may well be that the Policy gardens, which served the present mansion house and which were demolished in 1962 to make way for the school, were, in whole or in part, the gardens of the mansion house mentioned above. There were two square cottages with ogee roofs built into the wall of the gardens, which were about the same dimensions as the two pavilions mentioned in the survey, except that the height to the eaves was lower – it may be that the height had been altered.

On an estate plan of 1827, those two houses are marked, but are not listed as "houses", whereas another two buildings which stood at the southern end of the gardens, were marked and listed as "houses".

The height (to the eaves) of most of the houses was very low, and the total length of many of the terraced houses is of interest.

	James Duncan's Houses				
1	*Dwelling House*	*2*	*16 00*	*41 06*	*21 02*
	East Part of -do-	*2*	*16 00*	*13 01*	*21 02*
2	*A Barn*	*2*	*11 08*	*60 00*	*22 03*
3	*Another Barn*	*1*	*8 01*	*65 00*	*21 04*
4	*Other Office Houses*	*1*	*6 03*	*78 00*	*17 00*
5	*-do-*	*1*	*6 03*	*45 00*	*20 00*
6	*-do-*	*1*	*6 03*	*17 00*	*20 00*
7	*-do-*	*1*	*7 00*	*22 02*	*21 00*
8	*-do-*	*1*	*6 00*	*27 03*	*11 06*
9	*Houses on the West Side of Street just opposite to the former*	*1*	*8 05*	*49 09*	*19 02*
10	*South side of ye street bounded on the west by Mr Lumsden*	*1*	*5 06*	*41 05*	*23 00*
11	*-do-*	*1*	*7 06*	*45 07*	*19 10*
12	*-do-*	*1*	*7 00*	*29 05*	*19 00*
	(Yeards at this part of the Town)				
13	*North side of the street bounded by Mr Clerk on the west*	*1*	*6 00*	*63 09*	*20 04*

James Duncan's property was near the present entrance to the Causeway, from Duddingston Road West. The "street" was what is now called the Causeway, although it extended further (south-east) towards the mansion house, as already indicated, before becoming the Road to Niddrie

Plate 21 *Ogee-roofed cottages in kitchen garden*

This photograph was taken in 1912 and the young girl is one of the Gilchrist family, members of which lived in these two houses, the west lodge house and the old house at the Park gate ("Lochside Tavern"). The buildings were demolished, along with the old walls, in 1960.

(as stated above, erased by the Earl of Abercorn). There was no Old Church Lane; it was not established until early in the 19th century (*c* 1805, from Duddingston Road West to the church), about 40 years before the Queen's Drive was built. It was to be a further 60 years, however, before the section of road between the church and St Leonard's was laid. The distance from James Duncan's yards to "Duddingston Mills" was 663 yards.

	Robert Johnston's Houses	*No. of Floors*	*Height ft*	*in*	*Length ft*	*in*	*Widness ft*	*in*
1	*Dwelling House*	*2*	*10*	*09*	*51*	*04*	*21*	*10*
2	*Barn*	*1*	*9*	*03*	*51*	*04*	*22*	*03*
3	*Other Office Houses*	*1*	*6*	*09*	*35*	*06*	*14*	*04*
4	*-do-*	*2*	*11*	*03*	*15*	*06*	*19*	*07*
5	*-do-*	*1*	*6*	*06*	*19*	*00*	*19*	*09*
6	*-do-*	*1*	*6*	*04*	*56*	*00*	*19*	*09*
7	*North East corner of the town*	*2*	*13*	*00*	*27*	*03*	*19*	*08*
8	*-do-*	*1*	*7*	*06*	*19*	*00*	*17*	*03*
9	*-do-*	*1*	*7*	*09*	*17*	*08*	*17*	*00*
10	*South side of the street*	*1*	*7*	*03*	*26*	*00*	*16*	*05*
11	*-do-*	*1*	*6*	*01*	*28*	*02*	*19*	*03*
12	*-do-*	*1*	*6*	*06*	*27*	*08*	*16*	*05*

This Robert Johnston was not the same person who carried out the survey, but they were in fact friends. The surveyor was recommended to Lord Abercorn by the factor, because he was a friend of Mr Johnston, and because another "land-measurer", a Mr Burrell, failed to do it. The survey took six weeks and cost £30 sterling.

	Walter Johnston's Houses	*No. of Floors*	*Height ft*	*in*	*Length ft*	*in*	*Widness ft*	*in*
1	*Dwelling house*	*2*	*13*	*07*	*40*	*09*	*21*	*04*
2	*Barn*	*1*	*8*	*00*	*41*	*01*	*21*	*01*
3	*?*	*1*	*6*	*03*	*18*	*06*	*23*	*00*
4	*At North End of dwelling house*	*1*	*8*	*00*	*12*	*11*	*21*	*04*
	John Horn's Houses							
1	*Dwelling House*	*2*	*14*	*04*	*54*	*02*	*22*	*03*
2	*Stable and Byre*	*1*	*5*	*11*	*74*	*00*	*19*	*10*
3	*?*	*1*	*6*	*04*	*38*	*00*	*20*	*09*
4	*A Barn*	*1*	*8*	*06*	*51*	*05*	*21*	*09*
5	*Another Barn*	*1*	*7*	*09*	*31*	*09*	*22*	*00*
6	*Houses just on the opposite side of the street*	*?*	*?*		*58*	*09*	*13*	*09*
7	*-do-*	*1*	*5*	*08*	*39*	*09*	*20*	*00*
8	*-do-*	*1*	*5*	*08*	*70*	*09*	*20*	*00*
	A yard belonging to these							
9	*At east end of ministers barn*	*1*	*6*	*06*	*49*	*03*	*21*	*05*
	Another yeard							
	Andrew Horn's Houses							
1	*Dwelling house with some others in same row*	*1*	*8*	*00*	*78*	*02*	*19*	*11*
2	*Barn*	*1*	*7*	*04*	*74*	*07*	*19*	*00*
3	*Other office houses*	*2*	*8*	*05*	*35*	*04*	*18*	*08*
4	*-do-*	*1*	*6*	*00*	*47*	*03*	*18*	*06*
5	*South side of the street*	*1*	*6*	*02*	*34*	*09*	*16*	*05*
6	*-do-*	*1*	*8*	*03*	*20*	*08*	*17*	*03*
	Yeard belonging to these							
	William Horn's Houses							
1	*At the east end of the street north side*	*1*	*6*	*00*	*31*	*04*	*17*	*04*
2	*-do-*	*1*	*6*	*00*	*32*	*07*	*18*	*05*
	A passage betwixt these and Will. Duncan's feu – 6ft 2ins wide							
3	*West side of Alex. Johnston's feu*	*1*	*6*	*09*	*37*	*06*	*19*	*06*
4	*?*	*1*	*6*	*09*	*32*	*06*	*19*	*11*
5	*?*	*1*	*7*	*03*	*23*	*02*	*17*	*05*
6	*At the east end of that row sett to the washer women*	*1*	*6*	*06*	*56*	*10*	*18*	*09*
7	*South side of the street*	*1*	*5*	*07*	*19*	*06*	*18*	*00*
8	*-do-*	*1*	*5*	*04*	*27*	*06*	*19*	*09*

	Andrew Scott's Houses	*No. of Floors*	*Height ft*	*in*	*Length ft*	*in*	*Widness ft*	*in*
1	*Dwelling house*	*2*	*15*	*01*	*34*	*07*	*21*	*01*
	East part of -do-	*2*	*15*	*01*	*19*	*02*	*21*	*01*
2	*North most barn*	*1*	*9*	*06*	*51*	*03*	*22*	*08*
	South most barn	*1*	*5*	*03*	*55*	*00*	*19*	*09*
3	*Other office houses*	*1*	*5*	*09*	*20*	*06*	*16*	*00*
4	*-do-*	*1*	*5*	*09*	*77*	*09*	*14*	*07*
5	*Two pavilions same dimensions*	*2*	*13*	*07*	*21*	*01*	*21*	*01*
6	*Houses at his park at the west end of the town*	*1*	*6*	*02*	*93*	*05*	*19*	*06*
7	*-do-*	*1*	*5*	*03*	*54*	*10*	*18*	*03*
8	*-do-*	*1*	*6*	*05*	*40*	*07*	*20*	*06*
	Another yeard at the west end of ye town							

Andrew Scott's property (No. 1 to 5) was near the mansion house, i.e. on part of the area now taken up by Holyrood High School but further from the loch than the mansion house. Andrew Scott, son of Peter (builder of Portobello Hut), built Northfield Farm in 1761 (paid for by Lord Abercorn) and was the first of the Scotts to live and farm there as tenants. His grandfather, David, was a farmer at Easter Duddingston, as was his father, Peter, and Andrew's son, another David, presented the two silver cups (made in Edinburgh in 1682) as mentioned in William Cruikshank's book, to the Kirk. This David's son, another David (1808–82), was the last of the Scotts to farm in Duddingston. The 1881 Census indicates that the family lived at Meadowfield Farm, of which farm they were also tenants; David, aged 73, Fanny, his wife, aged 60, David, his son, aged 26 (he died aged 33) and Margaret, aged 23. They farmed "520 acres in whole, 320 arable, employing 13 men, two boys and six women (winter) and 15 women (summer)". The 1891 Census shows Fanny alone with two servants at Meadowfield, bringing to an end the Scott's long farming association with Duddingston.

There is a sequel, however; a few years ago, a descendant of the earlier members of the Duddingston Scott family, visiting from Australia, was shown the site of Northfield Farm. He asked about the neighbouring farm, Meadowfield, and was told the name and connection. He then said he would name his farm, in Australia, "Northfield", and one he was about to gift to his son, "Meadowfield". Some things never really end.

There is another far-flung member of the Scott family, this time in New Zealand, who has a sampler, framed in 1812, done by a young girl, daughter of Andrew Scott and Isabella Dickson. On the back is written, "The aunt of this little girl carried a letter in the lining of her shoe to Bonnie Prince Charlie on the eve of the Battle of Prestonpans". The aunt was Eupheme Scott, Andrew's sister, who was born in 1734, which means she was only ten or eleven when she did this. It is possible that she would have taken the message from this house near the loch, to the Prince at the tavern in the Causeway.

One of Andrew Scott's sons, another Andrew, married Elizabeth Rennie, a cousin of the famous engineer, John Rennie.

	Henry Brown's Houses	*No. of Floors*	*Height ft in*	*Length ft in*	*Widness ft in*
1	*Dwelling house*	*1*	*6 06*	*27 09*	*17 03*
2	*Barn*	*1*	*7 00*	*47 03*	*17 08*
3	*?*	*1*	*6 05*	*48 10*	*17 00*
4	*North side of the street*	*1*	*7 03*	*31 01*	*16 08*
5	*-do-*	*1*	*6 01*	*24 00*	*15 03*

	Thos Brown's House				
1	*Exactly opposite to Robert Johnston's*	*1*	*8 06*	*56 09*	*22 05*

	Mrs Cooke's Houses				
1	*Dwelling House*	*2*	*10 08*	*67 00*	*21 10*
2	*Barn*	*1*	*9 10*	*51 04*	*22 09*
3	*Other office houses*	*1*	*6 09*	*22 03*	*19 09*
4	*-do-*	*1*	*6 00*	*47 04*	*14 04*

Mrs Cooke was the widow of one John Cooke, who built this house prior to 1689. In 1699, he petitioned, via a solicitor, the Earl of Dysart, who then owned the Barony, as the Duchess of Lauderdale had just died, for compensation for the building of the house: "By the allowance of her Grace The Dutches your Lords mother I did build a house upon my farm room which Coast me Expenses upward of three hundred pounds Scots. But her Grace demurred to allow the same to me on regaird she thought I had built ane better house then was needfull for me to have as a Tennent."

He was allowed two hundred pounds Scots (one pound Scots = one-twelfth of £1 stg).

	Richard Robertson's Houses				
1	*Dwelling house*	*2*	*11 09*	*37 10*	*18 05*
2	*Byre*	*1*	*6 09*	*18 05*	*18 05*
3	*Stable*	*1*	*6 09*	*26 10*	*19 07*
4	*Barn*	*1*	*7 07*	*36 00*	*20 06*

	Some houses belonging to Mrs Cook & Mr Robertson conjunctly				
1	*West side of the street opposite to Jas. Duncan*	*1*	*6 05*	*28 09*	*19 02*
	Yeards belonging to -do-				
2	*A Smithy at the turn of ye street South side*	*1*	*6 06*	*18 01*	*18 03*
3	*Opposite to Andrew Scott's and north side of Mr Dallas bounds*	*1*	*6 03*	*54 07*	*19 02*

This smithy (blacksmith's) would seem to have been on the corner of the Causeway, at or in the grounds of the present "Hillfoot", which was built sometime between 1853 and 1876.

	William Duncan's Feu	*No. of Floors*	*Height ft*	*in*	*Length ft*	*in*	*Widness ft*	*in*
1	*?*	*3*	*17*	*09*	*49*	*01*	*22*	*01*
2	*?*	*1*	*6*	*01*	*42*	*02*	*20*	*00*
3	*?*	*1*	*6*	*01*	*77*	*02*	*21*	*09*
	A passage betwixt 1 & 2 7ft 9in wide							

	Archibald Duncan's Property							
1	*South side of the street*	*3*	*13*	*09*	*42*	*01*	*22*	*05*
2	*-do-*	*1*	*8*	*01*	*30*	*06*	*17*	*06*
3	*-do-*	*1*	*5*	*07*	*38*	*09*	*17*	*11*
4	*-do-*	*2*	*11*	*09*	*55*	*07*	*20*	*07*
5	*-do-*	*1*	*5*	*06*	*21*	*08*	*17*	*03*
	There's an oven at ye south end of No. 5							
6	*Houses at the south end of his bounds*	*1*	*7*	*05*	*67*	*00*	*17*	*09*
7	*-do-*	*1*	*6*	*09*	*102*	*00*	*20*	*00*

It is not certain what purpose this "oven" served; bread or iron-work? At that time, William and Archibald Duncan's houses were the only ones in the whole Barony, apart from those of the minister and landowner, which had more than two floors.

	Alex. Johnston's Feu							
1	*North side of the street*	*1*	*6*	*03*	*51*	*05*	*16*	*10*
2	*-do-*	*2*	*8*	*10*	*20*	*00*	*16*	*00*
3	*-do-*	*1*	*5*	*00*	*22*	*00*	*16*	*00*
1	*-do-*	*1*	*4*	*00*	*13*	*07*	*13*	*00*

	William Pringle's Feu							
1	*North side of the street*	*2*	*11*	*11*	*22*	*04*	*18*	*07*
2	*-do-*	*1*	*7*	*00*	*48*	*06*	*16*	*08*
3	*-do-*	*1*	*4*	*00*	*15*	*06*	*15*	*06*

	James Brown's Feu							
1	*Near the west end of ye street North side–Distance twixt -do- and Mr Clerk's No. 3 = 10ft 6in*	*1*	*6*	*04*	*60*	*10*	*18*	*07*
2	*-do-*	*2*	*10*	*07*	*28*	*08*	*18*	*11*

A yeard, on the north side of the street opposite to Arch. Duncan's Feu, belongs to Robert Johnston and William Horn.

	Mr Lumsden's Houses	No. of Floors	Height ft	in	Length ft	in	Widness ft	in
	First of these opposite to the entery betwixt Jas. Duncan's and Robert Johnston's bounds							
1		2	11	02	61	01	19	00
2	-do-	1	6	06	48	10	18	05
3	-do-	1	7	10	35	09	18	06
	An entery betwixt No. 1 & Thomas Brown's house is 4ft 3in wide							
4		1	5	00	22	02	14	00
	North side of the street bounded on the east by Willm. Duncan's Feu – a space betwixt these 1ft 1in							
5		1	6	09	43	03	18	06
6	-do-	1	6	00	17	01	15	00
7	-do-	1	8	06	31	09	17	00
	South side of the street – a space betwixt this and Jas. Duncan's is 1ft 7in wide							
8		1	6	01	38	02	14	05
9	-do-	1	5	08	36	06	18	05

	Mr Clerk's Feu							
	On the east by Jas. Duncan No. 13 & on the west by James Brown's							
1	East end of his house	1	7	08	16	11	21	07
2	Middle of -do-	2	12	06	28	00	21	07
3	West end of -do-	1	7	08	16	11	21	07

	Mr Dallas's Houses							
	On the east by the mansion house court & part of Andrew Scott's bounds on the north							
1		2	13	00	36	04	18	10
2	-do-	1	6	06	34	04	18	10
3	-do-	1	6	06	25	11	17	04

Andrew Scott's and Mr Dallas's property, together with the mansion house, were on the east side of the village, as has been said, where the Holyrood High School site now stands.

Space Taken up:	Acres	Roods	Falls	Ells
Mansion house, court and gardens	1	2	5	17
Washer's Row yeards	0	1	13	21
Houses and yeards – feus	8	2	2	
Other houses and yeards (Lumsden's, Clerk's and Dallas's although part of the Barony, these were separate "tenements")	1	0	39	22

Space Taken up:	*Acres*	*Roods*	*Falls*	*Ells*
Kirk and Church yeard	*0*	*1*	*9*	*33*
Space taken up by the streets, vacancies and by ways	*2*	*3*	*25*	*14*
The whole space taken up by the town	*14*	*3*	*16*	*18*

By 1770, the area of the village had been reduced by about five acres, and the present shape of the Policy at that corner had been formed, with Duddingston Road West continuing round by the loch, on the line of an earlier estate road to Cairntows and part of the road from Prestonfield to the church. The rest of the village, however, was little changed, except that a road from the manse and church led down toward the east end of the loch (Old Church Lane was not yet in existence), past the position of the current manse (built 1805) to what is now Duddingston Road West. Historically, this was a kind of interim arrangement, bridging the old and new layouts. The road which was replaced by this interim arrangement was referred to (in old Sasine Registers) as the "Kirkway" and a road which connected it to the main street ("High Street", or "King's High Road") was known as the "Tiend Wynd".

This was, then, the scene that the warriors from the north left on their way to Prestonpans. The next house to the east was part of the Mill Town – "663 yards away" – after which was a farm, where Duddingston Cottage was later built (now Southfield Square), then called (on Roy's map of 1753) North Mains (later called Midfield and, still later, Duddingston Cottage); next, away to the right toward Brunstane Burn (near Asda's Supermarket), was South Mains (later called Eastfield Farm) and, beyond that, Easter Duddingston.

Difficult as it may be to imagine, the only buildings in the Barony of Duddingston (and the lands of Figgate) at that time were at Easter and Wester Duddingston, the Mill Town, the two farms just referred to, those at the Magdalene salt pans (later called Joppa salt pans), Duddingston coal pit water-wheel (just to the east of the pans) and at Jock's Lodge. Although Mr Bennet says in his *Statistical Account* of 1794 that it was thought that Portobello Hut was built around 1742, this does not seem likely, as the statements on General Roy's map, the data for which appears to have been collected in the summer of 1753, seem to be quite dogmatic in terms of buildings and walls – all walls and buildings are marked in red and include isolated buildings elsewhere in the vicinity of Edinburgh. Baird was correct when he said that "it appears to have been built a few years after the Rebellion of 1745". This will be returned to later.

In addition, there was a farm called Easter Town Mains, which was between Magdalene salt pans and Maitland Bridge – almost opposite the east end of Seaview Terrace, but a little further east. Here is how Robert Johnstoun (as well as the Highland Army) would have seen Easter Duddingston:

EASTER DUDDINGSTON

	The Factor's Houses	*No. of Floors*	*Height ft*	*in*	*Length ft*	*in*	*Widness ft*	*in*
1	*House next the street*	*2*	*15*	*00*	*51*	*11*	*19*	*04*
2		*2*	*12*	*02*	*45*	*09*	*20*	*07*
3	*A stable*	*2*	*10*	*01*	*16*	*09*	*15*	*06*

The factor at this time, Robert Brisbane, lived at Brunstane; these houses would have been let.

	Mrs Horn's Houses							
South side of town								
1	*Dwelling house west end*	*2*	*13*	*05*	*32*	*00*	*23*	*11*
	East end of -do-	*1*	*8*	*06*	*39*	*09*	*20*	*11*
2	*A stable at the end of -do-*	*1*	*8*	*06*	*24*	*06*	*20*	*11*
3	*A Malt Barn*	*1*	*8*	*02*	*24*	*03*	*21*	*06*
4	*A Kiln*	*2*	*16*	*03*	*22*	*03*	*17*	*09*
5	*A row of houses - East end*	*2*	*10*	*02*	*39*	*02*	*19*	*00*
	West end	*1*	*7*	*00*	*42*	*05*	*19*	*00*
6	*A corn barn*	*1*	*5*	*08*	*45*	*00*	*19*	*03*
7	*A row of old houses*	*1*	*7*	*03*	*117*	*00*	*19*	*09*
8	*Another barn*	*1*	*5*	*07*	*34*	*11*	*17*	*00*
9	*A hen house*	*2*	*4*	*05*	*12*	*11*	*10*	*08*
10	*Another barn*	*1*	*6*	*00*	*47*	*06*	*19*	*09*
11	*A stable*	*1*	*7*	*02*	*35*	*00*	*15*	*10*
12	*A byre*	*2*	*7*	*02*	*37*	*05*	*20*	*00*
13	*Brew houses*	*1*	*6*	*02*	*27*	*00*	*22*	*00*
North side of town								
14		*1*	*5*	*02*	*49*	*00*	*16*	*03*
15		*1*	*6*	*03*	*45*	*05*	*18*	*04*
16		*1*	*5*	*09*	*39*	*01*	*15*	*04*
17	*A row on the north side*	*1*	*5*	*02*	*141*	*04*	*18*	*04*
18		*1*	*6*	*04*	*46*	*00*	*16*	*06*
19		*1*	*6*	*03*	*29*	*06*	*20*	*02*
20		*1*	*6*	*00*	*20*	*09*	*18*	*06*

Brew-houses were common at this time and the ale was sometimes sold further afield than the place of brewing. It is interesting to note that the hen house was not much smaller than many houses. Mrs Horn was probably the widow of William Horn, who was the previous tenant of the salt and coal works. Other members of the Horn Family lived in Wester Duddingston.

	Peter Scott's Houses							
South side of street								
1	*Dwelling house West end*	*2*	*11*	*08*	*15*	*07*	*17*	*03*
	East end	*2*	*9*	*04*	*40*	*00*	*18*	*01*
	South part	*2*	*9*	*00*	*11*	*03*	*17*	*06*

	Peter Scott's Houses	*No. of Floors*	*Height ft*	*in*	*Length ft*	*in*	*Widness ft*	*in*
2	*Brew house West end*	2	7	10	25	00	18	01
	East end	1	5	05	31	00	15	04
A passage betwixt -do- and ye stable 3ft 11in								
3	*Stable*	1	5	05	31	00	15	04
4	*North end the malt barn*	2	12	08	48	09	18	03
	Corn barn the south end	1	5	09	41	03	18	03
A kiln at the south end of -do- whole diameter is equal to the widness of the barns & the height of its walls 12ft 3in.								
5		1	5	08	108	09	19	09
6		1	6	02	64	03	12	06
7		1	5	01	39	03	17	05
8		1	5	01	63	01	17	05
9		1	5	01	42	06	16	03
10		1	3	10	13	06	17	08
North side of the town								
11		1	5	07	13	11	16	09
12		1	6	00	19	11	18	06
13		1	4	06	17	00	14	00
14		1	6	03	23	05	18	09
15		1	6	00	65	10	16	09
16		1	5	03	23	03	16	05
17		1	4	10	36	00	16	01

This is the Peter Scott who built Portobello Hut, or House. He was also a partner with William Horn in the coal tenancy. He married a Horn and therefore the two families had more in common than simply being the main Easter Duddingston tenants. He was born in 1703 and died in 1764.

As already said, his father, David, was a farmer here and his son, Andrew, mentioned above, built Northfield Farm in 1761.

A descendant of the Scott family, Andrew Scott, writing to the Estate Factor in 1829 (on behalf of the Governors of Cauvin's Hospital), requested financial assistance to clear up the "abominable and filthy state of the streets" (of Wester Duddingston) by laying "drains to carry off the stagnant water, and what comes from the higher grounds and a new and proper formation of the whole road and footpath in the village".

	Mr Biggar's Houses							
1	*North side of the town*	1	5	00	19	09	30	07
2		1	5	09	21	06	19	00
3	*At the east end of the town*	1	5	01	35	07	19	00
	Little yeard at the east end of school house north side of ye town	1	6	03	49	09	17	11

Mr Biggar, of Woolmet, took the salt and coal lease in 1746 and he dug the three-mile long coal level from next to the sea at what is now Joppa to the lands of Woolmet. As mentioned by Mr Bennet, the venture created extremely lengthy and expensive lawsuits and finally allowed the water to build up to such an extent that the whole coals were ruined.

The position of the school was central on the south side of the street (now under the tarmac of Milton Road East) and Baird states that it had a projecting porch over the doorway supported on two stout wooden pillars.

This period was before the lands were enclosed, i.e. they were still in the open, runrig system and the prince's army would not have found it difficult to stray beyond the confines of the narrow, dusty road on their way to Prestonpans. Whether the "damage" was caused by any such wanderings, camping arrangements or totally by their demand for food during their stay, the Highlanders' presence certainly resulted in a reduction in the Duddingston tenants' rents (about a third arising in Easter Duddingston):

List of allowance given to the tenants of Duddingston for loss sustained by them during the late rebellion. (given in 1748)

	£	s	d
James Duncan (Wester Dudd)	2	7	4
John Horn -do-	8	4	4
Robert Johnston -do-	1	18	3
Andrew Horn -do-	7	13	1
Peter Scott (Easter Duddingston)	7	3	3
Mrs Horn -do-	6	11	9
Widow Livingston (5 Bolls Barley)	2	19	3
She lived at what later became known as Duddingston Cottage, which place was on the route from Wester to Easter Duddingston			
William Horn (Wester Dudd)	5	4	0
Henry Brown -do-	4	7	2
	48	8	5

THE LANDS OF FIGGATE

Robert Johnstoun describes the area on which Portobello later blossomed as follows:

The Figget extends to . . . . 67 acres 1 rood 20 falls
This field is much the same quality with the Eastertoun Common (very sandy soil mostly overgrown with whins)

The distance, by the later High Road, from the west side of Figgate to the east side, was about 720 yards only. The lands of Figgate, at the time of Johnstoun's Report of 1752, contained no buildings and were bought by Baron Mure of Caldwell in 1763 and, from 1765 to 1771, sections were sold (among others) to William Jamieson, who feued about 40 acres as follows (Sasine Register dates are shown, not the purchase dates):

1. 7th June, 1765 (SRO REF. RS.27.169.204) – ". . . three acres of the lands of Figgat bounded by the Friggat burn on the west, the high road on the south and by a line at thirty feet distance from the flood mark on the north . . . wall to be built on the east . . ." Reference was made to *"tyle and paper works"* to be built by Jamieson.

(These three acres were later incorporated into the next lot purchased)

2. 26th September, 1766 (SRO REF. RS.27.174.348) – ". . . whole ten acres of the lands of Friggatt bounded by the friggat burn on the west, the high road on the south, the sea on the north and a wall to be built at the expence of William Jamieson upon the east parts upon the lyne already stalked out by Robert Robertson land measurer at the sight of partys for the purpose, all lying within the parish of Duddingston with the right (if any be) to the shoar and beach . . . lying nearest to the friggat burn . . . must build a wall of stone and lyme or brick and lime four and one quarter feet high . . . " Mure and Jamieson shared the *"sea wreck and ware"*, with Mure being allocated the west-most half and Jamieson the east-most, but Mure retained the *"privilege of fishing and the right to the oysters, or muslescalps"*.

(This ground is the top section of the lands of Figgate on Ainslie's Plan of 1787)

3. 28th September, 1771 (SRO REF. RS.27.195.39) – ". . . eight acres of Figget . . . high road to the north, by a straight line drawn in continuation of William Jamieson's wall now built on the north side of the said high road till it reaches the land then possessed by James Sherriff on the east, by a straight line drawn along the lands purchased by the said James Sherriff till it reaches the March of the Earl of Abercorn's ground on the south, and by the lands belonging to the said Earl of Abercorn on the west parts agreeable to a plan of the said eight acres of land . . . "

(This section is the land nearest to the Figgate Burn on the south side of the High, or Post, Road. James Sherriff, who at the time was a tenant at Brunstane, built a farm steading near Magdalene Bridge in March 1764, between the sea and the High Road. The specifications are of interest (see Plate 22, p 64):

4. 28th September, 1771 (SRO REF. RS.27.195.44) – ". . . the easter park of the said lands of Figget – 7 acres 2 roods 10 falls . . . great road on the north, by the Duddingston Common loan on the east, by the lands of Easter Duddingston on the south and by the ditch or water run along same from the other lands of Figget on the west . . . "

(This area was the south eastern corner of Figgate, the area which later became known as Mount Lodge, where a brick work is shown on Ainslie's Plan of 1787. The Common loan later became Hope Lane, after a tenant farmer who possessed Duddingston Mains, which was built at the south end of the Loan in the 1820s. The ditch probably related to the "lech" mentioned in the 15th-century charter previously referred to.)

5. (same reference details) – ". . . and wester park of Figget with the sand hills on the north side extending to ten acres two roods as the same was possessed by Andrew Guild, further bounded by the sea on the north, by the middle of a ditch

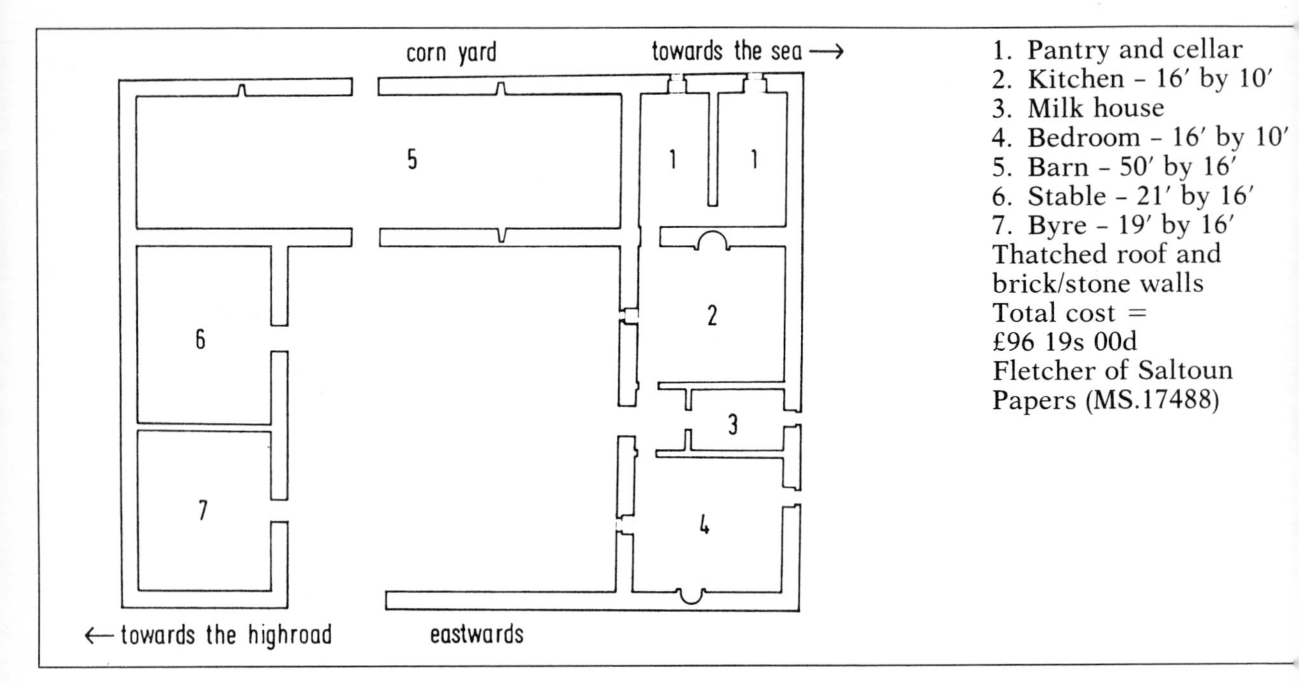

Plate 22 *James Sherriff's new farm steading, 1764*

separating the same from a park possessed by Andrew Guild on the east, by the high road on the south and by a brick wall . . . from the grounds formerly feued to Willam Jamieson on the west parts . . ."

(This ground is between the High Street and the sea, and between Bath Street and Figgate Street, approximately. The "sand hills" are represented on Ainslie's Plan of 1787 as "Bleaklaw".)

Neither Prince Charlie nor Robert Johnstoun could possibly have predicted that this wasteland was to become a thriving, popular community, with new industries and a rapidly increasing population, within a few years; or that rural Duddingston would survive more or less intact for almost 200 years, before being converted into bricks, stone and tarmacadam in an even shorter space of time than it took to "erase" completely the Figgate Whins.

CHAPTER 4
OLD WAYS - AND MEANS

EXPLORING THE OLD ROADS

The early roads in the Barony have been alluded to, but the subject requires further study. There were two basic types of roads - public roads and estate roads, used principally by the tenants; both types of roads fell into two categories - roads suitable for wheeled vehicles, and footroads.

Mention was made of an old court case of 1564. From this case, a rough sketch of the Wester Duddingston road and mill water systems of that time still survives (see Chapter 7). Mr H. M. Paton, in his *Book of The Old Edinburgh Club* (1940) article, "Notes on an Old Lawsuit about Duddingston Mills", grapples with the difficult task of making sense of the sketch which was drawn out of proportion and omitted the section of the road from Wester to Easter Duddingston (although it was mentioned in the process). As far as other roads were concerned, the following are shown; Niddrie to Restalrig (this supports the view mentioned in Chapter 2 that what became Willowbrae Road is a very early route); a road from this road to Wester Duddingston and one from a point further north on the Niddrie Road, up the hill, by the Park Dyke, toward the Park entrance at what became Muschet's Cairn. This road disappeared, probably due to the needs of later agricultural activities, but was, as will be seen later, replaced by one from Wester Duddingston to the same Park entrance. This process took place about 23 years after the commencement of the building of the Park Dyke and only three years after Mary, Queen of Scots, arrived at Leith.

Mr Paton concluded, quite reasonably, that the road to Wester Duddingston, from the Niddrie Road, was the present road from Duddingston crossroads to Duddingston Village and that the odd angle of it on the sketch was simply a part of the general mis-representation of scale evident on the drawing. This interpretation, however, must now be re-examined in the light of additional information.

BRIDGE UPKEEP BY THE CHURCH

Roads and bridges were kept in repair at the expense of the landowner, although, surprisingly, the Church seemed to pay for bridges in the early days, as two entries in Duddingston Kirk records indicate:

30th December 1688 - *Expence* (sic) *on ye bridge at the mill £30 8s 0d*
(This is where the Figgate Burn crosses Milton Road today)

12th October 1693 - *Expence* (sic) *on building ye Crannes Bridge £11 8s 6d*
(Where the road from Wester Duddingston to Niddrie crossed the burn, in today's Golf Course)

Plate 23 *Willowbrae Road 1909* (Reproduced with permission of Edinburgh University - Patrick Geddes Project)

This view of Willowbrae Road looks north west and the earlier Parson's Green Primary School (destroyed by fire in the 1950s) can be seen on the horizon, next to Whinny Hill. New Restalrig Church stands at Jock's Lodge and the field on the right of Willowbrae Road, towards Jock's Lodge, was called South Park. The field across the road from the camera was called Black Ridge and that which contains the tree stump, and which was being reduced to accommodate the widening of Willowbrae Road, was named Willow Head. It bordered the field called Waterpans at the right of the picture, where Northfield Crescent currently branches off Willowbrae Road. Northfield Terrace now stands on a line roughly where the tree stump is on the photograph. The wall across the road, and sloped bank above it, are still there as garden frontages, but are broken by the entry of Ulster Drive.

Then Road Trustee bodies were set up to administer repairs and alterations, with tenants being obliged to do the actual work ("Statute Labour"). For example, a John Shaw drove "channel", or gravel from the seashore at the Figgate to various parts of the roads in the Barony in 1744.

There is only one "proper" map, as far as is known, which shows anything of this older road system, and that is General Roy's military map of Scotland. Roy's military survey of Scotland was instigated by the Duke of Cumberland following the 1745 uprising; the whole of mainland Scotland was surveyed in the period 1747 to 1755 and the Duddingston area is thought

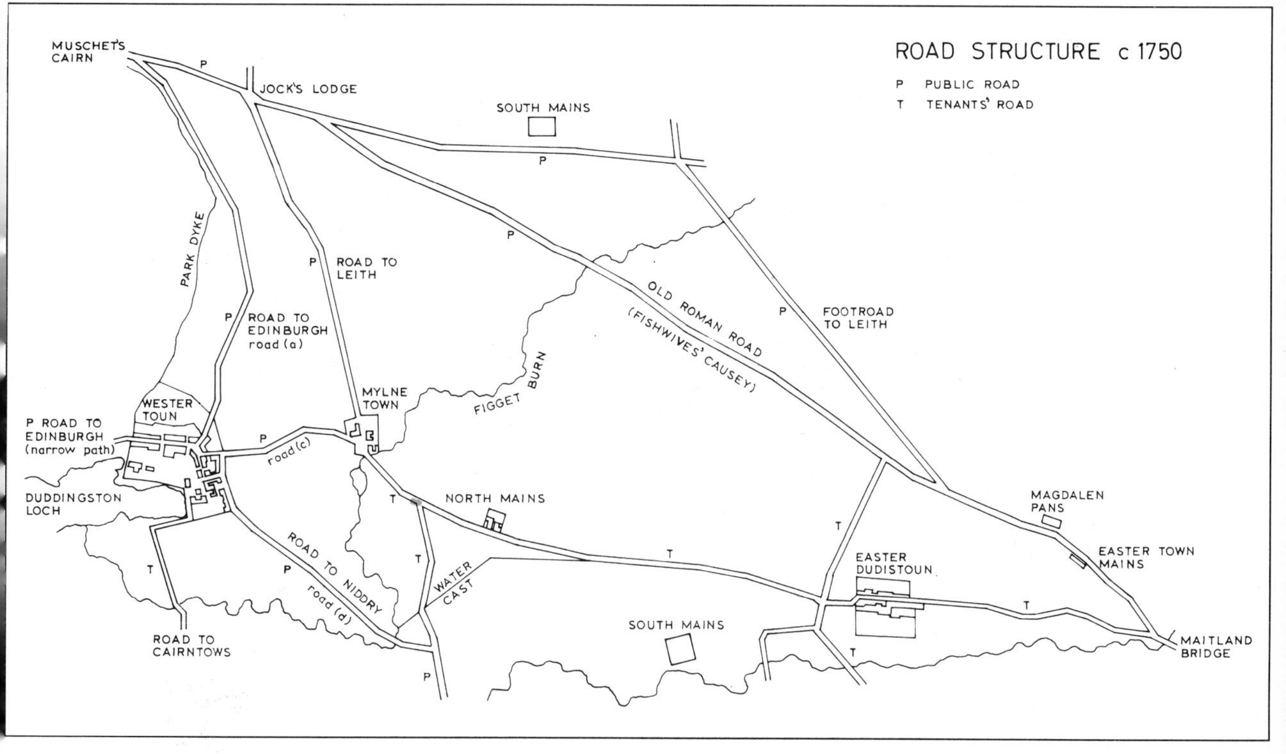

Plate 24 *Sketch of Roy's Map of the Barony - 1753* (By permission of the British Library)

All roads and no Portobello. This is the layout as it was when the Highland Army camped here in 1745 and when the fields were in runrig.

to have been surveyed in the summer season of 1753. There is also an undated Board of Ordnance map, which appears to have been copied from Roy's, and shows very little deviation from it, as far as Duddingston is concerned. A sketch of that part of Roy's map which pertains to the Barony of Duddingston is included here, but further elaboration is still required. Here are some quoted descriptions, from the Signet Library Session Papers, of these old roads, each one followed by further comments.

ROADS WITH "ENDS"

> *"There were four roads that passed through (Wester) Duddingston (which had ends) (a) by Wester Duddingston by the Parson's Knowe to Barbers Burn, (b) by Wester Duddingston by the Willowhead, (c) Wester Duddingston to Duddingston Mill and (d) Wester Duddingston on the south, very near to where Lord Abercorn's Offices are now built, to the Niddery Road, and all these landed on a public road."*

Plate 25 *Aerial view of Wester Duddingston – 7th December 1951* (Crown Copyright – RAF photograph)

The ancient cultivation terraces of Crow Hill are scratched in a timeless clarity. The Park Dyke marches up the hill, regardless of contour and, working from the lower right, the old fields of Sandilands, Backside Park, the Glebe lands and, following the Dyke, The Bank and Sowstripe can still be seen. At the base of the triangular, wooded area, which was once called the Haining, can be seen the reservoir (the stones of the walls are still to be seen today) which stored water on its way from the "Dunsapie Bog" area to Duddingston House. The army huts, which housed soldiers and, after the war, civilians, stand across the road from the beginnings of Meadowfield Gardens and Drive. The west lodge of the Policy can be seen opposite Meadowfield Drive, nestling between the Nissen huts. One can imagine the roads (a) and (b) leaving the village, on the north east side, and crossing the hill towards the Meadowbank entrance to Holyrood Park and Willowbrae respectively.

Plate 26 *The road through Easter Duddingston, looking west*

These were some of the houses in which colliers lived and the building which can just be seen on the left is part of what is now the King's Manor Hotel. The road is now known as Milton Road (after Lord Milton, who owned Brunstane) and if the cottages were still there, they would be well into the road.

These are four *public* roads. Referring to the map:

Road (a) leaving Wester Duddingston on its way to where the Meadowbank entrance to the Park now is, via the "Parson's Knowe" (later called Parson's Green) - there was a watering stone at this corner, just east of Muschet's Cairn, and beside the Barber's Burn (which took the water from the site of the present St Margaret's Loch). The road then forked; straight on to Edinburgh or right to Musselburgh - along to Jock's Lodge, before turning to the right (at approximately where the Abercorn Inn is now) along the old Roman road route, the Fishwives' Causeway, and directly across country to Magdalene pans and then Musselburgh. It was also the main public road from Musselburgh to Wester Duddingston, before the new Post Road to Musselburgh was made; which event also facilitated the growth of the future village of Figgate. At this time, however, the road to the sands (Portobello Road) was of very poor quality and the road along the sands (more or less on the line of today's promenade) was a footroad. As has been said, what became the High Street was not yet in existence, although it is thought that the eastern end of the old Fishwives' Causeway road line later became Abercorn Terrace, near Hope Lane (eastern border of the lands of Figgate).

Road (b) is not shown on Roy's map, but from various descriptions, it ran from Wester Duddingston (across part of what became Meadowfield Farm) to the Willowhead and on to Leith, i.e. it joined what is now Willowbrae Road, somewhere between the bottom of the present Paisley Drive and the top of the hill on Willowbrae Road. This was, apparently, the public road from Leith to Wester Duddingston; the section from this junction to the Mill Town was not yet a public road. The northward curve in the road between Wester Duddingston and the Mill Town could well be where this old road joined the road to Wester Duddingston, and could explain the bend in the present road, near the junction of Meadowfield Gardens and Duddingston Road West.

Road (c) is on Roy's map and runs from Wester Duddingston to the Mills (today's Duddingston Road West). The section of this road, from the old junction just mentioned (at Meadowfield Gardens), to the Mill Town, and from there to the old Willowhead junction also just mentioned (probably half way up Willowbrae Road), were "upgraded" from non-public roads to public ones in the early 1750s, at which time road (a) and the "missing" section of road (b) were "shut up". Lord Abercorn's "Offices", together with his new Duddingston mansion house, were built in the period 1763–8. It is of interest to note that Craig's plan for the New Town was submitted and adopted in this period.

Road (d) is seen leaving the south-east corner of Wester Duddingston, crossing what is now Duddingston Golf Course, and Duddingston Burn (by the Crannes Bridge), on its way to Niddrie. It is believed that this is the road shown on the 16th-century sketch, which also puts a new light on the position of the old Figgate Burn ("callit the Figget fra it cum fra Craigmillar") and mill lades, which subject will be returned to later. The section of the Niddrie road, from the junction east of the burn, north to the Mill Town, was then (1787) a non-public road, and was possibly not suitable for carts.

This meant that the public road from Niddrie to Edinburgh was via Wester Duddingston and Muschet's Cairn (there was only a single-file rocky path from Wester Duddingston through the Park, via Samson's Ribs, to Edinburgh), and that, to go from Wester Duddingston to Leith, one had the choice of using road (b) (by-passing the Mill Town, via "Willowhead") to Jock's Lodge, or taking road (a), over the Parson's Knowe, to Muschet's Cairn and the Watering Stone, then turning right to Jock's Lodge. The decision would have depended, probably, upon the weather, and the state of the road, for it is assumed that they were both cart roads.

The road from Wester Duddingston to the Maitland Bridge, via Easter Duddingston, was not at that time a public road and, as has been said earlier, deviated from the line of the present (West and East) Milton Road at both ends. It was used for the tenants going about their daily business, including carrying coals to Wester Duddingston, and for going to Duddingston Kirk.

The road from the crossroads, just west of Easter Duddingston, to the Fishwives' Causeway, starts at the southern end of the present Brunstane Road, but ends at where Morton Street now meets Joppa Road. This road line appears to have been altered, in about 1760, to create the present "Brunstane Road" and to make way for the new "Fire Engine", mentioned by Mr Bennet in his *Statistical Account* of 1794. This engine was built on the south side of the Musselburgh Road where Morton Street, which was a much later development, now meets Joppa Road. It is interesting to note, however, that the access "road" into the main Joppa Quarry (Quarry Park), created in the first half of the 19th century, took the same line, from the Morton Street/Joppa Road junction towards the crossroads formed by Brunstane Road and Milton Road East.

ROBERT JOHNSTOUN'S VIEWS ON THE ROADS

Robert Johnstoun's report (1752) supports the Signet Library quotation almost completely:

> *The road next the Kings Park leads from Duddingston to Edinburgh* (road (a)); *the one next to that from Duddingston to Leith* (road (b)), was not shown, as the survey, relative to this part of Roy's map was carried out, it is believed, in the summer of 1753, by which time the road had been "shut up"*; that one which passes by the Milne Town & by the east end of the Inclosers is a portion of the Road 'twixt Leith and Dalkeith.* (roads (c) & (d)). "He goes on to say, "*The rest of the roads are principally for the use of the Tennants except that one which passes thro' the Easter Town Common* (Figgate Whins area i.e. the lands of Figgate) *which is a portion of the Road 'twixt Edinburgh & Musselburgh all that part of which west from the Road going in to the Sands* (Kings Road) *was made March 1752.*

The road going into the Sands was at the eastern end of today's King's Road (at today's promenade), and the part to the west was the road from Jock's Lodge to that point. The reference to this road being "made" in March 1752, means, not made from "scratch", but made into a proper main road, as this road, which previously served mainly as an access road to the sands for building materials and so on was now to become part of the Post Road to London, thereby replacing the Fishwives' Causeway. The part of the Post Road to the east of "King's Road" was, in March 1752, not yet on the line of today's High Street, as already mentioned.

The "Inclosers" referred to were part of the walled areas on the eastern side of Wester Duddingston (site of the present Holyrood High School). It may be that the walled kitchen garden, or Policy garden, demolished *c* 1960, was part of this complex.

The actual detail of the layout of Wester and Easter Duddingston is not too clear on the sketch, as it was taken from a fairly small photograph of Roy's map, on which grouped detail (buildings) is quite small. Buildings in the sketch are about the right size, except some of those outwith the two "touns"; they are shown simply to demonstrate the position of those places.

The road to Cairntows (and Craigmillar) was a small road, but suitable for carts, at least in good weather. The water-cast, previously mentioned, carried water from the Duddingston Burn to supply Easter Duddingston, the salt pans and a "water engine" (water wheel), mentioned by Baird, which was of the "chains and buckets" type, and which drained the coal pit by lifting the water up the "engine pit" in its buckets.

TENANTS' VIEWS ON THE ROADS

Michael Watson, of Cairntows (between Wester Duddingston and Craigmillar) – "marching" with Lord Abercorn's Pleasure Ground – *"As far back as before the Rebellion of 1745 I was in use of driving a cart from Broughton, eastwards to Pinkie and Tranent. At that time the present (1787) Musselburgh Road* (i.e. Portobello Road/High Street/Joppa Road) *was not made and the part of those lands lying nearest to the present road* (line of future High Street/Joppa Road) *was all in whins and sheep-gang for a good way up."* He would have travelled along the old Fishwives' Causeway, before the Portobello Road/High Street/Joppa Road line was established.

George Kinnaird, of Niddrie Mill, in 1787 – *"I remember in my youth,* (he was 64) *of brewers' carts from Edinburgh coming for clay at Adams Laws* (field later called Brickfield) *for clay* (shows that clay was taken from here before Wm. Jamieson's time at Figgate). *There were also roads called the Sandilands road, and Musselscape road, which came off by the watering stone, or Barbers Burn, that is, the Musselscape road which passed along the hill side to Wester Duddingston, and the Sandilands road, came off at the Willowhead, or height, to the west of the road from Jock's Lodge to Duddingston Mill, and so on to Wester Duddingston."*

The Musselscape road was road (a) above, and the Sandilands road was road (b) above. The name Musselscape, or Musselscaup, means mussel-bed and presumably reflects the broken, rocky surface of the road on its way over the hill, near the Park Dyke; or even evidence of actual mussels, as this area is a "raised beach". Alternatively, it may refer to another "Fishwives'" route to Edinburgh, via Easter and Wester Duddingston. Road (a) ". . . goes over a steep Craggy Rock, which rises no less than 130 foot perpendicular height. This road is only used for foot and horse passengers, empty carts, and for giving access to dung your Lordship's ground which lye to the westward of the Road . . .", according to a report dated 1754 (Abercorn Papers, D 623/A/49/30).

Sandilands, as already said, was the name of a field west of Duddingston Crossroads and this fact also fits in with the supposed route of road (b).

In his *Cromwell's Scotch Campaigns*, W. S. Douglas refers to Leslie's (Scottish) Troups, "... wound round the gentle eastern slope under Dunsapie Craig, wheeled through Duddingston, and, skirting along under the very shadow of Samson's Ribs, debouched through Prestonfield and Cameron" (1650). It is likely that they rode along road (a) on their way to Duddingston, before going down the "lane" into the Park. The English army was positioned near Niddrie.

Alex Galbreath, carter, 40, of Brunstane – *"... a long time ago, and before the road was laid betwixt the two Duddingstons."* This was said in 1787, and refers to the alteration of the road from Wester Duddingston, via the Mill Town, to Easter Duddingston, from a footroad to a properly-constructed road capable of taking wheeled vehicles.

The following quotations relate to what was a farm road – for the tenants to use for access to crops and to dung their runrig fields and so on – but there was a dispute between the Earl of Abercorn and William Jamieson and others of the new Village of Figgate, concerning the right of way on this road, which throws much light on the topography of the area for several decades prior to the time of the legal case which occurred in 1787. The quotations given above were taken from the Session Papers relative to that case and John Ainslie's plan, created for the case and part of which Baird included in his book, is shown in Chapter 1.

THE FIGGATE AND THE CAUSEWAY

Easter and Wester Duddingston - in 1673, erected into a Barony by Charter by Charles II in favour of John Duke of Lauderdale and his Duchess (whose daughter became the Duchess of Argyll). In 1745, the Earl of Abercorn purchased from Archibald, Duke of Argyll, 'ground in good cultivation and very little enclosed'. In 1764 or 1765, Mr Baron Muir purchased from Lord Milton the lands of Figget, the whole of which amounted to about 60 acres of rugged, waste, bent hills and sand, interspersed with a little green pasture upon which no improvements had ever been attempted.

Baron Muir set about improving the lands of Figget, which he feued out between 1767 and 1772. Mr Jamieson, by different feu contracts with Baron Muir, acquired right to about three-quarters of the whole lands of Figget, part of which Mr Jamieson sub-feued to Mr Cunninghame and others (Mr Cunninghame built 'the Tower'). *Mr Jamieson retained land and built brick and tile work and other manufacturies and houses for himself, servants and labourers. Before this* (and 1765) *there were no houses on the lands of Figget, except one small cottage, called Porto-Bello, which had been erected as an accommodation for his shepherd, by one of the tenants of Duddingston, who had the pasturage of the lands of Figget.*

Mr Jamieson bought Figgate lands from Mure in the period from 1765 to 1771 (see Appendix III for details) according to the account books of Baron Mure and the Sasine Register, and Baron Mure eventually wrote to Jamieson pointing out that he (Jamieson) must erect more buildings in accordance with his feu charter; this would presumably attract more feu duty income for the benefit of Mure, the Superior of the lands.

Between the time of Roy's map, (1753) and this court case in 1787, much had happened to the layout of the lands. Abercorn had enclosed all his lands, the runrig farming system had been entirely replaced, the Pleasure Grounds of Duddingston Policy had absorbed the eastern section of Wester Duddingston, as well as old field structures, and some of the old roads had disappeared. As far as the Fishwives' Causeway was concerned, it had been dissected at both ends. The western end, to Jock's Lodge, was cut off when, in 1756-7, Mr Ronald Crawford, of Restalrig, enclosed his lands, which included at that time a section at Jock's Lodge. The Fishwives' Causeway was then diverted northwards to meet the Portobello Road, as it does today.

The eastern end disappeared, or was improved, about 1753, when the Musselburgh Road was made, including the forming of the new line of what became Portobello High Street. There was, however, a kind of interim stage, as can be gleaned from the following. The dispute arose because Jamieson and Cunningham insisted that a road, from Fishwives' Causeway to the

Duddingston Mill Road (Willowbrae Road) via Northfield Farm, could be used by them (see Ainslie's plan in Chapter 1).

Before the Post Road (Musselburgh Road) was made out there was an old road, known by the name of Fishwives' Causeway, which led from near to where the Fishwives' Bridge upon the Post Road presently is, towards Edinburgh.

It seems that this adjustment to the Fishwives' Causeway (which created the present position of its eastern end) was carried out prior to the main Post Road being complete, i.e. the Causeway was diverted to this point from its line from Jock's Lodge to Magdalene pans. The old section from here (through the village of Figgate, to roughly Hope Lane) was removed, and a new line of road was formed, to become the (later) High Street and to run to the Figgate Bridge and to the new "Seafield Road/Kings Road" junction, before turning left to Edinburgh. Prior to 1753, the eastern end of "Kings Road" (i.e. at the "sands"), joined the only direct route from Musselburgh to Leith, which was on the line of today's promenade.

THE BUILDING OF NORTHFIELD FARM

John Allen, *assisted in driving the stones* (for Northfield Farm - from "Lower Joppa" Quarry) *through the whins by the house called Porto-Bello, cross a ford in the burn a good way above the place where the old Fishwives' Bridge stood and across a ditch and up to the road which led to Northfield, on a sort of temporary road.*

George Luttit; *the direction in which the stones were driven was by the south side of Porto-Bello, through a ford a good way above the old Fishwives' Bridge, and straight up through the farm of Northfield till they came to a ditch which ran north/south, which was not possible by a cart till Mr Scott* (Andrew) *rendered it so. He had heard that the ditch was made by John Horn to drain the Fishwives' Causeway. If he had been to pass from where the Figget Bridge now is, to Niddery, he would have been obliged to go by Easter Duddingston, or by Lord Milton's dove-cot and Hunter's Hall.*

The old Fishwives' Bridge (carrying the Fishwives' Causeway) could well have been about where the present Abercorn Bridge crosses the Figgate Burn (Baileyfield Road); The point being made in the last sentence is that there was no road here (from Willowbrae to Fishwives' Causeway) since "beyond the memory of man", for which case the "incomers" were arguing. Abercorn's case was that (a) there was no road through to the Fishwives' Causeway and (b) there were no people who could have used it "since time immemorial"! One would, they said, have had to have gone (in 1787) through the Village of Figgate, up the Black Road (by now the new "Brunstane Road") and either along towards Wester Duddingston to what is now Duddingston Row (although the line of the road to Niddrie was then in the back gardens of the houses now on the Golf Course side of Duddingston Row - formerly Bingham Road), or down "Brunstane Road South" toward Brunstane House, past the dovecot, which was on the right, then to the right again towards what is now Newcraighall. Hunter's Hall was a small farm steading and Hunter would have been the tenant.

Plate 27 *Aerial view of Northfield – 19th May 1962* (Reproduced with permission of Hunting Aerofilms)

From Willowbrae to the sea, with Mountcastle Drive elbowing its way through the lands of Northfield. The housing scheme, built c *1920, is on the lower left, with the old farm in its very last days. The "pre-fabs" are still in neat formation, Gordon Smith's "Right Wing" is quite new, as is Duddingston Primary School. The "new" Portobello High School is being laid out in the former playing fields, the Mountcastle housing scheme has only just progressed from the 1930s bungalows, the new Telferton Industrial Estate area has not yet changed from a coal deposit area. Railway activities have yet to undergo change and these two hallmarks of "modern" Portobello – the Power Station and Open Air Pool – are still dominant.*

PORTOBELLO HUT OR HOUSE

Peter Scott, brother of Andrew, mentioned a small field called Eastlees, which was enclosed and a small, enclosed field on the burn - enclosed in the Duchess's time, before continuing: *Two foot-roads formerly passed; one of them to the Fishwives' Bridge and the other led by the south side of Porto-Bello (house) to the Figget Burn ford and from that passed up the north side of the ditch that took the water off the Fishwives' Causeway. After passing Lord Abercorn's grounds* (he was referring to travelling from the east side of the village of Figgate) *these two roads ran through the grounds now belonging to Mr Jamieson; one on the one side and the other on the other side of the place where Mr Jamieson's house now stands - one very close to the house. The Fishwives' Causeway was regarded as a footroad only.* These two roads were an old section of the Fishwives' Causeway (south side of Portobello House) and a recently formed footroad which was to form the line of the future High Street (to the Fishwives' Bridge). (In 1756, Portobello House - the only house - stood 1,400 feet east of the Figgate Burn and 725 feet from the eastern border of Figgate, at Hope Lane.)

Before the great Musselburgh road was made (in 1752–3) *travellers from the east to Edinburgh, when prevented from going the ordinary track by the tide, were in use of passing by another road which entered Mr Jamieson's south east corner, went westwards, then crossed the burn before turning north to where the Fishwives' Causeway joined the Musselburgh road (which junction was created in 1753).*

Again, this is the old eastern section of the Fishwives' Causeway coming from the east, and again, reference is made to a turn north to join the Musselburgh road; this was the interim road system referred to above. This interim link northwards, and the footroad which later became the High Street, are not shown on Roy's map, because it is thought that this section of the map was surveyed in the summer of 1753 - after the road from Jock's Lodge to the sea was "made", but just before the new road (later High Street) was formed into part of the London Road.

The Fishwives' Causeway was described as a break-neck road and it was acknowledged that the east end of (what was left of) *it was now part of Jamieson's garden and pleasure ground. In 1753, when the Musselburgh Road was made, the new Figget Bridge was built* (where the present one is on the High Street), *a "good many yards below" where the old bridge stood. The old one, which was only for foot-passengers, was then taken down. Andrew Scott, of Northfield, took up the stones of the Causeway* (in the field called Adam's Law) *and gave them to Jamieson.*

Adam's Law was previously used for sheep pasture and the commonty was held by Peter Scott, John Horn, Robert Johnston and Walter Johnston; after 1745, the commonty was divided but the whole of Adam's Law became part of Northfield Farm. Formerly, the whole north side, and part of the south, of it was in whins until 1761, when Andrew Scott, Peter's son, burned the whins and improved the land.

William Scott (brewer), *Andrew's brother, who went to Leith in 1748, said that his carts brought ale to the lands of Figget and that Porto-Bello and stable were built by his father as a shepherd's house and a place for retailing ale.*

The names of all these tenants should be becoming rather familiar by now. There are no apparent clues in the Session Papers as to the identity of one George Hamilton, who lived in Portobello House by 8th October, 1753 (there was an advertisement in the *Edinburgh Evening Courant* on that date referring to a horse race; " . . . articles of the race to be seen at George Hamilton's at Porto Bello . . . "); or who actually applied the name to that house. From the dates and information now available, however, it is probable that George Hamilton - who is traditionally supposed to have been an ex-sailor, retired from the navy having been involved in the taking of Puerto Bello, Panama, under Admiral Vernon in 1739, and the person who applied the name to the house - was Peter Scott's shepherd. It is also possible that Portobello was built, or completed, in 1753 - between Roy's survey and the date of the *Courant* advertisement - in order to retail ale to the users of the new Post Road to London, as well as to serve the purpose of being a "shepherd's house".

Andrew Fletcher, Lord Milton, purchased the lands of Figgate in July 1753. So, in the summer of 1753, we trace in Figgate a new landowner, a new main road and the first written record of the first house. It is known that the house was built by Peter Scott, tenant farmer in Figgate and Easter Duddingston, as a place for his shepherd and to "retail ale". It is reasonable, therefore, to conclude that George Hamilton was a sub-tenant of Peter Scott and that Portobello House was built in 1753, between the time of Roy's survey, thought to have occurred in the summer of 1753 (not on Roy's map) and 8th October, 1753 (mentioned in *Edinburgh Evening Courant* on that day). It is just possible that the influence of the enterprising Lord Milton was behind the building of the house near the new road to London, the introduction of the ex-sailor, George Hamilton, and even the naming of the house.

DEVELOPMENT OF THE ROAD FROM JOCK'S LODGE TO JOPPA - A SUMMARY

No single, specific record of the detailed development survives for the period 1740s to 1762, but the jigsaw can be assembled by combining information from various sources, as above. In addition, all the basic map sketches shown in this book have been re-scaled by computer to a common scale and, although it is not possible to show examples in this book, overlaid comparisons have been done, which confirm the statements made concerning the relative positions of various roads. For example, the coastal road on Plate 24 looks as though it is on the High Street line, but, when compared by the overlay method, it is seen to be on the line of the promenade, even after allowing for possible map and input errors. This position is supported by the statement above, "... travellers ... when prevented from going the ordinary track by the tide, were in use of passing by another road (Fishwives' Causeway) . . .".

POSITION BEFORE 1752

1. The Fishwives' Causeway was part of the old London road, between Jock's Lodge and Magdalene Pans. Its west end came to Jock's Lodge.
2. The old road from Jock's Lodge to the sea (at present Portobello Road and King's Road) was used as an access road for obtaining building materials from the shore.
3. The only direct road from Musselburgh to Leith was via the line of today's promenade.

POSITION FROM MARCH 1752

1. The road from Jock's Lodge to the sea was improved to the status of main road. As we shall see later, however, there was still room for even further improvements.
2. This road on Plate 24 (Roy's map of 1753) shows this position.

POSITION IN THE SUMMER OF 1753

1. Temporary footroad on line of future High Street made into main road.
2. The old Fishwives' Causeway was altered at its east end - turned north-east to join the new Musselburgh/London Road (later High Street). This is its present position also.
3. The old Fishwives' Causeway cut off east of field called Adam's Law, i.e. it no longer entered the lands of Figgate.

POSITION FROM 1756

1. Fishwives' Causeway altered at its west end - turned north-west to join the "Post Road", as it does today.
2. A later chapter deals with this road again, from 1762.

SHEEP-MILKERS AND THE BUGHTS

The common loan by the herd's house, Pike-a-Plea, was mentioned (1787), and can be seen on Ainslie's plan in Chapter 1 as being the first house a traveller from the east, on the new "Great Musselburgh Road", would meet upon entering the village of Figgate.

> *Another common "road" to Porto-Bello, was one the sheep-milkers used to go to the bughts* (small inner folds for milking ewes) - *from Wester Duddingston, down by the burns - not all the way to Porto-Bello, but after a certain length, they crossed at the brock-holes and fought their passage any way to Porto-Bello, where there was but one thatched house. The tenants had a flock-rake for sheep, which belonged to all mutually, before enclosing.*

The reference to more than one burn here is possibly related to the rivulet that came down from Dunsapie (before it was a loch) and joined the Figgate Burn just below the (lower) mills, at the bend in the burn (this still occurs underground). Another idea on the burns, however, is presented in a later chapter. The brock-holes were some kind of rubbish, or compost, holes (possibly old clay-pits), and the flock-rake was an area of ground for sheep; a kind of pen. In 1801, there were "distillings" on the Figgate Burn, in what is now the Figgate Park, and near where Mountcastle Drive crosses the burn.

MR SCOTT'S ROAD PAST NORTHFIELD FARM

> *John Shaw was herd to Arch. Duncan, tenant in Duddingston Mill, and herded his cattle in 1737 upon the grounds called Cowden's Wells, much about the same place where Northfield Farmhouse now stands* (Northfield Park now). *The east-most part of the lands of Northfield were in tillage - a place called "Make Him Rich"* (part of Adam's Law nearest to the sands). *The farm road from the Duddingston Mill Road* (Willowbrae Road), *down to Adam's Law was called, prior to the building of the farmhouse in 1761, Bleaklands Road* [see Ainslie's plan in Chapter 1 for "the Bleaklaw" in Mr Cunningham's property]; *it was then called Mr Scott's road. He remembers carts coming down to the "Saughs"* (Willows) *near to Mr Scott's house* (Northfield Farm) *and taking horses down from Wester Duddingston by the Broomy Balk and down to Cowdens Wells, and then to the Fishwives' Causeway.*

Although Mr Scott's Road was predominantly a farm road, there is no doubt that there was some sort of occasional access for a lot of people. Here is a list of non-farming uses mentioned by tenants:

> *to go to sea-bathe*
> *go to a field of turnips on Mr Skirving's ground (next to Portobello House - see Ainslie's plan in Chapter 1)*
> *get to church - weddings, christenings and funerals*
> *wash horses in the sea*
> *get to the coal hills*
> *get to the "south country"*
> *seek birds' nests*
> *get sand from seaside*
> *get "channel" from seaside*
> *get whins for drying corn at Duddingston Mills*
> *get salt water*
> *hunt*
> *lead the coals necessary for Jamieson's brick works*

THE BIRTH OF THE TOWN OF PORTOBELLO

The following factors explain why William Jamieson came to the Figgate Whins and form, in essence, the basis of the decisions which created Portobello the village and, later, town:

> *At the time of first feuing the 40 acres from Baron Muir, the lands, naturally barren, were altogether uncultivated. But, besides their vicinity to Edinburgh, they had several advantages;*
> *1. A stratum of clay, which, not only by being mixed with the sand, was capable of bringing it to a state of fertility, but was proper for the manufacture of brick (Hugh Miller's Brick Clays), tile and earthen ware.*

2. A considerable command of water from the Figget Burn, which falls into the sea in the lands of Figget.
3. A short and easy communication to the coal of Niddry, the free-stone quarries (he was a mason) of Craigmillar, and the whole country to the southward, as well as the Church of Duddingston, in which parish the lands lay.

Having been induced by these advantages to pay a high feu duty for ground which was in a state of absolute barrenness, scarce producing a blade of grass, Mr Jamieson immediately established a manufacture of brick, tile and earthen ware, built houses and erected mills of different kinds, particularly a paper mill, in the neighbourhood of his dwelling-house.

From time to time, others obtained feus of the whole contiguous parts of the lands of Figget, so that the buildings and inhabitants have gradually increased until the lands of Figget, which, till the year 1764, were a mere waste, are now well inhabited, and the Village of Figget is far from being contemptible.

Some years ago, Mr Jamieson, at great expence (sic), *brought hands from England, and established a manufacture of white stone or Staffordshire ware. But he is sorry to say that his undertakings have been cramped, and the profits he expected from the natural advantages of the lands, diminished, in consequence of the proceedings of the noble Lord (Abercorn).*

The first dispute respected the water of the Figget Burn, great part of which was many years ago carried off for ponds in the Earl's pleasure grounds, and a much greater quantity led off from the natural course of the burn eastwards through the lands of Duddingston, for the use of salt-works belonging to the Earl, near to his engine, and there passed into the sea, instead of being allowed to run into it through the lands of Figget. Two feuars of the paper mill have been ruined through the expence (sic) *of Process against the Earl.*

Jamieson did not actually "discover" clay at Portobello, as it had been used for other purposes at much earlier dates; for example, it was used in the 17th century to build dam-heads at the pit water-engines, and was required by brewers, as already mentioned. It is not known why Jamieson did not obtain his coal from Duddingston or Brunstane; it may have been a question of price, availability or even personal relationships!

The second dispute, concerning access through the lands of Northfield, formed this court case (1787) which has made our glimpse of 18th-century life possible, and difficult as it must have been for Mr Jamieson and his fellow "settlers" to tackle the might of the Earl of Abercorn, we can only be grateful that they did. They lost the case, however, and a public right of way from the Fishwives' Causeway to Willowbrae Road was never established. In fact, it took another 38 years before Portobello got the first part of its direct road to the Kirk at Wester Duddingston (Duddingston Road) . . . but not without another dispute!

Plate 28 *William Jamieson – the "Father" of Portobello*

CHAPTER 5
FIELD STUDIES IN DUDDINGSTON

THE FIELDS OF OLD DUDDINGSTON

One of the unfortunate features of the list of street names (Appendix II) is that *none* of the complete names has been taken from the many rich and varied names which used to be attached to the fields. Names which came down from at least the 17th century, and some from medieval times, either disappeared in the transition from one agricultural system to another, or in the change to a suburban environment.

This is not simply the fault of those who allocated names to streets; it is mainly a result of the fact that certain information was probably not available to them (indeed, some has yet to emerge) – the maps and plans of the old fields were previously held deep in the recesses of hidden archives. In any case, it was the fashion in days gone by to use names connected with famous people and events. Building "local history" names into posterity is more common now, especially in that area on the west side of Portobello (part of the lands of Craigentinny), on the sites of the Power Station and potteries and so on, where all the new street names reflect the former activities, and people associated with that area.

The 1801 sketch map, which shows the position after the runrig system had been abandoned, is the principal reference to the names about to be studied. The earlier versions of the names will be considered also – when runrig was in vogue – and more lovely old words of Lowland Scots will emerge, along with their meanings, where possible.

The names, acreages and crop examples of the fields are as follows, in the field order shown on the map:
(1 Acre = 4 Roods; 1 Rood = 40 Falls)

THE FARMS IN 1801 (REFERRED TO BELOW)

FARMS	TENANTS (1801)	CURRENT LOCATIONS
M = Meadowfield	Miss Duncans	Paisley Drive
N = Northfield	Andrew Scott	Northfield Park
S = Southfield	John Johnston	Duddingston Row
DE = Eastfield	Mrs Andrew Black	Nr Brunstane Burn
E = Earlsfarm	Louis Cauvin	Woodlands Grove
J = Jock's Lodge	Louis Cauvin	Jock's Lodge
DH = Duddingston Hall	Widow Black	Durham Rd Sth
ED = East Dudd	Andrew Bennet	Musselburgh Rd
S = Snubnuik	Andrew Bennet	Musselburgh Rd
MD = Midfield	Thomas Scott	Southfield Square

Plate 29 *The Barony in 1801 - places*

1 = *Wester Duddingston Toun*
2 = *Duddingston House*
3 = *Duddingston Hut (later "Earlsfarm" and later still, "Woodlands")*
4 = *Meadowfield Farm*
A = *Musclescalp Planting (shown on Estate Plan of Meadowfield dated 1827 - confirms name of road, "Musselscaup Road" mentioned in Chapter 4).*
B = *Pannie Clump (shown on Estate Plan of Meadowfield Farm dated 1827 - site of Abercorn Sports Club).*
5 = *Jock's Lodge*
6 = *Mill Town (including mill)*
7 = *Mills*
8 = *Mills*
9 = *Northfield Farm*
10 = *Southfield Farm*
11 = *Duddingston Cottage*
12 = *Duddingston Hall*
13 = *Eastfield Farm*
14 = *Village of Figgate*
15 = *Rabbit Hall*
16 = *Old Engine*
17 = *Joppa*
18 = *Easter Duddingston Toun*
19 = *Hardy Flatt Farm*
20 = *Old Salt Pans*
21 = *Bunkers Hill*
21a = *Salt Pans and Harbour*
22 = *Easter Duddingston Farm*
23 = *Maitland Bridge*
24 = *Brunstane Mill ("Farthing Haugh")*
25 = *Old Engine*
26 = *Brunstane Dovecot*

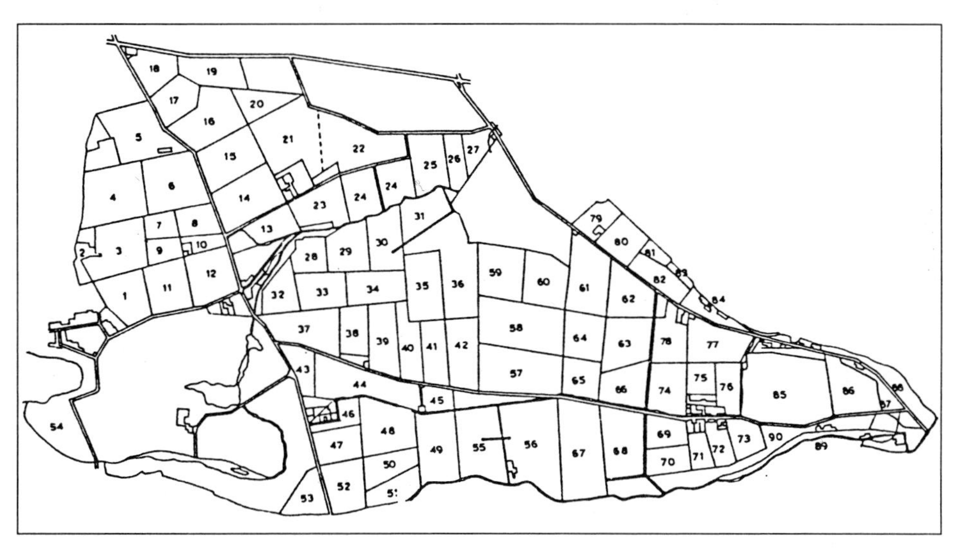

Plate 30 *The Barony in 1801 – fields; see text for details*

WESTER DUDDINGSTON

No.	*Name*	*Farm*	*A*	*R*	*F*	*How Cropped in:* *1800*	*1801*	*1802*
1.	Backside Park	M	11	00	05	Wheat	Barley	Oats
2.	The Bank	E	1	00	06	Wheat	Barley	Oats

(The three areas between The Bank and No. 4 – Longswift – are Steelhead Planting, South Steelhead and North Steelhead respectively. These names appear on the Estate Plan for Meadowfield Farm dated 1827. The word "steelhead" may refer to a metal casting which carried the excess water, under the Park Dyke, from the Dunsapie area. The unmarked area to the west of No. 5 – North Park – was called Musselscalp (or scaup) Planting and the unmarked area between Wester Duddingston and The Bank is the Minister's Glebe. The name Musselscaup was applied, as already seen, to an old road to Edinburgh which previously passed that way.

No.	*Name*	*Farm*	*A*	*R*	*F*	*1800*	*1801*	*1802*
3.	Sowstripe	M	14	02	02	Grass	Grass	Pease/Potatoes/Oats
4.	Longswift	M	16	01	10	Oats	Potatoes	Wheat
5.	North Park	M	19	00	20	Wheat/Potatoes	Turnip/Oats	Barley
6.	Black Ridge	M	15	00	03	Potatoes/Pease	Wheat	Barley/Grass
7.	West Meadow Lees	M	4	01	00	Wheat	Oats	Potatoes
8.	North Meadow Lees	M	5	01	14	Barley	Oats	Potatoes
9.	South Meadow Lees	M	3	02	23	Oats	Potatoes	Wheat
10.	East Meadow Lees	M	1	03	32	Pasture	Pasture	Pasture
11.	Sandilands Park	M	11	01	21	Potatoes	Wheat	Grass
12.	Mill Park	M	11	01	37	Wheat	Grass	Oats
13.	Mill Park	N	8	02	16	Pasture	Pasture	Pasture

No.	Name	Farm	A R F	*How Cropped in:* 1800	1801	1802
14.	Willow Cleave	N	14 03 38	Wheat	Wheat/Turnip	Turnip/Barley
15.	Willow Head	N	12 02 10	Grass	Oats/Wheat	Potatoes/Barley
16.	Waterpans	N	13 02 00	Grass/Potatoes	Grass/Wheat	Wheat/Grass
17.	South Park	J	7 01 22	Barley	Oats	Grass
18.	Barn Yard Park	J	7 00 38	Oats	Grass	Potatoes
19.	Dixon's Park	N	8 01 22	Grass	Grass	Wheat
20.	Angle Park	N	6 01 08	Turnips	Barley	Grass
21.	Crooked Furtcheons	N	19 00 29	Barley/Oats	Pease/Barley	Wheat/Oats
22.	Causey Gates	N	16 03 39	Barley	Pease/Oats	Wheat/Fallow
23.	West Blacklands	N	11 01 15	Potatoes/Barley	Barley/Oats	Pease/Potatoes
24.	East Blacklands	N	15 03 22	Pease/Bean/Wheat	Wheat/Oats	Barley/Potatoes
25.	West Adams Lawn (Law)	N	11 01 10	Oats	Potatoes	Wheat
26.	East Adams Lawn (Law)	N	4 02 12	Oats	Barley	Grass
27.	Brickwork	—	5 00 00	(Ex Adam's Law - now as named)		
28.	West Langlands	E	6 00 00	Barley	Oats	Potatoes
29.	East Langlands	E	10 00 03	Barley	Oats	Potatoes
30.	Langlands	S	9 01 38	Bean/Fallow	Wheat	Barley
31.	Broom Hills	S	14 03 07	Oat/Wheat	Potatoes/Barley	Wheat
32.	Mill-brae Head Park	E	5 00 06	Oats	Potatoes	Wheat
33.	Mid Langlands	E	9 03 38	Oats	Potatoes	Wheat
34.	Horns Park	MD	9 01 16	Grass	Oats	Pease/Beans
35.	Muir Park	DH	12 03 28	Oats/Grass	Pease/Oats	Wheat/Potatoes
36.	Whinnie Park	DE	13 00 38	Wheat/Pease	Barley	Grass
37.	Garbrage	E	13 00 21	Potatoes	Wheat	Grass
38.	Garbrage	MD	6 03 13	(no details - part of "Midfield"		
39.	East Park	MD	11 01 31	or "Middleton" or "Dudd. Cott")		
40.	East Park	S	7 02 38	Potatoes	Wheat	Grass
41.	West Lees	DH	8 01 18	Barley	Grass	Oats
42.	East Lees	DE	10 01 15	Wheat	Pease	Oats
43.	Muir	S	5 01 04	Bean/Pease	Wheat	Barley
44.	Back of the Cast	S	15 00 03	Barley	Grass	Potatoes/Oats
45.	House Park	DH	4 03 28	Oats	Potatoes	Wheat
46.	Cow Park	S	4 01 37	Pasture	Pasture	Pasture
47.	Foreshott	S	7 02 10	Barley	Wheat	Barley
48.	Clays	S	13 01 38	Grass	Wheat/Barley	Grass
49.	South Park	DH	14 02 02	Oat/Wheat/ Pease/Barley	Potatoes/Barley/ Wheat/Oats	Pease/Oats
50.	Bear Furlongs	S	8 01 29	Oat/Wheat	Wheat/Barley	Grass
51.	The Burns	S	5 02 04	Wheat	Potatoes	Wheat
52.	Willow Pool	S	9 02 22	Barley	Potatoes	Wheat
53.	Cranvas Park	S	6 02 21	Oats	Oats	Potatoes
54.	Bawsinch	E	11 00 08	Grass	Grass	Grass

These formed the approximate shape of Wester Duddingston at that time. The remaining fields were (approximately) those of *Easter Duddingston.* The word "approximately" is used because the "border" of the two Duddingstons seems to have varied, in accordance with the varying field structures and ownership of Easter and Wester Duddingston. The crop details are not available to the same extent, as they survive for the leased farms only.

EASTER DUDDINGSTON

No.	Name	Farm	A R F	How Cropped in: 1800	1801	1802
55.	West Park	DE	22 00 03	Barley/Wheat/ Pease	Barley/Oat/ Pease	Grass/Oats/ Bean/Potatoes
56.	East Park	DE	21 02 16	Barley/Oats Grass	Barley/Wheat Grass	Grass/Barley Wheat
57.	Upper Langlands		18 01 19			
58.	Under Langlands		21 01 31			
59.	West Brown Hill		11 03 11			
60.	East Brown Hill		10 02 11			
61.	Broad Lee		11 03 05			
62.	Laigh Sandy Lee		7 02 00			
63.	Sandy Lee		12 00 21			
64.	Thorn Tree Park		9 03 25			
65.	Wester Clays		8 03 30			
66.	Easter Clays		9 03 26			
67.	The Bank		18 00 17			
68.	Lone Dub		12 03 23			
69.	Back Park		5 02 23			
70.	The Bank		5 02 15			
71.	East Bank		3 01 14			
72.	South Park	ED	3 03 17	Grass	Grass	Oats
73.	East Park	ED	5 01 21	Wheat	Oats	Potatoes
74.	Head of the Town		10 00 18			
75.	Baron Maule's West Park		4 02 08			
76.	Baron Maule's East Park		5 03 29			
77.	Wardlands		11 00 28			
78.	Old Engine Park		8 01 30			
79.	Rabbit Hall		5 01 26			
80.	Rabbit Hall		7 03 32			
81.	Links		1 02 32			
82.	Links (not named)		6 00 15			
83.	Links -do-		1 01 11			
84.	Joppa		4 03 09			
85.	Hardy Flatt	ED	28 02 32	Wheat/Potatoes/ Barley	Same	Oats/Barley/ Wheat Potatoes/Grass
86.	Snub Nuik	S	10 02 33	No Account	Wheat/ Oats/Grass Potatoes/Pease	Barley/Pease/Oats/ Wheat/Potatoes
87.	Bank	S	3 03 38	No Account	Barley	Oats/Grass
88.	not named		5 00 09			
89.	(Old Engine area)		1 01 25			
90.	not named		16 00 00			

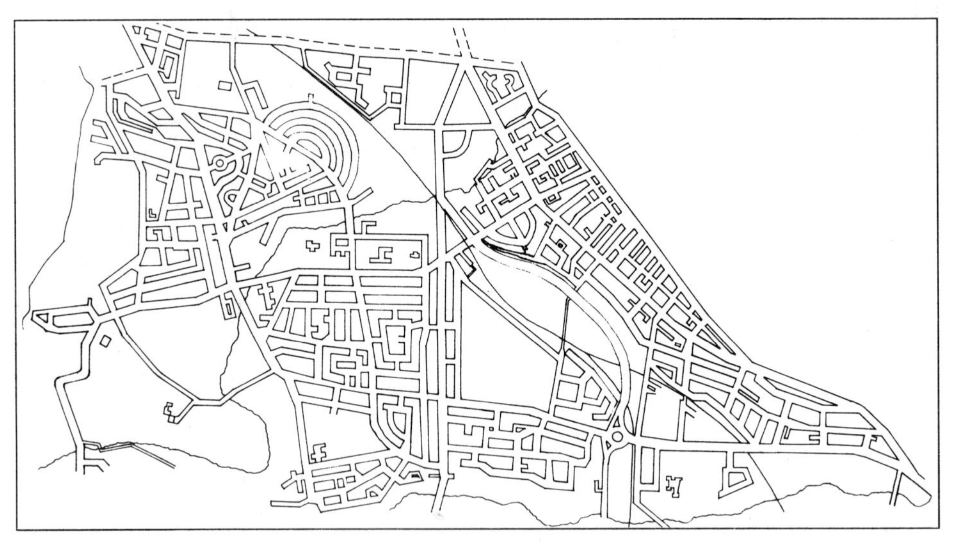

Plate 31 *The Barony in 1986 – same scale as Plates 29 and 30*

Comparing this sketch with the 1801 drawing (Plate 30) *gives a good idea of the development of the "Barony" since 1801, as well as a guide as to which field one may live in!*

The 1801 map may be compared with the 1986 one, to see, as closely as possible, in which old field any particular street now stands and what was grown there in the period from 1800 to 1802 (if shown above). The Village of Figget, Figgat Freegate or Figgate, which had now become a growing Portobello, was still contained within its original boundaries.

According to George Robertson's *State of Agriculture in the Lothians*, written in the first half of last century, potatoes appear to have been first cultivated in the Lothians about the year 1746, by a man named Henry Prentice.

The fields were "dunged" at the rate of 25–35 cartloads (or cubic yards) per acre per year.

OTHER TENANTS – NOVEMBER 1800

Part of East Duddingston	*Mr John Thomson*	Near Eastfield
Rabbithall	*Mr John Thomson*	East of Figgate
Lands of East Duddingston	*Mr Andrew Bennet*	Near E. Dudd.
Brunstain House and Lands	*Mr Andrew Bennet*	Present location
Duddingston Mills	*Mr William Laing*	Present location
Brunstain Mills	*Mr Archibald McDowall*	Near Eastfield
Policy and Mansion House	*General Campbell*	Present location
Duddingston Salt Pans	*Mr William Horn*	Joppa
Houses at Joppa	*Mr William Young*	Joppa

Plate 32 *The out-woman and her cow*

A dairy maid (Mrs Black) and her charge, and hens, in the field between Duddingston Village (dairy) and the Park Dyke – c 1930.

Houses at Old Engine	*Mr Alex. Robertson*	Joppa
Clark's Feu	*Colonel Graham*	Duddingston Vill.
Site of Brunstain Engine	*Mr Richard Hill*	Brunstane Burn
Brick Work	*Mr William Young*	Baileyfield Estate
Stone Quarry	*Mr William Young*	Lower Joppa
Duncan's Feu	*Mr Lewis Cauvin*	Duddingston Vill.
Brown's Feu	*Mr Lewis Cauvin*	Duddingston Vill.

TRACING THE FIELD NAMES PRIOR TO 1801

The field names will now be compared over a period of time. Here is a list showing the above names on the 1801 map, together with the respective names in a) Robert Johnstoun's Report of 1752 and b) Estate Papers of 1707 (Fletcher of Saltoun Papers). From this comparison, one can obtain an idea of the way words changed, as well as the development of the field layout. It has to be borne in mind that field names were sometimes "moved" to different fields and that acreages varied at different times. The same numbers used above are listed here also – the base map here is again the 1801 map – and some possible derivations are given in brackets, for the more obscure names.

WESTER DUDDINGSTON

1801	1752	1707
	(Name/Field not always same as later year in table)	
(* = name not used in a later year in table and exact position not necessarily known)		
1. Backside Park	Backsides	Backsides
		*Kibhill
	(possibly Kip - a jutting point on a hill)	
		*Kirk Green
	*Calf Ward (south and west of church yard)	
	*Haining	Haining
	(ground enclosed by a fence or hedge)	
2. The Bank	Fore Bank	Northbank
		*Neather Bank
		*Upper Bank
3. Sowstripe	Sows Trype	Southstripes
	(south or sow; narrow piece of land)	
4. Longswift	Lang Swift	Longswift
(may refer to a drain, now covered, from Dunsapie to Willowbrae Road - opposite Northfield Crescent; or it may refer to the wind or to the steep angle of the ground - in 1829, the tenant farmer of Meadowfield Farm requested a reduction in rent due to the fact that he had to keep an extra pair of horses to cope with the "slopes of Arthur's Seat")		
	*Torbie side	Torbey side
	*Dorvies haugh	Dorvies haugh
	*Websters back	
	(possibly tenants at one time)	
		*Plummie lands
	(from fruit of potato plant or plum trees)	
5. North Park		
6. Black Ridge	Black Riggs	Blackrigs
	(rigs = cultivation beds)	
7. West Meadow Lees	Meadow Lees	Meadow Lees
8. North Meadow Lees		
9. South Meadow Lees		
10. East Meadow Lees		
		*Gallow Law
	(obvious meaning, but reference not known)	
11. Sandilands Park	Sandy Lands	Sandilands
(refers to thick layer of dark sand about a foot under the soil)		
	*The Floors	Floors
		(low lying)
	*Carin Buck	Carnbuck
(cairn = heap of stones; buck = gush, pour or gurgle. May be reference to boundary stones. This field covered an area from the present dam towards Wester Duddingston and consisted of about 30		

Plate 33 *The kye coming home*

Cows making their own way along the Causeway, Duddingston Village, on their way home to the dairy. They came on to the street via the old lane which used to be one of the routes from Wester Duddingston to Edinburgh.

	1801	1752	1707
	acres; but in 1599 it was applied to an area of only one and a half acres "between the crofts of Wester Duddingston")		
		*Crooked Acres	
			*Cuninger (rabbit warren)
12.	Mill Park		
13.	Mill Park		
14.	Willow Cleave		Willow gate
	(cleave-cut; possibly for fencing, or refers to land on slope or bank. Field included steep slope between Northfield Broadway and the eastern end of Northfield Crescent. An area near Northfield Farm was called The Saughs - another word for willows)		
15.	Willow Head	Willow:head	Willow Head/Cleave
16.	Waterpans	Watter Pans	Waterpanns
	(may refer to stratum of clay under the soil which would have been impervious to moisture. A 1906 deed refers to the "lands of Water-pans" and "Slockendrouth" - both names refer to drinking and this area is surrounded by ditches on Roy's map (1753), and later maps.)		
17.	South Park		

No.	1801	1752	1707
18.	Barn Yard Park		
19.	Dixon's Park		
	(tenant of ground)		
20.	Angle Park		
	(shape of field)		
			*Cowden wells
		(from "cow-den", cows hollow, near Northfield Farm)	
			*Clerks acre
21.	Crooked Furtcheons	Crooked Furtcheons	Crooked furtchoins
		(may be "the crooked chains which run forth")	
22.	Causey Gates	Cause:way:gates	Cassey Gate
	(refers to Fishwives' Causeway - paved Roman road)		
23.	West Blacklands	Black Lands	Wester Blackland
		(probably refers to soil colour)	
		*Meadow	Meadow head
		*Nor Meadow Burns	Nor Meadow Burn
			*back of Davi gregs (one-time tenant)
			*Crooked Tiker (difficult soil?)
			*Green Dykes
			*Jannets park (tenant)
24.	East Blacklands		Easter Blacklands
25.	West Adam's Lawn (Law)		Adam's (Edam's) Lawes
26.	East Adam's Lawn (Law)		East Laws
		(Law - probably refers to sand-dunes)	
27.	Brickwork		
	(Jamieson's brickwork)		
28.	West Langlands		
29.	East Langlands		Easter Langlands
30.	Langlands		
31.	Broom Hills		Bloomrooll hills
32.	Mill-brae Head Park	Mill:brae:head	Mill Brae dam head
33.	Mid Langlands	Lang Lands	Longlands
34.	Horn's Park		
	(refers to the Horn family, mentioned elsewhere in this book)		
35.	Muir Park		
36.	Whinnie Park		
	(the lands of Figgate were often described as "the Figget Whins")		
37.	Garbrage	Gare Breads	Garb roads
	(possibly "thinly coated" ; Johnstoun (1752) described it as "gravlie".		

	1801	1752	1707
	Next to roads to Niddrie and Easter Dudd.)		
		*Mid Liverins	Midliberans
		(not known)	
			*Wester Midliberan
			*back of Pat Ligton
			(tenant)
			*Easter Midliberans
38.	Garbrage		
		*Gooseberry Vintage	
39.	East Park		
40.	East Park		
41.	West Lees		
42.	East Lees		
43.	Muir	Muir	Little Moore
		*Muir Dales	Moore Daills
			*Merkle Moore
	(this area used to be the eastern part of the Burgh Muir. Merkle may refer to an earlier rental system related to the Merk (5.5 pence stg)		
44.	Back of the Cast		
	(the stone water cast which carried water from the Braid Burn to Easter Duddingston and the "water engine" at Magdalene Pans. It crossed the Niddrie Road near the entrance to the old Southfield Farm, which was situated in the north-western corner of the present playing fields of Lismore School.)		
45.	House Park		
	(Duddingston Hall, built about 1770 and removed early in the 19th century, when Southfield and Duddingston Mains were built, about 1830)		
46.	Cow Park		
47.	Foreshott		
	(shot = ground cropped rotationally - late 16th century)		
48.	Clays	The Clays	
	(obvious reference to the "foundation" of Portobello)		
		*The Corslit	Easter Corslet
		(possibly "cross" and "armour-shaped")	
49.	South Park		
50.	Bear Furlongs	Bear furlongs	Bear furlains
		(not the animal, but the vegetable - barley)	
51.	The Burns		
52.	Willow Pool	Williow pooll	Willow pooll
53.	Cranvas Park		Cranies (Crany)
	(the word cran has several connections with water. A cranny is a small opening, or chink. Cranvas Park (now Bingham Way area) is where the road from Wester Duddingston passed on its way to Niddrie, after having crossed the burn over the Crannes Bridge. Chapter 8 looks at this area in the 1560s, and it will be seen that this		

Plate 34 *Thatched cottage in Northfield Broadway c 1910*

This building housed two families and the house on the left was once that of Thomas Horsburgh, in whose name Duddingston Forge still operates today (but owned by Mr G. Mackie). The cottage stood in the middle of today's Northfield Broadway, approximately where the bus stop is, next to Northfield Community Centre. The late Mrs Christine Egan, who lived in the house when she was about seven, and who was a daughter of Mr Horsburgh, is quoted in a later chapter. The front faced south and stood in the north east corner of the field called Water Pans. The building belonged to Northfield Farm.

1801 1752 1707

is possibly where the "original" mill dam was. The name, therefore, possibly refers to the old sluice system.

*Cow pasture Common
*Sheep Pasture Common
*The Inclosures

Plate 35 *Ploughman in Lone Dub*

This view is looking west and what is now "Milton Road" is behind the hedge on the right. Today's B & Q Superstore and the new by-pass to Musselburgh stand not far to the east of this spot. The field belonged to Duddingston Mains (Hope Lane) at that time.

1801	1752	1707
	*Firr Park (latter two near site of Holyrood School)	

54. Bawsinch
(suggests a reference to ball-games, but may be to do with keeping horses. Inch (island) could be related to the fact that this triangular field is surrounded by Duddingston Loch on the north, a drainage ditch on the west and a road on the east. In fact, there used to be another ditch beside the road leading to Forkenford. The name first appears about 1800, but the field used to belong to Prestonfield and was "given" to Duddingston because that estate had "encroached"

1801	1752	1707

upon it and Dick of Prestonfield simply regarded it – then called the Gushet (triangular piece of land) – as part of Duddingston, in order to avoid a lawsuit and for the sake of peace and quiet. This actually reversed a previous transaction – see Chapter 2).

EASTER DUDDINGSTON

1801	1752	1707
55. West Park		
56. East Park		
57. Upper Langlands	Lang Lands	Longlands
58. Under Langlands		
59. West Brown Hill	Broom Hills	Broomhills
60. East Brown Hill		
61. Broad Lee		
62. Laigh Sandy Lee (low-lying)		
63. Sandy Lee	Sandy Land Lee	
64. Thorn Tree Park		
65. Wester Clays	The Clays	Wester Clayes
66. Easter Clays		Easter Clayes
67. The Bank		
68. Lone Dub (wet area near farm track – now site of the B & Q Superstore)		
69. Back Park	Back sides	
70. The Bank		Bank
71. East Bank		
72. South Park		
73. East Park		
74. Head of the Town		
75. Baron Maule's West Park		
76. Baron Maule's East Park (Member of the Exchequer who lived in Easter Duddingston – site of present Queen's Bay Nursing home. Charles Jenner, founder of the Princes Street store, lived here.)		
		*Crofts
		*Narlins (northlands?)
		*Gilies Haugh (probably tenant)
		*Mercat Gate
(presumably a field beside the "market street" of Easter Duddingston)		
		*The Lady Park
		*The Lady Park bog
(The "Lady" was the Duchess of Lauderdale)		

	1801	1752	1707
77.	Wardlands	Warr Lands	
	(enclosed land for pasture)		
78.	Old Engine Park		
	(refers to Lord Abercorn's "Fire Engine" - see Chapter 7)		
79.	Rabbit Hall		
80.	Rabbit Hall		
	(farm built at the end of the 18th century, to the east of the old Figgate "border" - name refers to large numbers of rabbits which used to inhabit the area)		
81.	Links		
82.	Links (not named)		
83.	Links (-do-)		
	(stretch of undulating, open sandy ground, covered with turf, bent-grass or gorse)		
			*Grass Common
			*East Maitland Common
			*Wester Links Common
			*Easter Magdalen Common
84.	Joppa		
	(name first shown on site of brickworks - not salt pans, which are further east. One of several biblical names introduced to the Edinburgh area)		
85.	Hardy Flatt	Hardy Flatt	Hardflett
	(describes the land - Johnstoun (1752) describes part of it as "very barren")		
86.	Snub Nuik		
	(probably a description of the shape of this nose-shaped field at the eastern corner of the Barony)		
87.	Bank	Bank	
88.	not named		
89.	(old Engine area)		
90.	not named		
		*The Flashes	Flashes
		(swampy, or waterlogged land)	
		*Holm's Acre	
		(possibly a tenant)	
		*Grizles Acre (actually 2.5 acres)	
		(sounds odd, but possibly a tenant)	
		*Auld Dam head	Old Dam Head
		*Inclosures	
		*Easter Town Mains	
		*Common	

According to an estate plan of 1827, Duddingston Policy consisted of many component parts, but the largest areas were Cairn Buck (from the Dam area to Holyrood School); Front Park (that area east of the mansion house

Plate 36 *Skaters on Duddingston Loch, c 1900*

The winters must have been harder then. The lands to the west and south of the Church include grounds that used to be called the "Orchyard", the "Calf Ward" and the "Butts".

and the eastern entrance road); West Park (that area west of the road from Duddingston Village to the mansion house); Pasture (on the east side, on both sides of the entrance road) and House Park (the area near the mansion house and the land down to the Braid Burn).

OTHER NAMES AND LAND DEFINITIONS
(Appendix III for land/ownership lists)

Other names, or definitions of names shown above, which used to be in vogue here in the dim and distant past are to be seen in some of the old Laing Charters:

> *No. 1113 - 18th March, 1586 "... parcel of land called Orchard ... between the church and the yard occupied by Gilbert Blak and John Hil on the north, the 'Butts', belonging to the late Robert Lawson of Humbie, occupied by Richard Cairns and John Lambert, on the east, the Loch of Duddingston on the south, and the 'gerse' (grass) yard with dovecot on the west. ..." (This seems to indicate that the beautiful garden area created over the last 20 years by the Drs Neil was once part of both the 'Orchard' and the gerse yard.) A dovecot apparently stood on the site of the Curling House (built in 1825), as older plans indicate a round building once stood there.*

Plate 37 *Part of the "Orchyard" today*

The Drs. Neil have transformed this barren slope into a magical garden, which blends beautifully with the surrounding scenery.

No. 1377 – 1st June and 10th July, 1599 "... the whole Kirk lands of the Vicarage of Duddingston, lying on the east side of the town and territory of Wester Duddingston namely: Eleven rigs of land in the Langlands of Wester Duddingston, fifteen rigs of land lying between those two ways, the one leading from Duddingston to Nudry, and the other leading from Duddingston to Musselburgh; six rigs lying in the 'clayis' or 'claggis'; and one and a half acres lying between the crofts of the said town, called 'Carnebukis', extending in all to fourteen acres." (The "two ways" are described in Chapter 4 and the 15 rigs of land were somewhere in the north-west corner of today's Golf Course. The Clays and Carnbuck are shown above.)
In 1751, the Roup and sale of Sir John Home of Manderston's Lands included both the above descriptions, except that Home had nine rigs out of the fifteen "between the two ways" and did not have the acre and a half in "Carnebukis". The roup included ... "Houses, Biggings, Yards, Dovecotes, Tofts, Crofts, Pendicles and Pertinents thereof whatsomever, and that free from all Payment of the Parsonage-teinds therof, as they have been possessed and enjoyed in Time past ..."

(Biggings = buildings: Tofts = homestead and its land: Pendicles = subsidiary land: Pertinents = all things on the land covered by the agreement: Teinds = one-tenth of produce to landowners, formerly church)
No. 2449 – 13th December, 1653. Mention made of Adam's Law and "Quhythauch"; Quhyt = wet; hauch = level ground on river bank.

LANDS INCLUDED IN THE TITLE DEEDS OF DUDDINGSTON AS AT 1673

In legal terms, the lands of Duddingston used to consist of more than simply Easter and Wester Duddingston; the title deeds of the Lands and Barony of Duddingston demonstrate this, and also repeat the definitions of the areas mentioned in the old charters shown above. It is interesting to see the same definitions of land and previous ownership being preserved by many generations of charters and deeds.

WHAT THE OLD TITLE DEEDS COVERED IN 1673

1. The Towns and Lands of Easter and Wester Duddingston, with mill and coal rights and all buildings and right of patronage of the parish church.
2. The Burgh of Barony of Wester Duddingston, with power to appoint Bailies, Burgesses and Artists, to erect a Tolbooth, a market cross and to hold Friday markets and hold Burgh courts.
3. All such lands, mill teinds, right of patronage, Burgh of Barony and so on, were erected and incorporated into a free Barony called the Barony of Duddingston and conform to a Charter under the Great Seal in favour of John, Duke of Lauderdale, dated at Whitehall 5th September, 1673.

LANDS EXCLUDED FROM THE OLD TITLE DEEDS OF DUDDINGSTON (AS AT 1673)

Certain areas of land, however, were outwith this arrangement (and were disponed by Archibald, 3rd Duke of Argyll to Andrew Fletcher of Milton, Lord Justice Clerk, on 5th February, 1747 along with Brunstane) Lord Milton was a nephew of the celebrated Scottish patriot, Andrew Fletcher of Saltoun. He became a judge in 1724 and, through Archibald's influence, was appointed Chief Justice Clerk from 1735 to 1748.

1. "that oxgate and half an oxgate with the pertinents acquired by the deceased Richard Lawson of Humbie from deceased Richard Morum lying in the Town and territory of Wester Duddingston on the south side of the said town betwixt the lands belonging to the deceased Laird of Kippo on the West and the Lands of deceased Henry Hunter on the east parts."

(An oxgate = area ploughed by one ox in a day - about an acre. If this Laird of Kippo was one John Berclay of Kippo, then the period covered by this clause is dated prior to 1473, as this gentleman was quoted in a Charter of Confirmation and Mortification by King James the Third in that year. It concerned donations to the Blackfriars and said, "also that gift which the late John Berclay of Kippo made to the same church and friars of an annual rent of ten shillings of usual money of our Kingdom, to be levied and uplifted annually from the lands of Dudingstone and husband lands thereof").

2. "that other oxgate and half an oxgate of land of the said Lands of Wester Duddingston with the pertinents acquired by the said deceased Richard Lawson from the deceased John Martin lying in the said Town and territory of Wester Duddingston on the north side thereof betwixt the lands of the deceased Laird of Kippo on the east and west parts."

3. "that other oxgate and half an oxgate of land of the said lands of Wester Duddingston acquired by the said deceased Richard Lawson from the Daughter and Heirs of deceased James Young with the pertinents lying in the Town and territory foresaid, on the east side of the said Town betwixt the lands of the said Laird of Kippo on the east and west parts. . . ."

These four and a half oxgates (or bovates) of land, with sundry houses, biggings, yards and orchards had their own teind sheaves, i.e. one tenth of the produce was given to the church.

4. The Vicarage, Kirklands of Duddingston (12.5 acres):
Lying in the town and territory of Duddingston upon the east side of the said Town with houses, biggings, dovecots, yards, tofts, crofts, pendicles and pertinents thereof whatsoever free from all payment of the parsonage teinds thereof as they were possessed and enjoyed in former times.

Eleven rigs of land in the Langlands of Wester Duddingston, fifteen rigs lying between the two roads whereof the one leads from the Town of Duddingston towards Niddry and the other from the Town of Duddingston to the Town of Musselburgh and six rigs lying in Clays.

(As can be seen, this definition of the Kirklands of Duddingston differs from that given in Laing Charter No. 1377 (shown above), in that "Carnebukis" is no longer part of the Kirklands and the total area therefore reduced from 14 acres to 12.5 acres).

5. These parts and portions of land called Orchyard lying in the territory of the said Town of Duddingston upon the south side thereof between the Kirklands and yard of old possessed by Gilbert Blak and John Hil on the north, the lands called Butts of old belonging to Robert Lawson of Humbie on the east, the Loch upon the South and a grass yard and dovecot upon the west parts.

(The lands in Nos. 4 and 5 above were called, in 1747, the West Mains of Duddingston.)

LANDS LEGALLY UNITED FOR THE FIRST TIME

The excluded lands were united and annexed to the Barony of Duddingston and declared to be proper parts and portions of it, and a Sasine was taken out at the Wester Town of Duddingston by delivery of earth and stone of the ground of Duddingston in 1747.

Another Charter under the Great Seal was drawn up, in favour of James, Earl of Abercorn, and was dated 27th July, 1747. This Charter combined all the lands of Duddingston, for the first time, although the Kirk Lands were a "separate tenement" and remained in the ownership of Lord Milton until they were disponed to the Earl of Abercorn with the lands of Brunstane (and some other lands), in 1767. The Lands of Figgate, and other small "parcells" of land, were "separate tenements" within the Barony of Duddingston also.

TYING UP LOOSE PARCELS

Some of these "parcells" were bought by the Earl of Abercorn, while he was laying out his Policy and re-shaping Wester Duddingston, and some remained the property of others. Examples of such purchases on the part of Abercorn are:

> *1. In 1759, from Margaret Clark and Mary Bell to Abercorn . . . "east side of the Loch of Duddingston the unarable Bank betwixt the same and the Loch containing 3 Roods 9 Falls and 18 Ells (about 0.75 of an acre) . . . that piece of ground called the Backsides upon the east side of the Pavillions containing 2 Roods 23 Falls and 22 Ells . . . and Ground called the Willace Park near the road to Niddery Milne containing 1 Acre 1 Rood 9 Falls and 24 Ells . . . parcell of ground called Bear Furlongs joining to the Marches of Niddery, 3 Roods 10 Falls and 4 Ells . . . Cow Pasture joining to the road by the two southmost Pavillions, 2 Roods 4 Falls and 3 Ells extending in measure the foresaid parcells of ground . . . in whole to 4 Acres 23 Falls Scots measure . . ."*

(Apart from Bear Furlongs, the other "parcells" were all on the east side of Wester Duddingston, between the loch and the road to Duddingston House via Holyrood High School.)

> *2. In 1787, John Duncan's property . . . . "three quarters of an acre of land . . . bounded by Vennel of Teind Wynd on the east, the way called the Kirkway on the south, the Butt of Land sometime pertaining to deceased John, Duke of Lauderdale and then Abercorn, formerly possessed in common amoung the tenants in Duddingston, on the west, King's Highway on the north . . ."*

(This layout again illustrates part of the old Wester Duddingston, and the land referred to was probably near where the east end of Old Church Lane is today; the "Kirkway" no longer exists and the "King's Highway" was what is now the Causeway; the Teind Wynd was probably a lane which linked the two.)

> *3. In 1798, from Alexander Ormiston to Abercorn . . . "tenement of 2 houses and yeard at the Bank of Wester Duddingston . . . bounded of old as in the original Rights of Infeftment thereof and then bounded thus – the High Street of Wester Duddingston on the south; the Vennel that leads from the said street to the head of the yeard on the east; the south end of the ridges of cornfields at the head of the said yeard belonging to His Grace John Duke of Argyll and possesd by William Johnston coalman there as subtenant to his Graces Tacksman of the said cornfield on the north; and that house and yeard possesd by Adam Conquergood coalman there his subtenant to Archibald Duncan farmer in Duddingston Mill also belonging to the Duke of Argyll on the west parts . . ."*

This property was on the north side of the Causeway ("High Street"), near the east end – possibly where Hawthorn Cottage now stands, as that piece of ground was once feued by a Duncan, according to the old feuing plan mentioned below. The "ridges of cornfields" were possibly that field which stood just to the west of "Backside Park" on the "1801" map, and which now

Plate 38 *Aerial view of "Middle" Duddingston – 15th April 1946* (Crown Copyright – RAF photograph)

This fascinating map-like view shows, yet again, the fields being replaced by houses. Northfield, Meadowfield and Southfield Farms, the Mill complex, the chemical works and Duddingston Cottage are all there. One of the clay pits has been transformed into the Figgate Pond, the semi-circle of the Mountcastle area is awaiting completion (the drains are laid), and the "prefabs" have not yet been built. Duddingston Golf Course holds the key to the locations of some of the old, "lost" fields.

belongs to the Church of Scotland and is currently rented, appropriately, for the purpose of keeping horses. A feu condition relating to a property in this part of the village, dated 1814, included the burden . . . "No brewing, tan work, brick work, soap work, distilling and other manufactory or chemical process . . . must build a neat and ornate house, with stone wall and gate like lots 23-25, or a lower wall with iron rail". Lots 23-25 represent the ground on which are built the last four houses but one at the top of Old Church Lane.

By 1800, members of the old tenant families of Duddingston were no longer living in Wester Duddingston, and the village was "re-drawn" and mainly feued to new people who were attracted to invest in such properties. During the 1760s and 1770s, the Scotts ("originally" from Easter Duddingston) moved to the new Northfield Farm; the Johnstons to the new Southfield Farm (the first one); the Duncans to the new Meadowfield Farm and the Horns ("originally" from Easter Duddingston) apparently left the Barony. The new feuing plan of 1805 shows property divisions which can still be traced in today's layout and the original "Lotts" which comprise today's "Hawthornbrae", were feued by William Scott, brewer in Leith; Robert Wright, builder in Edinburgh; David Handyside, baker in Edinburgh; Andrew Handyside, merchant in Edinburgh; William Handyside, Writer to the Signet; William Bennet (the third to live in Duddingston), tenant farmer at Brunstane and Guthrie Wright, the factor for Abercorn.

LANDS OF RABBIT HALL

These lands were on the north side of the High Road to Musselburgh, between the lands of Figgate on the west and the part of Easter Duddingston Links which became known as Joppa (around 1770), on the east. The first part of the lands of Rabbit Hall to be feued, which name simply reflects the fact that a small farm was built on ground which was previously densely populated with rabbits, was as follows (Sasine Register):

> *Piece of ground being part of Lands of Rabbit Hall lying to the east of the Village of Portobello and upon the north side of the Highroad leading from Edinburgh to Musselburgh but under the burden always of being divided into such number of Lotts as may occupy the whole of said ground none of the said Lotts exceeding one eighth of an acre and to be divided and built on upon a plan to be approved of . . . and extending the said piece of ground to 270 feet in front of the Highroad or thereby and running backwards to a narrow point on the seashore 720 feet bounded partly by a stone wall running from the Musselburgh Road down to the sea and which is the March betwixt the property of the Marquis of Abercorn and that of Mr John Rae Surgeon in Edinburgh and partly towards the north end of that wall by an ideal straight line drawn from a marked point on that wall from its south extremity and extending north to the seashore.*

The feuars of the largest part of this ground were Thomas Scott WS (Sir Walter's brother, who was the estate factor) and Robert Buchan. This feu was 4.4 acres, instead of the normal one eighth of an acre, and it seems that the factor and Buchan jointly bought the ground for development purposes. Is this Thomas Scott's "unfortunate spirit of speculation" that the Marquis complained of (mentioned in the Abercorn Papers)? The original feu plans were made out by Robert Brown, land measurer, in 1801 and this was the beginning of the change in land use as demands grew for land in the country and by the seaside.

The lands of Rabbit Hall were treated as two parts; the western part ran from what is now Marlborough Street to Bellfield Lane (mentioned above) and the original plan was to have another lane and a street in between, running from the Highroad to the sea. The street became the western part of Bellfield Lane and the other lane did not materialise. The eastern part of the Rabbit Hall lands, stretching from Bellfield Lane to Lower Joppa, originally contained Melville Street (now Bellfield Street), Pitt Street, divided by circular gardens (did not materialise, as Abercorn Park was laid out as a square, without any central access from the main road), John Street, James Street, Thomas Street (Brunstane Road North) and another street not named (near Joppa Terrace).

By 1807, however, problems in feuing the eastern section emerged, and it transpired that the factor, Thomas Scott, did not include in the missives and feu charters a condition that the feuars a) build houses and b) do so in accordance with the plan, i.e. houses to be in the centre of the plot, set back from the front of the plot with the height of each to be uniform. The result was that some feuars did not build at all, others built beyond their plot, others did not build in the centre of their plot and others built "on hillocks or in hollows", i.e. on and around sand dunes.

Legal advice pointed out that the feuars were really only bound to build within a reasonable time but those whose land contained hollows could build a basement level to maintain uniformity in height; feuars could not exceed the limit of their feu and were not confined to building houses. By 1807, Thomas Scott was no longer the factor and commissioner for the Marquis of Abercorn.

LOST PROPERTY

Duddingston Policies, or Pleasure Grounds, which now comprise Duddingston Golf Course, Holyrood School and Portobello School playing fields, grandly surrounded the mansion house of Duddingston House. When the house was finally built in 1768, after a period of five years, the grounds were nearing completion also. Breathtaking as they would have been in their heyday, the act of their construction, combined with the absence of any older plan of the area containing names, removed from our knowledge the layout of some of the old fields and pastures of Wester Duddingston. Names like the Willace Park, Floors, Cuninger, Merkle Moor, Liberans and the exact shape of the "original" Carin Buck, for example, may never be put into their proper perspective, unless a revealing, long-lost estate plan is yet to slip from its hiding place.

CHAPTER 6
DUDDINGSTON ON EDGE

IDENTIFYING COAL SEAMS AND PIT SITES

If Hugh Miller's "Coal Measures" are now considered, it will be remembered that he described the relatively flat area on the north and east sides of Edinburgh as being the surface of a deep basin filled with clay, sandstone and, to an extent, coal seams. The coal seams in the Barony of Duddingston are to be found only on the east end, i.e. east of a line which runs from Bingham Broadway to Pittville Street. Why is there a cut-off point? The line just described represents the approximate location of a geological fault, called the Pentland Fault, which means, in simple terms, that the land on one side of the fault has "slipped", resulting in a mis-match in strata on both sides of the fault, i.e. the eastern side has slipped and the older rocks and material on the west of the fault have been eroded on the surface, leaving no coal there.

Between John Street and the old Pinkie Salt Works (east of Maitland Bridge), there are 41 beds of coal, plus limestone and other beds, all of which run roughly south-west to north-east.

These seams of coal are on their "edge", i.e. they are sloping into the ground, from north west to south east, at an angle of about 45 degrees. This means that we can imagine lines, representing these layers, running inland away from the sea, which indicate, just like a geological chart, the depths of each original, horizontal layer, before the land was subjected to the tremendous upheaval which altered the angle by about 45 degrees. Therefore, from John Street to the Maitland Bridge, we have the following general "chart" of the original horizontal beds of decaying vegetation which formed the coals of Duddingston (seams on the west therefore lay originally at a lower level than those on the east).

SEAM NAMES FROM THE 18TH CENTURY

(Current Geological Map) East from John Street	Seam thickness	(1766 Plan) (RHP 600)	(1760 Plan) (RHP 33)
North Greens coal	48″	North Greens	North Green
Rough Parrot coal	30″	Vexom	Rough Coal
Niddrie Vexhim coal	30″	Rough Coal	Rough Coal
Blue coal	30″	Blue Coal	Blue Coal
Blackband coal	30″	Real Carelton	Not shown
Carlton coal	48″	Carelton	Not shown
(Junction of Abercorn Terrace/Brunstane Road)			
Coal	36″		
Corbie coal	48″	Real Corbie	Not shown

(Current Geological Map)		(1766 Plan) (RHP 600)	(1760 Plan) (RHP 33)
Peacocktail coal	42″	Big Splint	Peacocktail
Niddrie Little Splint coal	32″	Little Splint	Splinty
Stinkie coal	39″	Little Corbie	Not shown
Blackchapel coal	57″	Corbie Craig	Corby Craig
Little Gillespie coal	27″	Little Gillespie	Sm. Gill.
Gillespie coal	48″	Gillespie	Gillespie
Stairhead coal	57″	Stairhead	Stairhead
Great Seam coal	78″	Great Seam	Great Seam
(Morton Street)			
Laverock coal	36″	Laverock	Not shown
Not shown	—	Rumble (24″)	Roumles
Flex coal	48″	Flex Coal	Fleck's
South Parrot coal	29″	Parrot Coal	East Splint
Wood coal	30″	The Wood Coal	Wood Coal
Allan's coal	21″	Not shown	Not shown
Seven Foot coal	96″	Not shown	Seven Foot
(Just east of Joppa Salt Pans)			
Pinkie Four Foot coal	42″	(Seams to east	Four Foot
Fifteen Foot coal	90″	Not shown)	Fifteen Feet
Nine Foot coal	54″		Nine Feet
Salter's coal	36″		Not shown
Glass coal	18″	(Actual	Foul Coal
Quarry coal	18″	(Positions Unknown)	(Mount Starling)
Cowpits Five Foot coal	48″		Small Seam
Little Splint coal	6-48″		Not shown
Coal	20″		Not shown
Coal	18″		Not shown
Coal	24″		Not shown
Golden coal	36″		Not shown
Musselburgh Jewel coal	38″		Jewel Coal
Diamond coal	4-48″		Not shown
Beefie coal	42″		Not shown
Rough coal	28″		Not shown
Splint coal	60″		Not shown
(Between Eastfield and Maitland Bridge)			
Clayknowes coal	30″		Not shown
(East of Maitland Bridge)			
Thin coal			Not shown
Thin coal			Not shown

All interspersed with beds of limestone, blaes, sandstones, fakes, and fireclays. All coal seams between South Parrot and Seven Foot lie on the coast and do not travel inland, as do the others. Most of the seams run as far as Woolmet (Geological map).

Plate 39 *Joppa Rocks* (Reproduced with permission of Cambridge University)

This 1967 aerial view shows clearly the "geological lines" containing stone, coal and other material, all lying on their "edge". The area covered by this photograph includes the sites of two old salt pan complexes and about six coal pits. Most of the area between Musselburgh Road and Milton Road East contained the old field called "Snubneuk". This section of Milton Road East used to curve to the right, near the old cottages (site of an old "Steam Engine"), before turning back to its left, to drop down to the coast road.

It is not certain when mining began in the area, but, as Baird points out, coal is mentioned in old charters dating from the 15th century. The earliest records which give any detail date from the 17th century (Tollemache Papers) but another rich source is, again, the Session Papers of the Signet Library.

WATER AGAINST WATER

A problem the "coalliers" had to contend with (apart from terrible conditions, slavery, "bad air" and sheer hard work and long hours) was water build-up. "Edge coals" were also a problem, as the beds were not horizontal, as has been said above. There were six early stages of man's solution to this problem in Duddingston, by using a) a water-gin, i.e. a water wheel which simply worked a rope or chain attached to buckets to raise water, as well as the coal, up a vertical pit, or shaft, (b) a "horse-gin", which had the same effect as the water-gin, (c) a "level" mine, which drained water away from a seam, towards the sea, (d) a water-engine; a water wheel which was capable of working pumps, in order to drain the water from the mine up a vertical shaft, or pit, (e) a steam, or "fire" engine, which worked pumps but could not wind and (f) by the ingenuity of James Watt, an improved steam engine, or "fire" engine, which could both pump water and raise coal. Interestingly, there was a windmill pump (at or near the Gillespie Seam) near Niddrie and just east of the Wisp.

All these types of machines (apart from the horse-gin and windmill) had to have a supply of fresh, running water. This was, of course, not a problem where the machine was next to the Brunstane Burn, but where did the water for the machines on or near the coast come from? Remember the water cast which came from the Duddingston Burn? Such a cast had been made at least by 1686, and there appears to have been various sections added to, and removed from, it in the vicinity of Easter Duddingston and Magdalene salt pans - depending upon the location of the current water wheel, or later, steam engine. It also served the salt works at Magdalene pans.

PIT SITES

In order to determine where some of the various engines, pits, and the largest level were, several sources should be referred to. A complete picture of the old pit positions is not possible to re-create, as pits were "sett" and filled as and when required by progress along a coal seam. Baird tells us that, in the 1730s, when Duddingston Coal was owned by Argyll and let to William Horn, chains and baskets (water-gin) were used to raise water from a great depth; that, in 1745, John Biggar, of Woolmet, dug his drain (level), which ran from the sea to Woolmetbank and was an incredible three miles long; that, about 1763, the Earl of Abercorn erected a powerful engine (steam or fire engine) at Mount Pleasant (between Joppa Road and Dalkeith Street, next to Morton Street), the shaft of which went down 52 fathoms - flooded on 20th March, 1790; that about 1790, an engine of even greater power (probably a fire engine that could wind) was erected on the Duddingston/Brunstane border, which worked to a depth of 60 fathoms, through the 7 foot, 9 foot and

15 foot seams (it can be seen from the list above that the order is shown to be 9, 15 then 7, and that it would have gone through the Pinkie 4 foot seam also; but it appears that the names of some of the seams, in addition to being out of step with the thicknesses shown on the Geological map, have been applied to different seams at different times); that about 1842, a Miss Ellis built a powerful engine, where Coillesdene House is now, that it was unprofitable, and was finally demolished about 1852. Baird, without indicating types of engines, and locating the pits only in general terms, supposed the pits to have been:

—one immediately south of Mount Pleasant
—one west of Brunstane Road, near Argyle Crescent
—one east of Joppa pans (north of road)
—more than one south of Easter Duddingston on the way to Brunstane House
—(no specific mention of any pit on the site of Coillesdene House by the Geological Survey map but Baird refers to Miss Ellis's engine, and therefore a pit, on that site. This site previously housed part of the salt pans complex, as shown on the 1801 map).

The Geological Survey map, referred to above, shows 13 pit sites in the Barony of Duddingston, but even this source probably depended upon, to some extent, word of mouth, resulting in some doubt still remaining as to the exact locations, and types, of pits. According to that map, the pits were:

1. Morton Street/Dalkeith Street corner, marked "Approximate site of Duddingston Pit". Agrees with Baird, but see below.
2. Corner of Brunstane Road/Joppa Road, marked "Old Water Mill Pit". See "1766 case" below.
3. East end of Seaview Crescent, just south of Joppa Road, marked "Old Water Mill Pit". Baird, however, says "north" of the road.
4. South-east of this site, towards Coillesdene Avenue, marked "North Pit".
5. Eastfield Gardens, marked "Old Water Mill Pit".
6. East of this site, near angle of junction of Milton Road East/Musselburgh Road, at the side of Milton Road East, marked "Small Knowe Pit" - 22 fathoms (under Eastfield Garage).
7. Just north of Brunstane Burn, and on a line south of Milton Terrace, marked "Great Fire Engine Pit" - 60 fathoms. The one Baird says was built about 1790. (Incidentally, army barracks stood near here - just south of the burn - in the 1730s (shown on later plan, RHP 14979/2). The "sodgers" laboured in the lands of Brunstane for Lord Milton.)
8. A little further upstream, marked "Bye Pit" - 50 fathoms. (On the same plan of Brunstane, dated 1761, a well named St Anns Well is shown, just south of the burn and north of Brunstane House.)
9. Further west, and south of Portobello Cemetery, unmarked.
10. On site of Joppa Quarry (west of South Morton Street), marked "Quarry Pit".
11. On site of new by-pass (approx.), to the rear of Duddingston Mains Farmhouse, marked "No. 2 Pit".
12. Immediately behind Duddingston Mains Farmhouse and behind Duddingston Mains Cottages, unmarked.
13. Just south of Brunstane Burn, near roundabout on new by-pass - unmarked - 32 fathoms. (Called Glen Pit on late 19th-century plan).

Baird was right when he mentioned the pit "east of Joppa Pans, north of the road", because as mentioned in the minutes of the Post Road District (in 1801), "a large sett (pit) of an edge seam of an old wrought coal the property of the Marquis of Abercorn fell in on the side of the road near the third milestone and runs across the road at no great depth from the surface". The third milestone was just east of the pans. (The third milestone was actually the fourth from Edinburgh, but the third within the Post Road District).

Due to the angle of the "edge" seams, the pits were sunk some distance from where the seam was nearest to the surface of the ground (shown by a line on the map).

Neither Baird nor the Geological Survey indicate the position of Mr Biggar's level. There are, however, plans of it in the Scottish Record Office, one of which is dated 12th March, 1760 (ref RHP 33) and the level is called "The Gillespie Coal Level". It ran approximately from the north side of Joppa Road, opposite the foot of Morton Street, directly under the Brunstane Road/Milton Road East crossroads, and into the "lands of Brunstane, Niddry, Edmonstone and Woolmet". An "engine house" is shown on the south side of the Musselburgh Road, with an "engine pit" a few yards to the south and a "Bye pit" a few more yards to the east of the engine house. The level ran "under" the main road and split channels carried the water into the sea - one under Morton Street North and the other about 30 yards to the east. This level, which Mr Biggar had started in 1746, had "reached about 500 yards south-west of the Brunstane Burn by Whitsunday, 1754".

This map shows "Brunstane Road" ("Black Road" then) in its current position, although a re-scaled comparison with Roy's map (1753) shows it running from where the engine house was in 1760, (i.e. where Morton Street now meets Joppa Road) to where Brunstane Road meets Milton Road East. This seems to indicate that the road line was shifted to the present Brunstane Road line in order to make way for the steam-engine house and pit.

The following items, from the session papers of the Signet Library, are sorted by the sequence in which the events mentioned by the witnesses appeared to have occurred - not by the dates shown, which are the dates of the legal processes in which the statements were made.

1770 case - "The coal in Duddingston was wrought assiduously for 50 years before Horn's entry" (he "entered" in 1738).

1768 case - Janet Gordon, 79, "remembers when there was no coal-mill (no engines of any kind) upon Duddingston, but that it is many years ago since the first coal mill was erected; she remembers to have gone to see it and at that time she was a fine bit lassie".

1779 case - "Horn got his tack (lease) in 1738 and used a water engine near the sea, upon the road leading to Musselburgh - engine had chain and buckets".

1766 case - "John Biggar of Wolmet got his lease of Duddingston coal in 1745".

1770 case - "Duke of Argyll sold to the Earl of Abercorn in 1745, and the Rebellion coming on immediately after, the coal lay unwrought till 1746".

1781 case – "John Biggar (son and heir of Wm. Biggar, the former proprietor of the estate of Wolmet) died in 1753; his brother, Andrew Wallace, continued working on the level; he died in 1764; his nephew, Captain MacDowall next, then he made over the right to his brother-in-law, Sir Archibald Hope, Baronet".

1770 case – "Biggar's tack (lease) contracted him to pay one-tenth of the value of the coal, plus £48 6s 0d sterling in money".

1781 case – "Measured water flowing into the level, at the Niddery March, from all seams of coal which have been wrought in Niddery and Woolmet = 36 tons per hour; Niddery Burn rate was 1,200 tons per hour".

1770 case – "Biggar's level discharged into a place near the sea called Chapman's Hole, from whence the water was brought up to the surface by means of a water engine with chain and bucket, which was then kept going".

(A kind of sump appears to have been dug for this purpose, from which the water was discharged into the sea.)

1766 case – "Water engine on march (border) with Niddery; erected about 1748 and pit 22 fathoms deep" (pit No. 13 above?) Name suggests that machine used pumps, as opposed to buckets. – "fire engine lately erected" (Baird says "about 1763"). Probably pit No. 1 above and probably of the pump type, as Watt's improved "winding engine" had not by that time appeared. This suggests that a water wheel, perhaps Horn's, was actually used to raise the coal – this could explain the "Bye Pit" shown on the 1760 plan (and perhaps the place of the Water Mill is misplaced on the Geological map, because of confusion between the altered position of "Brunstane Road", i.e. it could have been a "Bye Pit"). Or the coal may have been raised entirely by the "coalliers" – "level ran beside the Gillespie Seam" (agrees with 1760 plan).

1770 case – "Horn and his partners, Peter Scott (the builder of Portobello House) and Angus Beaton, were obliged to work to a depth of 32 fathoms below sea level, which was as far as a machine wrought by the Duddingston or Freegate Burn could draw the water". The water from the Duddingston Burn, it will be remembered, was conveyed by a water cast from a point in the burn which is near the Bingham corner of Duddingston Golf Course.

1770 case – "Mr Horn's machine stood idle for about a third part of the year for want of water to move it, and another third was consumed in drawing up the water from below ground so as to make it workable therefore any machine depending upon the Duddingston Burn alone, would be entirely insufficient". At first sight, this passage does not make total sense, but it seems that a) it lay idle because there was insufficient water in the water cast from Duddingston Burn and b) the water drawn up from below the ground may have been pumped by the "fire" engine, which would then have applied it to the water wheel in order to raise the coals from the pit. If so, the two machines would have been fairly close together – could it have been the "Bye-Pit"? If this theory is correct, the coal-bearers may have been saved at least from the task of carrying the coals to the surface at this particular juncture.

1770 case – "By 1761, Mr Wallace had placed upon Niddry's coal a water engine which worked with pumps". Mr Wallace was Mr Biggar's brother.

Plate 40 *Sketch of typical water gin*

1766 case – "Lord Abercorn intends, with engine, to work two other seams to the east, i.e., the Great Seam and Stair Head". Implies that the fire engine was, by 1766, only working the Gillespie Seam.

1767 case – "James Ferrier and Robert Hunter, at the desire of Walter Scott, WS (factor for Abercorn and father of Sir Walter Scott), visited, measured and inspected the level-mine from the sea to Niddry March, in the seam of coal commonly called the Gillespie – 'and first we went down into a pit in Niddry ground, near to the Brunstane March (No. 13 above), to measure the level-mine from Brunstane March to a pit immediately upon the north side of the road (agrees with Baird) leading from Edinburgh to Musselburgh, to the east of the Earl's fire-engine and found the same to measure 541 fathoms or thereby. And we found the coal for 1,000 feet in length in the said level from Brunstane March to measure about four foot thick' " (fathoms of length, not depth).

1769 case – "That the water from the Forked-Ford (now Forkenford, just north of where the line of the "Innocent Railway" crossed Duddingston Road West) takes its course till it comes near to Niddery Road (adjacent to Duddingston Row), and then there a part of it goes by a formed lead to Easter Duddingston, for the use of the town and the fire-engine, and that the remainder by another lead to Duddingston Mill. That there is a sluice upon that part of it which goes down to Easter Duddingston to give more or less water as it's wanted, which sluice is a good way within my Lord's lands about 200 yards from the road or thereby (presumably where the water course left the burn, within the Policies)".

1778 case – "Reports from so able an engineer as Mr Watt (*the* James Watt), that the expence (*sic*) of erecting and upholding such an engine

Plate 41 *Remains of a typical "Newcomen" atmospheric steam engine*

This is probably the type of engine that was erected in 1763, where the corner of Morton Street and Dalkeith Street is now.

Watt's type), during the nine years that the level continued upon, would not have exceeded a third of the money spent in executing and completing the level".

To substantiate the statement above that "Duddingston coal was worked assiduously for 50 years before Horn's entry" (in 1738), here are quaint but informative extracts from the opening report relative to the Account Books of the new tacksman of the coal and salt works, dated 1688, followed by an extract from the account books of the "Coale Workes at Duddingstoun and Brunstane" for the week beginning 30th December, 1688 or 1689 (from the Tollemache Papers). This report was written only about six years after tea was first tasted in Edinburgh and about 14 years after water was first piped the three and a half miles from Comiston to Edinburgh:

DUDDINGSTOUN AND BRUNSTANE COALE WORKES – A REPORT DATED 1688

(Explanatory comments follow)

R1 William Marstane Oresman under Alex Steel.

THE COAL MINES

R2 Charles Murray (previous tacksman) *left the work when he hade wrought so much Coal and made the Roomes large, that the stoops being made too thin by ye same became too small to suport the Roof. Then did the water break in, by which there was two Roomes lost which was all the Dammage the work did sustain, in Prejudice to Charles Murray whose termes in his take bearing such a price to be allowed for each roome made his proffit the greater the larger the Roomes ware to her Grace Loss the more.*
R3 . . . after Charles Murray did leave it untill the Burn did break in upon it, and Soe lost it wholy The Occasion of which wass from a Neglect in not setting down a Sink of Ayre and Stair upon ye Great Seam . . .
R4 They have pierced the Dyke at the 7 foot Coal and there they are setting down a Sink for Air and stair. Then they will runn a Myne from ye 7 foot Coal to the Level Room, by which they will find the 5 foot Coal which is all the Seams that will be gott att the Pans, and which two Seams will hold in work ten men and their servants, which is 10 Roomes, the just number that was allowed to Mr Charles Murray when he took his tack of the Coal and the Salt. The 10 Roomes att 450 Strlg and the Salt Pans being 4 in number at 250 sterling in all 700 sterling. This Coal may continue 5 years to come untill the same is wrought up till ye Back Burne.
R5 All the Seams doo Lye at the Cloven Breays, what is in Lockhead just at ye back of Duddingstone. (Probably the braes at Brunstane Burn.)
R6 . . . there must be two (sinks) sett down the one may seem to carry away the water. The sink which is sett down there will be most for her Graces proffitt the Deeper it is.

The stoops should be 10 quarters in thickness and 6 Ells long some of the stoops where the Level is Drayning ar 4 Ells thick and 6 Ells long Mr Charles Murrays stoops not one Ell in thickness, in Patersons time ye stoops ware 9 quarters in thickness.

The stoops broak just in Mr Charles Murray's time then did he support the Roof with timber soon after ye Burn lost 2 Roomes and Charles Murray gave up his Tack. Mr Paterson made the Roofe good by raising it higher with more timber and Recovered the work after which tho the Burn broak in and Drown'd the work in which Condition Mr Callender did find it.

THE COAL ACCOUNTING SYSTEM

R7 In all the time that both Mr Charles Murray and that Mr Paterson hade ye mannagement There did 10 men and their servants work and each man did bring in one week 120 Load of Coales which is with his man 240 Loads and from 20 men 2400 Loads Each week.

Lastly the 3 Men at Brunstane made each man 100 Loads per week which is 300 Loads till they did Run upon the Dyke. (Sandstone "fault" at Brunstane Burn). *A good Coal ought to make 30 Tickets Every day.*

Plate 42 *Sketch of a stair-pit and coal bearers*

Two bearers, each climbing the stairs twice, resulted in the accounts of the coal tacksman effectively showing an entry such as "paye to her Grace 4/- Scots" (1.6p). The Duddingston hewers and bearers received 0.8p in total.

Mr Callender did Employ 4 Men from Preston Grange to sink this great sink down, they did run the sink wrong soe those men are discharged, and now her Grace own men are sett upon the same sink, and are to sett the sink Right. (This was the year after Newton's "Principia" defined the Laws of Gravity.)

R8 There does 14 tickets belong to her Grace to be paid Every week which is 2 tickets from every man. Besides ye 2 pennes and a Candle for each Load which

14 Tickets are due to her Grace even tho there ware noe more but one dayes work from the men.

The Rake is 2 Coal Bearers when they goe up and down the Stairs togither. they bring up 1/2 ticket everytime of small Coal (which is the Coal the next to the Pan wood).

For that 1/2 ticket they pay her Grace 3 Counters.

When they goe 2 Rakes it is 1 ticket which to her Grace payes 6 Counters every Counter is 8d Scots. 6 Counters is 1 ticket and 1 ticket is 1 Load. 6 Counters is 6 Atchisons 24 Bodles. 6 Counters is 4/2d Scots.

There are 3 sorts of Coal { *the great Coal*
the small Coal
and the Pan wood }

The weekly account setts down the loads or tickets allowing 6 Counters to the same. But if the Rakes fall soe that the number of the Counters, exceed soe many tickets then the number of the Counters placed in the account as they are found to be given in by each of the colliers and at the end of the whole number of Loads those Counters are alsoe reckoned, and each six Counters are added to ye tickets, and soe many Counters as are more but falls short of 6 to make a ticket are alsoe placed in the weekly summ'd product.

16 Penney burthens payes 2 Counters
12 Penney burthens payes . . .
8 Penney burthens payes 1 Counter

They would bring 12d burthens and pay as for 8d which is only 1 Counter. Hector will have them pay either for 16 peny of 8 penney Burthens in which he does Right.

James Murray is for the same.

COAL ACCOUNTS DATED 30TH DECEMBER 1689

DUDDINGSTON

	tickets		£	s	d
John Cunningham	51:0				
Robert Broune	43:1				
Robert Tyler	38:0				
John Mar	5:0				
Thomas Baukes	54:4				
John Baukes	34:0				
John Anderson	22:0				
	247:5	@ 4s 2d per ticket is	51	12	06
Deduct 14 tickets for oncost					
Rest 233:5 @ 2s per ticket for hewing and bearing			23	04	08
		Rest	28	07	10

BRUNSTANE

	tickets				
William Marstane	161:2				
John Black	61:4				
James Paterson	108:4				
Alexander Lugget	78:3				
John Young	109:4				
	519:5	@ 4s.2d per ticket is	108	05	10

Deduct 10 tickets for oncost			
Rest 509:5 @ 1s 8d per ticket for hewing and bearing	42	08	04
For Her Graces fire to the Lodginge, 41: tickets to the mill 6 tickets	9	16	00
	52	04	04
Rest	56	01	06
Both Products	84	09	04

Oncost:

Oversman	4	16	00
Grieve	3	00	00
Cheques	4	00	00
Wright	3	00	00
Redsman	2	08	00
John Levestane	2	00	00
For 10: Bearers carrying Rubbish to fill up the pit in the seven foot Coale	2	00	00
For 2: men filling to the Bearers	0	14	00
For 5: fathome of the Levell of the great Seame	6	00	00
For 1: upset in the 4: Foot Coale	0	13	00
For 1: upset in the 7: Foot Coale	1	00	00
For 4: C/weight of Steele	1	00	00
For 6: men 1: day for the cast	2	00	00
For 7: men 1: day at the Wheele	2	06	00
For the Myne from the 4: foot to the 7: foot	6	14	00
Small Coales Loaded to the Pans 136: Bolls By £ s			
From Duddingstoun 48: @ 1s 10d per Boll)			
From Brunstane 88: @ 2s 8d per Boll)			
Loading and Bearing	16	02	00
Oncost	57	13	00
Both Products	84	09	04
Rests	26	16	04

EXPLANATORY NOTES ON THE COAL REPORT AND ACCOUNTS

1. The names shown against the tickets are those of the colliers; some of them, Christian names as well as surnames, can be seen on a list (shown below) of the Duddingston colliers, dated 1744 (in Fletcher of Saltoun's Papers), demonstrating that generations of "bonded slaves", as Hugh Miller effectively called them, actually existed in Duddingston.
2. Section R8 of the Report section (above) explains the word "ticket". It seems strange that the five Brunstane hewers (and bearers) were paid a lower rate than the seven hewers (and bearers) at Duddingston, especially as their output was more than twice that of Duddingston.
3. The word "oncost" means expenses.
4. "Rest" means gross or net nominal coal "value". The final figure of £26 16s 04d (Scots) was shown as income in the salt account for the same week. The salt pans were about 50 years old at this point.
5. The "oncosts" for both Duddingston and Brunstane were two tickets per collier, i.e. 8s 04d each (42p). (See section R8 of the Report section).
6. Her Grace was the Duchess of Lauderdale and the Lodging was Brunstane House. (She then owned the whole of Duddingston and Brunstane).
7. The mill was that at "Duddingston Milne Toun".
8. "Redsman" was the person who tidied up.
9. Myne means mine; Oversman means manager and Grieve means foreman.
10. Small coals loaded to the Pans means small panwood coal for the salt pans.
11. The reference to seven men spending one day at the wheel, and six men spending one day at the cast means construction work on the water-gin and the associated waterway. Janet Gordon's testimony (above) now seems doubtful (or suggests that she mis-stated her age somewhat!).
12. The "upsets" and "steele" refer to mine adjustments (following a seam deviation). The progress in the first week of 1689 was two fathoms in length, and the standard rate of cost was £1 4s 0d per fathom. The "level" (drainage tunnel) was seven and a half feet high and four feet wide.
13. The great seame, four foot and seven foot coals were just east of the Magdalene salt pans. (The names "shifted" over the centuries).
14. The pit in the seven foot coal, being filled in, could be that which Baird says was on the north side of the road "east of the pans". Remember that the bearers were usually women and children; their rate of pay appears to have been four shillings each, whereas that of the two men who filled their creels, as they would with a packhorse, was seven shillings each.
15. A boll was about one and a quarter hundredweights (about 140 lbs.).
16. The "Levell of the great Seame" related to the 15 foot seam at the pans and was not the level excavated by John Biggar (near Morton Street) from 1746.

Plate 43 *Sketch of a coal bearer deep in a mine*

Plate 44 *Sketch of a typical horse gin*

17. Miscellaneous examples of coal-related expenses in the years 1686–7 are as follows, without amounts (additional comments are in brackets):

- *Stones to the Levell* (stone-lined floor)
- *1 stone* (of) *Candles for the use of the worke* (imagine carrying a cwt. of coal up a pit-shaft - by candlelight)
- *Running the mynde to the Bottome of the Sincke in the hard Flatte to the Crop of the foure foot coale* ("hard Flatte" became the field name of Hardy Flatt; the sincke was pit No. 7 in the list at the start of this chapter as it was next to the 4 feet coal).
- *900 Flooring Nailles* (Plenchers) *for ye Staire att Brunstan* (for constructing a wooden staircase from the mine to the surface).
- *To the wright for Setting downe the Staire at Brunstane 2 days and an halfe att 8d per day.*
- *Carrying forward the Levell of the 4 foot Coale and casting on the Coale upon the pavement* (at least the bearers had a stone-lined pavement to walk on).
- *2 Pound of tallowing for the use of the mill* (water-wheel).
- *Taking out of the timber out of three Sinkes and* (to the men) *ane gallone of Ale for the fastning of the Gugett of the water wheele* (the Ale was for drinking and the Gugett was the housing which held the outer end of the wheel axle.
- *Two Stone 2 pounds of Roops* (ropes) *for the use of the water-mill.*
- *John Mar at the Wester Clewse and Dam Head* - 4 days (clewse=sluice, which reflects the diversion of water to the water wheel from the Figgate Burn. The Easter Clewse would have been near Eastfield).
- *Mending the geate* (gate) *from the pitt to the Pans* (indicates a close proximity; probably refers to the pit in the north side of the road).
- *1 Lock and key to the Dore* (door) *att the Hardiflatt Pitt* (possibly pit No. 7 in the list shown earlier in this chapter).
- *To the men foure pintes of Ale.*
- *David Scott for loading stones and sand to the Wester Clewse* (the father of Peter (builder of Portobello House in about 1753 and the Figgate Bridge) and farmer at Easter Duddingston. He was the first of the Scott Family to farm in Duddingston; his father, Patrick, was a Writer in Chancery. David Scott was 42 at this point in time. On the south wall of Duddingston Church there is a pedimented tabernacle to David Scott and his (first) wife, Margaret Gourley who died in 1693).
- *Levell of the 4 foot Coale att the Pans* (There was a water level on each of the three main seams at the pans).

- *The Notar att preston for extracting the instrument against Preston Grange for Coalehewers and Bearers* (legal action to bring back hewers and bearers belonging to Duddingston).
- *Taking timber out of the pitt att the Blackhouse tree. This name was given to rigs of Brunstane land halfway between Brunstane Mill and Brunstane House (Fletcher of Saltoun Papers – MS17477).*
- *For* (the) *cutting off* (of) *whins to mend the Horse gate* (even the whins had a part to play).
- *2 Gallons Ale given to ye Collyers for helping on with the Horse Gin Chaine* (at last, evidence of a horse-gin. It is not clear where it stood, but it was obviously at the pans or the Brunstane Burn).
- *1 man and horse going to penstoun* (at Tranent) *about the Rods to boare one Downe sett and 2 Dayes boaring* (relates to making the pit shaft).
- *For 15 dozen of picks sharping.*
- *To the men that helped to fasten the pannelling of the water-mill* (wooden boards which lined the housing).
- *1 Double tree to the Horse mill to bring the Pannelling on* (wooden beams for the boards to be nailed on).
- *Draught of Timber from Brunstane to the Pans; 4 draughts of old Timber from the old Sinckes* (pits) *to the pans* (new wood from Brunstane and old from used pits).
- *40 Deales* (boards) *to bee for the use of the wheele* (water wheel).
- *For bringing from Edinburgh to the pans 15 stone of Skrews.*
- *1 Cart and horse loading clay to the Damhead* (early use of clay).
- *For 3 women carrying stones 1 day to lay the Levell* (to lay the "pavement" in the water level, or drain).
- *1 small Rope to bee 1 pooleing string – 20 fathom.*
- *21 Bags of Lyme to paynt the Sclathouses* (slate-houses).

COAL TACK OF 1746

Moving on some 60 years, here are some relevant extracts from the actual tack between Biggar and Abercorn, dated 1746.

> *. . . together with the salt-works of Magdalen-pans, with the haill houses, girnels, and office-houses, belonging to the said coal and salt-works at the Magdalen-pans, and in Easter Duddingston; particularly the houses possessed by the colliers and their servants, and the salt-grieves houses, with the change-house, office-houses, and haill pertinents thereto belonging, at Magdalen-pans, as the same were lately possessed by the widow of Andrew Horn . . . with the sole and exclusive privilege of sutlery and brewery, and of importing ale, bread, candle, and other necessaries, into the said barony; and that . . . for the use and behoof of the colliers and salters, and their children, servants, and others, employed about and resorting to the works; and to be under astriction to any person for furnishing the same : together also with six acres of the ground of the farm of Easter Duddingston next adjacent to the said Magdalen-pans, as the same was possessed under the tack of the said coal and salt works granted by the late Duke of Argyll to William Horn; (reserving always forth of this tack the houses possessed by Agnes Beaton, which is part of that house commonly called the baillie's house, and these in Easter Duddingston which are possessed by colliers, but belonging to the tenants farms).*

Girnel=salt store-house; change-house="business-house"; the six acres is the ground surrounding the pans (on both sides of the Musselburgh Road);the farm of Easter Duddingston was to the east of the pans, on the south side of the road. Agnes Beaton was the widow of one of the partners of Andrew Horn in the coal operations and her house was in the salt-work complex.

> *... to dig and bring out the said coals from the pits lately or formerly wrought by the said William Horn, or from those to be hereafter set down by the said John Biggar, or his foresaids; together with the free use of the* harbour *at Magdalen-pans; and with power to him, and his foresaids, to improve the same as they shall think fit, upon their own proper charges and expences; and likewise to set down new sinks or coal-pits, make coal-hills, form coal-roads to and from the said coal-pits to any adjacent highway, lay waggon-ways, drive levels, make water-courses, dams, and dam-heads, and erect engines . . . and search for, dig, and win, limestone, freestone, clay, gravel, sand, or any other materials useful.*

This is the first written reference to a harbour; it was on the west side of the salt pans and can be clearly seen on the map dated 1801.

> *... the said Earl assigns and makes over to the said John Biggar, and his foresaids ... all right, pretention, or property, he has in and to the colliers and salters, and their children and servants, the colliers being twenty-one in number; with full power and liberty to him, and his foresaids, to employ them as he thinks fit, in working the said coal allenarly; and also to punish them for misdemeanors or neglect of their work, as the case shall require, according to law.*

DUDDINGSTON COLLIERS IN 1744

The number of colliers reduced, as two years earlier the Duke of Argyll owned the following colliers: (Fletcher of Saltoun Papers.)

IN DUDDINGSTON
James Brown & Jean Cunningham his wife, James Brown, Abraham Brown and Robert Brown his sons.
IN LONGSIDE
John Black and Jean Dobie his wife and John Black his son
Alexander Anderson and George Flucker
IN WINTON
George Nelson and Marion Flucker his wife and Joseph Nelson his son
John Hunter and Marion Clark his wife
Robert Tayler and Jean Wilson his wife
John Bauke and Elspeth Flucker his mother
IN BONNOCKRIDGE
Archibald Bauke and Kathrine Wat his wife, Eupham Bauke, daughter
John McClean and Janet Black his wife, Janet McClean, daughter
William Brown and Alexander Brown
IN GILMERTON
John Flucker and Eupham Miller his wife
Richard Brown and Elspeth Pearie his wife
William Mark and Janet Blaik his wife
Robert Flucker and Mary Leslie his wife

James Flucker and Christian Groundiside his wife
Alexander, George, Archibald and Angus Hamilton
William Wilson and Bessie Smith his wife
IN NIDDRIE
John Hamilton and Isobel Tayler his wife, & Robert Tayler
Andrew Tayler and Margaret Bauke his wife
IN ENGLAND
John Bauke, Mary Gullen his wife
Robert Paterson and Christian Duncan his wife
COAL BEARERS
Mary Brown, Nellie Smith, Isobel Geddiss, Janet Baukes, Mary Black, Elspeth Bennet, Janet Anderson, Betty Mark, Kathrine McClean, Helen Baukes.

Also . . . "Memorandum for the Lord Justice Clerk (Lord Milton). Sir John Baird begs the favour your Lordship would give him ane order for 3 of the D: of Argyll's Colliers at Duddingston that have been *offering* there service to him they having no work from the Duke, just now, and a receipt will be given to return them when called for."

James Brown, Andrew Taylor, Robert Taylor

Perhaps we should spare a thought for these colliers and bearers, who were unlucky enough to be born into such circumstances. Was this part of the price they had to pay for well-intentioned job security willingly entered into by their ancestors (this theory is being investigated by a member of St Andrews' University)? An American, Mr L. S. Reeks, whose mother comes from the parish of Newton, has written a book, *Scottish Coalmining Ancestry*, which includes many genealogical details of Duddingston colliers.

Biggar's tack goes on:

. . . with full liberty to remove or carry away any engines, coal or water gins, tools or utensils, waggon-way timber, coal waggons or carts.

. . . right to the free, undisturbed, and uninterupted use of all the water-courses, and water, which the deceased Duchess of Argyll used in working the said coal . . . with respect to the corn-mill of Duddingston; and to the performance of which, John Biggar is bound . . . that so much of the water shall at all times run down through the town of Easter Duddingston, as shall be necessary for supplying the use of the town with water.

. . . to pay and deliver to the said Earl . . . the tenth part of whatever coal shall be wrought of the seams within the said lands; and that as well great coal and small as panwood; excepting only such part of the said coals as shall be consumed by any fire-engine, and if such be necessary, and used for drawing the water from the said coal-seams, and of which the said Earl is to have no share.

. . . to work the said coal regularly . . . leave sufficient stoops, middlings, and pillars, at proper distances, for supporting thereof, and the sides of the seams of the coals he works, and thereby prevent the falling in of the surface of the ground, commonly called coal-fits, and also that he shall fence and fill up the coal pits to be made by him whenever they become useless, so as persons and cattle may not be in danger or hurt by falling into them.

. . . if he or his foresaids shall at any time take the water from the corn-mill, so that there shall not remain a sufficiency for working the said corn-mill, that then the said John Biggar . . . shall either satisfy the master of the corn-mill for his damages, at the sight of two honest men to be mutually chosen, or shall

become tacksman of the corn-mill, dam-heads, and leads, now used in working thereof, and of the two houses presently possessed by the miller at the said mill, and of the thirlage used and wont, and the four acres of mill-lands.

This is the mill at Duddingston. There were more than two houses in the Mill Town.

... John Biggar binds and obliges himself, and his foresaids, at the issue of this tack, to restore and return to the said Earl, and his above-written, all the colliers and salters hereby assigned (at least those he gets possession of), if alive; and that in case of the death or desertion of one or more any of them, he or they shall intimate the same to the said Earl and his foresaids, or their baillie or factor for the time, who may, if it is their pleasure, *provide others to supply the vacance or vacancies.*

The remaining two extracts are taken from Biggar's tack with Lord Milton (Andrew Fletcher).

... these six seams of coal, called the Corby craig, Black Chapel, Stairhead, Great seam, Rumbles, and Flecks ... to work all the said seams (except that called Black Chapel and Corby Craig) down to the sea level, which seams, the said John Biggar ... hereby empowered to work so deep as his engine may or shall require.

The Flecks (flakes) is obviously the Flex coal, and they can all be seen in the list of seams at the start of this chapter.

... binds and obliges himself, to put in sufficient repair the road leading from the mansion-house of Brunstain down to the links, and to keep and maintain the same in the like repair during the time he ... shall use the said road for conveying and transporting the said coal.

This would appear to be the old road from the top of today's Brunstane Road to the bottom of today's Morton Street (at Joppa Road), as the date of the tack is about the same as that of Roy's map.

WHAT HAPPENED TO THE DUDDINGSTON COAL MINING INDUSTRY

As already mentioned, Baird records the last Duddingston coal operations as taking place at Joppa between the years 1842 and 1852, at the end of which period a Miss Ellis closed her pit, which was said to have been on the site of Coillesdene House, after finding the business unprofitable. Baird also mentions that the earlier Duddingston coal works, at Mount Pleasant, were "rendered useless and the pits were altogether destroyed on the 20th March, 1790, the whole of the working seams being flooded and choked through this communication of the level with the higher grounds".

Was this the end of Duddingston coal works? The "Eastern Division" of the Barony of Duddingston was sold to the Benhar Coal Co. in 1875. Did that company extract coal? It may be that Miss Ellis's efforts in 1842 were the last attempt, as Benhar wanted the land for the extraction of minerals, but no significant (new) operations were apparently carried out and the company got into financial difficulties about ten years later, and their lands were sold by the Receiver.

There is a report in the Abercorn Papers (D.623/D/10/13), however, which sums up the position of the coal mining activities in Duddingston and Brunstane as at 5th February, 1808. This report, written by John Grieve, of Ramsay Garden, Edinburgh, also throws additional light on the coal structure, economics of extraction, the possibility of making an "iron rail road" to take the coal to the Jock's Lodge area of the Barony, on its way to Edinburgh, and raises the possibility that there was some mining activity in Duddingston after the date of the report.

REPORT OF THE STATE OF THE COLLIERIES OF DUDDINGSTON AND BRUNSTANE - 1808

These Collieries are thought to be amongst the oldest in Scotland and the first that were opened for the supply of the Edinburgh market - This considered it is wonderful that they are so little exhausted, the Duddingstone Coals are only wrought to the depth of 45 fathoms below the sea level, or high water mark, and the Brunstain Colliery to the depth of only 30 fathoms.

Duddingstone Colliery was overflowed with water in March 1790, by an operation of Mr Wauchope of Nidery the adjoining Proprietor against which a Protest was taken at the time, but as this operation was upon Niddry's own ground and as an encroachment upon him by the Duddingstone people had given him the opportunity of communicating his water to them, the Protest was not followed out by any consequent legal steps – A proposal has lately been made to Niddry for doing away the effects of this encroachment by considering the Whinstone Dyke which is near the (Niddry) March.

(This "Protest" has been referred to earlier, in the form of Papers held by the Signet Library.)

Of the 17 workable seams in Duddingstone Colliery the Engine level is communicated with 14 of them, and it follows that these 14 are subjected to the waters of the Superior Collieries of Niddry – but the Parot and the Wood Coals on the south of the 14, and the North Green Seam on the north of them, are not subjected to these waters.

(Superior means "upper", not "better".)

It would have been better not to have communicated so many seams with one another, but to have put a movable Fire Engine upon a few of them, and when these few were wrought out then to have removed the Fire Engine to another Class of Seams; this may be had in view when the 14 seams shall again be opened, by putting dams in the Engine Level between the Classes to prevent their communication. In the meantime a moveable Fire Engine might be put to drain the north Green coal and the Limestone accompanying it, or might be put to drain the Parot or the Wood Coal, for there is no communication between any of those and the 14 seams, which are at present subjected to Niddry water.

In 1790, when Duddingstone Colliery was given up, Coals were selling for 3.5d per cwt - the present price is 7d per cwt. This advance of price is a strong inducement for reopening the Colliery - there is another inducement; an iron rail road may be had from it to Piershill Barracks nearly on a dead level, all on the Marquis's ground, by which Coals could be led for less than half of the cost of leading them in carts, and there is not another Colliery in the Neighbourhood of Edinburgh that can have the advantage of an iron level rail road.

(The point about the iron rail road was a proposal, not a fact. A number of old wooden wagonways were in operation in Scotland during the eighteenth century, one of the oldest (if not the earliest) taking coal from the Tranent area to the coast at Cockenzie. Many of them, relaid with iron rails, continued well on into the nineteenth century. A railway, with "moving" engines, did not appear in the Barony until 1846, although the "Innocent Railway" passed along its southern border from the early 1830s.)

In the Duddingstone Colliery there are 17 workable seams amounting in all to about 20 yards in thickness; the length from the great road from Edinburgh to Musselburgh under which road there is a Dyke in the Coal through which the workings have not yet passed, is 1,100 yards, west to the March with Niddry.

The Duddingstone Engine Pit was 50 fathoms deep; supposing it came only to be sunk 25 fathoms deeper this would drain about 35 fathoms or 70 yards additional breadth of Coal and if half of this be deducted for pillars and refuse Coal the other half would yield 770,000 Tons of Great and small Coals, and would last 60 Colliers working at the rate of 20,000 tons per year for 38 years.

Besides this there is a great deal of Coal yet to work in the old or upper Colliery for the Engine seldom could take down the water to the bottom of the pit and they were obliged to fly to the crop and leave the deep Coal unwrought - and besides all this there is from the said Dyke under the Musselburgh road, the east field of coal which runs under the Sea none of which is yet touched - there seems to be no reason why this field should not be wrought as well as the Coal fields of Whitehaven and Workington which are wrought to great extent under the Sea - In this view therefore by sinking the Duddingstone Engine pit 25 fathoms deeper, it would drain a field of Coal to last 60 Colliers, turning out 20,000 tons a year probably 100 years.

(It is possible that today's "Eastfield" derived from the coal context.)

Brunstain Colliery is about half a mile to the south of Duddingstone Colliery but the iron rail road above mentioned can very well be communicated to it - Brunstain Colliery may be also said to have been drowned by a Niddry operation - this happened in October 1794 when Niddry attempted to pour the water drawn by his Whitehill Engine into Brunstain Colliery, but had the smallest Colliery skill been exercised at Brunstain it was impossible for Niddry to have disturbed them - Brunstain Colliery is in a manner already fitted, for its Engine pit of 60 fathoms deep, and its bye pit of 50 fathoms deep are arched over at top and ready for opening at any time, nothing is wanting but the Machinery of a Fire Engine, the Engine House being already built.

(It is possible that these pits are still "arched over" see No. 25 on Plate 29.)

It appears that there are 6 edge seams of Coal in Brunstain Colliery the thickness of them in all is about 12 yards, that the stretch from the Sea side on the east, to the March at Whitehills with Niddry on the west is 1,600 yards.

On an average these seams have been wrought 30 fathoms under Sea level and as the top of the 60 fathoms deep Engine pit is 5 fathoms above Sea level, the depth of the Coals to be won by this Engine is 25 fathoms, and this by the inclination of the Seams (45 degrees South East) gives a breadth of 70 yards in each of them. From the Sea side therefore to the March with Niddry, the Coal to be won by the present depth of the Engine pit amounts to 1,344,000 cubic yards or tons and deducting half to be left in pillars and refuse Coal the remaining 672,000 tons will last 33 years at the rate of 20,000 tons a year, and this without following the Coals on their easter stretch under the Sea – The Edge seams of Brunstain should yield nearly the same Royalty as the Duddingstone edge seams, which cannot well be less than £500 a year.

The flat seams of Brunstain are as distinctly separate from the Brunstain edge seams as these are from the edge seams of Duddingstone – the flat seams of Brunstain make therefore a Colliery of themselves; they are 6 in number their total thickness 9 yards, the breadth of them to be had by placing an Engine on them in the South East corner of Duddingstone Links is 220 yards – there is no danger in following these flat seams to seaward, for they do not crop out to the surface, on the contrary their out crops are defended by a thick cover of Clay impervious to water – now every 100 yards that they are followed under the Sea will give 5 years work at 20,000 tons a year, and as they may very well be followed 600 yards, this gives 30 years work without reckoning anything upon their stretch to landward, or westerly, and without reckoning that their Sea stretch must become broader than 220 yards, which I think it will do.

These flat seams should be tried for by a boring in the S. E. corner of Duddingstone Links, the Expence (sic) *of winning them could then be ascertained – The probability is, that they will be as valuable as either of the other two Collieries and will also like them yield not less than £500 a year royalty. So that in the Marquis of Abercorn's grounds of Duddingstone and Brunstain, three distinct Collieries may be formed yielding together at least £1,500 royalty yearly.*

(This "boring in the S. E. corner of Duddingstone Links" probably refers to pit No. 6 mentioned at the beginning of this chapter, i.e. in the eastern corner of the field called "Snubneuk". If this is the case, it demonstrates that further coal mining activity did take place in Duddingston after the date of the Report and before Miss Ellis attempted it in 1842.)

It can therefore be seen that the Duddingston Coals were extensively worked, expertly reported upon, but not exhausted due to the problem with water drainage and the angle of the seams. Geology has both provided and withheld this valuable commodity in Duddingston.

The subject of the coal mines will be left with a verse from what Baird called "The Coal-Bearer's Lamentation":

When I was engaged a coal bearer to be,
When I was engaged a coal bearer to be
Through all the coal pits
I maun wear the dron brats.*
If my heart it should break,
I can never won free!

(* dron=buttocks; brats=coarse apron)

CHAPTER 7

THE BOTTOM LINE ON THE NEW HIGH ROAD

Extracts from the Minutes of the Trustees of the Post Road District 1762-1806 - 44 years of Activities Surrounding the High Road

THE SYSTEM

The Trustees of each Road District, including the Post Road District, had to report to a General Committee for approval of major decisions and had, initially, to rely on a few toll bars for their District's income. In 1762, for example, when these surviving minutes begin, there were no toll-bars in the Barony or, surprisingly, at Jock's Lodge.

The Post Road District, as far as the "Barony of Duddingston" was concerned, covered the new High Road, which was made in 1752 and 1753 (see Chapter 4), and ran from Jock's Lodge to the Maitland Bridge, via what we know as Portobello Road, Portobello High Street and Joppa Road, and included some bye-roads, or "cross roads", such as the road from Jock's Lodge to Duddingston Mill.

The much-needed work was carried out, as previously mentioned, by tenants having physically to contribute to whatever work was laid down by the "overseer", who was appointed by the Trustees, and men from outwith the Barony often worked within it. In 1762, the overseer was Thomas Dickson. The Committee generally met a few times a year, at John's Coffee House, Edinburgh.

Various extracts, depicting the conditions of the roads, problems confronted, and action taken by the Trustees, and road-building methods, are given below and are followed, as usual, by qualifying comments. Again, the quaint styles of expression are also of interest.

1762

At this date, the section of the Post Road which travelled through the Barony of Duddingston had replaced the Fishwives' Causeway and its line, as already seen in Chapter 4, had been "re-formed" about nine years earlier. (The words in italics are extracts or notes (or both) from the Minutes.)

STATUTE LABOUR ACTIVITIES

Carriages in the parishes of South Leith and Duddingston employed in repairing that part of the Post Road betwixt the east corner of Clockmill Park and the turn of the road which goes towards Portobello and all the carriages in Fisherow that could be got were applied to that part of the Road which lies near to the Magdalene pans. This was not sufficient to make the repair complete on this part of the road and another coat of gravel was laid upon it in the summer.

At this time, the eastern road from Edinburgh to London left the Canongate, curved round the Palace by lower Abbeyhill, past where Elsie Inglis Hospital was, over the Clockmill Bridge at Clockmill Lane, continued to the present entrance to Holyrood Park (at the Watering Stone and the Barber's Burn), and took the present line to Jock's Lodge, Portobello, Joppa and the Maitland Bridge. In 1712, the Stage Coach to London took 13 days, but only four days in 1773 using this route.

(Incidentally, in Thomas Johnston's *Plans of all the Roads of the several Districts in the County of Midlothian - 1777*, the Figgate Burn is wrongly shown as Barber's Burn.)

The "turn of the road which goes towards Portobello" is at the present King's Road Roundabout and the Magdalene pans were what became known as Joppa, or Duddingston, salt pans. The "carriages" is a reference to the statute labour from the two parishes.

FIGGATE BRIDGE PROBLEMS

The parapets or legens of the bridge over the Figget Burn is too laigh and that to heighten them about 3ft will require about 50 cart loads of stones and 30 bags of lime. (This was accepted, but bricks were to be used, not stones).

Laigh means "low". This bridge was at the site of the present one, near the site of the recently-removed Open-Air Swimming Pool.

DUDDINGSTON MILL BRIDGE PROBLEMS

The bridge at Duddingston Mill stands also in great need of repair - 5 bags of lime and 3 carts of stones to make it sufficient.

This was not the bridge the Kirk repaired in 1688, as that one "fell down" in 1750 and had to be repaired (at the orders of Lord Milton, who lived at Brunstane). Naturally, it was a much smaller and lower affair than the present bridge and it stood at a right angle to the burn and marks the point where the Braid (or Duddingston) Burn becomes known as the Figgate (Figget) Burn. The bridge which carries Duddingston Road over the Figgate Burn, to Portobello, was built much later, in 1825.

REPAIR COSTS IN 1762

The Post Road affecting the Barony of Duddingston

	£ s d	
Jock's Lodge to Figget Bridge	*12 11 11*	(in the Village of Figgate)
Figget Bridge to Magdalen Pans	*12 16 02*	(i.e. Joppa Salt Pans)
Legens of Figget Bridge	*10 09 01*	(parapets)
Duddingston Mill Bridge	*3 07 04*	(on the Milton Road)
	£39 04 06	

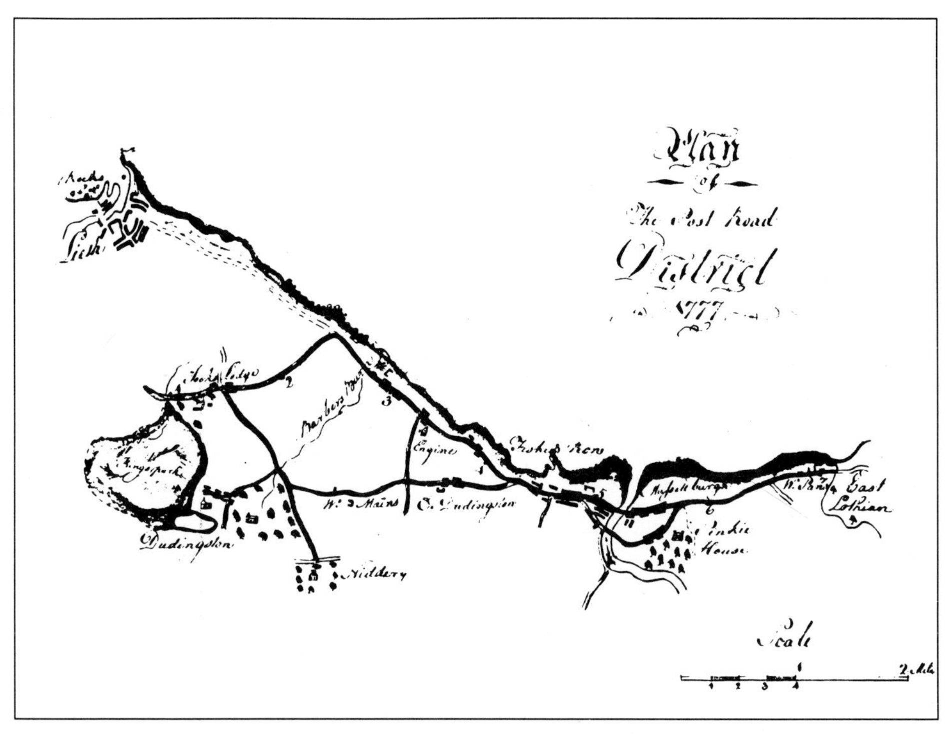

Plate 45 *Plan of the Post Road district in 1777* (Reproduced with permission of Signet Library)

The Figgate Burn is incorrectly marked as "Barber's Burn". Barber's Burn was near Muschet's Cairn at the Meadowbank entrance to Holyrood Park. The numbers mark the miles from Edinburgh.

1763: TRUSTEES REQUEST MORE POWER OVER SPENDING

> *Agreed to apply to Parliament for an Act to empower the Trustees to act in accordance with proposed requirements, therefore moneys from tolls on Post Road could be used for bye-roads also.*

Bye-roads in the Barony, under the jurisdiction of the Post Road District, as opposed to the landowner, were the roads to Duddingston Mill from Jock's Lodge, from Jock's Lodge to Niddry, and "Brunstane Road".

1764: INSUFFICIENT STATUTE LABOUR

> *Eighty roods of Post Road east of Jock's Lodge repaired; hard stones from Mr Crawford's quarry. Dickson said, "2,000 cartfulls of gravel at least would be required to put it in condition to withstand the winter and that supposes the whole statutory carriages of Duddingston and South Leith to come out regularly*

and perform their whole work upon it, they will only amount to 1,420 cartfuls and therefore there must be an allowance of money to make up the deficit. It will also be necessary to have the liberty continued of taking materials from Mr Crawford's quarry near Jock's Lodge".

One linear rood was about seven yards. The use of stones from a neighbouring quarry was apparently free. The conclusion that money would be required (from the General Committee) was a significant one, and was possibly a first step away from the statute labour system.

Notices regarding statute work were put up on church doors.

1765: MORE PROBLEMS

Jock's Lodge and the middle of the Figget Whins done. Yet to repair towards the sea, although it looks at this time of the year indifferently well, yet being a bit thin of the gravel, having no stone bottom, it cannot stand a winter without a filling yearly. Also great need for a small bridge to be made through the road at the east end of the Long Sands where the water crossed the road to the sea. The bridge at Duddingston Mill is in a very dangerous condition of falling. Dickson and his men supported, and awaiting orders to repair. Jock's Lodge to Niddrie not repaired.

Jock's Lodge was, of course, a hamlet stretching from the present crossroads at Willowbrae Road/ Smokey Brae eastwards to just beyond the Abercorn Inn site. In the Ordnance Gazetter, 1884 (much later than the date of this extract), it is described as "... extends somewhat stragglingly a quarter mile along the road; consists chiefly of a spacious cavalry barrack and two lines of dwelling houses and has a Post Office with a money order, savings bank and telegraph department, a soldiers' home and a police station. The barrack on the north side (of Jock's Lodge) was built of Craigmillar stone in 1793 and comprises a quadrangular, enclosed area (500 by 300 feet), containing accommodation for a regiment of cavalry and includes a neat, comparatively recent Episcopalian Chapel".

The Figgate Whins still only contained Portobello House and by 1765, a few new buildings erected by Jamieson.

The Long Sands was a footroad along the line of the present Promenade and the water crossing the main road could well have been coming out of Biggar's coal level which was made to drain some of the Duddingston, and other, coal mines. The public road from Jock's Lodge to Niddrie was, by now, a direct one, via the Mill Town as in the 16th century, and by-passed Wester Duddingston.

IMPOSITION OF FINES

Eighteen pennies to be collected from every householder and other person residing in Musselburgh, Fisherow, Inveresk and Newbiggin who shall fail to perform their statutory labour. Dickson had trouble getting paid.

A desperate measure to keep up some sort of standard of road surface.

Plate 46 *Jock's Lodge in 1955*

The tram lines follow the line of the old Post Road and Willowbrae Road takes the old route, to the right, towards Niddrie.

OVERSEEING THE WORK

To repair that part of the Post Road betwixt the Magdalen Bridge and Lord Abercorn's Coal Engine. Jock's Lodge towards Niddry, by Duddingston Mill; Earl of Abercorn - 6 carts; Robert Young - 2 carts; Wm. Brown - 2 carts; Joseph Berry - 1 cart; Wm. Brown - 1 cart and John Kirk - 1 cart. To be done under Abercorn's direction, failing whom - Mr Dickson.

Between Eastfield and Morton Street is the first section referred to and Mr Dickson "delegated" the job of overseeing to the landowner, as far as cross-roads were concerned.

Received Petition from Andrew Scott regarding his late father's (Peter) costs in building the Figget Bridge.

So Peter Scott, who built Portobello House for his shepherd in about 1753, also built the first stone bridge in Figgate. The previous bridge (the "old Fishwives' Bridge", made of wood) was probably near the place where the present Baileyfield Road crosses the Figgate Burn. The bridge referred to was built about 1753, when the new Post Road was made and when the present line of the High Street was formed from what had become, a few years earlier apparently, a temporary footroad.

1766

Last summer, the road betwixt the east side of Abercorn's Coal Work and Magdalen pans and several other places west towards Jock's Lodge. Also, a second coat of gravel. Part of the Post Road to the west side of Abercorn's Coal Work which never as yet got a firm laid bottom which in winter is excessively bad and requires much to be laid with stone and gravel. The road betwixt Magdalen pans and Magdalen Bridge which never was made and part of that piece of road stands both summer and winter in a loch of water. It requires a very large conduit or little arch through the road.

Andrew Scott to oversee statutory work in Easter Duddingston and Brunstane.

Brunstane Road and the road through Easter Duddingston. In 1746, Biggar's Tack obliged him to keep the Black Road (Brunstane Road) in good repair between the Links and Brunstane House.

1767

Andrew Scott was paid for the work his father, Peter, did in building the Figget Bridge.

Two years after requesting it. Bureaucracy was slow then, too.

John Johnston, soapboiler in Canongate got toll for Abbeyhill toll-bar (roup).

That is, he rented the toll. This is mentioned, as this was the way tolls were later to operate at Jock's Lodge and two other points within the Barony of Duddingston.

1768: MOVE TO CONTRACT-OUT THE WORK

Dickson is to present proposals regarding the yearly cost of upkeep for the Post Road from Barber's Burn to Maitland Bridge.

This was another milestone in the development of road upkeep; the concept of leasing, or renting, the tolls was now applied to the whole upkeep of the Post Road in the Barony.

A petition from tenants of Duddingston and Restalrig was received regarding the Abbeyhill Tolls on all carts, laden or unladen (Bill of Suspension).

Changes did not always come easily.

1769

Dickson was stopped from taking stones from Miss Crawford's quarry at Parson's Knowe.

What was allowed by Ronald Crawford, owner of Restalrig, was now disallowed by his heir.

> *Dickson is to arrange for "the blowing of stones on the road to the westward of Maitland Bridge" - 40 shillings stg yearly.*

Eastfield area - presumably this means manually hammering the stones to make the surface more even.

1771: SUNDAY TOLLS AND "BRIDGE MONEY"

> *Alex Sliven, mason, to quote for the repair of the Figget Bridge. The north land breast has been undermined by the water and has given way so far. Dickson repaired it temporarily and the other breast is to be checked daily. The arch is in order, if it be properly taken care of it may stand for these 100 years to come. It is 15 foot in span. The retaining walls are to be repaired. It was suggested to the general meeting that a sum be granted out of the bridge money for the county for repairing it and that application ought to be made to Parliament for a Sunday toll on wheel machines and saddle horses. Sliven built a bridge at Dalkeith. His estimate for the Figget Bridge was £70 stg.*

We have seen statute labour, money requested from the General Committee, the addition of tolls for unladen carts, fines for not carrying out statute duties, contracting out the road maintenance and now we see a "County Bridge Fund" being used and Sunday tolls. The readiness of the Committee to apply to Parliament is interesting.

> *Some years ago, this road (Post Road) did not require that expense to keep it up as is now necessary. It was not then confined by Dykes or Hedges on each side as at present. There was near two miles of it through Link ground which needed no repairs at all. Ground materials were also to be had in plenty at the seaside where now a cartfull is not to be got. Two Coal Works and two brickworks have lately been erected in this quarter and these with the drawing of sand from the seaside for the new building about Edinburgh and the great increase in chaises and wheel carriages of all sorts do now occasion such destruction to this road that the small toll of a halfpenny on each cart and the statute work which is perfectly trifling are not sufficient with the best Economy to keep it longer in tollerable Condition. The committee requested the Sunday toll to be applied to the Police Bill going through Parliament.*

The dykes and hedges were part of the "land enclosure" idea carried out by landowners. This was becoming a popular way of contributing towards the efficiency on the farm, but obviously had disadvantages on the roads. The "two miles of Link ground" were through the Figgate Whins and this is a reference to the old Fishwives' Causeway, which was paved, and therefore required "no repairs at all". The two brickworks were at Adam's Law (west end of the village) and the new "Joppa" complex, just west of the pans. The two Coal Works were near the present Morton Street/Joppa Road junction and (at this time, possibly) on the north side of the road, east of the pans, at today's "Joppa".

1772

The road betwixt the Salt pans and Maitland Bridge is in exceedingly bad repair, particularly at one place which is for the most part covered with water. To make a drain or syver.

This section of the road had not yet been "made" and was obviously causing many problems.

MORE BRIDGE PROBLEMS

Got £50 and lodged it with William Cuming and Son, bankers in Edinburgh. Considered the advice of Deacon William Jamieson, mason. Approved of a proposal by Thomas Dickson (overseer) re Figget Bridge. Two buttresses on south-west of bridge at two and a half feet in thickness for the old wall until it should be half way up then take down old wall and bind them with a course of strong, long stone then raise the height of both on one - £19 Stg. William Jamieson to oversee and the actual bill was £30 12s 11d, as the basis was "daily wages", but it had a guarantee of 10 years.

This is an interesting reference to an early Edinburgh bank. Jamieson was now involved in "shaping" the road development in Portobello.

Dickson also built a small "bridge" on the Post Road near Abercorn's new salt pans. An arch, 30 inches wide, 50 feet long and 3 feet high, lain in strong flaggs - "so a man may go in and clean it". The stone came from either Cairntows or Restalrig quarry and cost £10 stg.

The "new" salt pans were either the ones on the south side of the High Road or new buildings on the old site, by the sea on the north side of the road. Note the quarries at Cairntows (between Craigmillar and Wester Duddingston) and Restalrig, as well as the Parson's Knowe (near Jock's Lodge), the east end of the King's Park and Salisbury Crags, mentioned earlier. Stone was quarried at these quarries for road building, but not necessarily for buildings.

1773

Dickson repaired base of east abuttment of Freegate Burn, and floods washed away the earth. A Wm. Rankine feued a piece of ground there on which he had built a Milne, deepened the channel of the water below the bridge, taken away the stones formerly there and made a miln dam or lead with them. Repairing road betwixt Portobello and the Coal Engine.

There appears to have been no end to enterprise in early Portobello.

Trustees suggested to General Committee - apply to Parliament regarding additional tolls on coaches, chaises and saddle horses.

Even more financial aid was necessary to combat the bad state of the roads.

1776

The clerk advertised, in July 1775, in the newspaper for a contractor for keeping up that part of the Post Road from Comely Garden at the Barber's Burn to the Magdalen Bridge. Dickson and Rbt. Skirving of Wallyford were considered.

Probably advertised in the *Mercury* or the *Courant*.

OPTING OUT OF THE STATUTE LABOUR SCHEME

Duddingston and South Leith Parishes were being allowed to opt out of the statute labour by paying a sum of money in lieu, based on the number of ploughs, acres or carts held: a selection is shown below:

	Ploughs	*Acres*	*Carts*	*Conversion*		
				£	*s*	*d*
Earl of Abercorn for Duddingston lands	*4*			*1*	*16*	*00*
James Duncan, Wester Duddingston	*2*		*4*	*0*	*12*	*00*
John Horn, Duddingston Mill	*1*		*3*	*0*	*13*	*06*
Andrew Scott	*4*			*2*	*00*	*06*
Peter Horn	*3*		*6*	*1*	*11*	*06*
Mr Hamilton for Brunstane	*3*			*1*	*07*	*00*
Charles Aitken, Wester Duddingston		*7*		*0*	*01*	*06*
Baron Maule		*6*		*0*	*01*	*06*
William Jamieson for the Figgate		*30*	*3*	*0*	*09*	*00*
Thomas Hill for the Figgate		*10*		*0*	*02*	*00*

A total of 22 people were involved, totalling £23 13s 00d. The tenants, and other residents mentioned on the list, agreed. Dickson got the job of contractor for the Post Road.

Mr Hamilton was at that time the factor for Abercorn. Charles Aitken (tenant) may be an ancestor of the Aitkens (James and Robert) who were millers in Duddingston Mill (and Brunstane) for many years until it (Duddingston Mill) stopped operating in 1950. Baron Maule lived in Easter Duddingston and Messrs Duncan, Horn, Scott and Horn were all tenants. Opting out of statute labour by payment in lieu was another important historical development concerning the District's roads. The collective decision on the part of the inhabitants would not have been a great surprise. Jamieson had sold about ten acres by this time as he owned about 40 acres in Figgate by 1771.

1780: ASHES TO ASHES

Ashes from the Salt pans were turned over into the road, confining it and Daniel Murray, the new undertaker for the Post Road was to keep road clear, without depriving the public of the liberty of taking these ashes for the benefit of the roads.

Murray had apparently replaced Dickson as undertaker (contractor) for the Post Road. If statute labour was difficult to achieve, the idea of the public voluntarily taking the ashes to repair the roads indicates that people must have been motivated by desperation.

Abercorn asked to give orders to solve the salt pans "ashes" problem.

1783: TOLL TACK

8th August 1783 – a Toll Tack between the Trustees of the Post Road District and Wm. Thomson and Arch. MacDowall, Merchants in Edinburgh:
15 years. Petty Customs or Duties exigible upon Carriages and loaded horses on Post Road, i.e. Clockmiln Bridge to Magdalen Bridge. (Musselburgh Magistrates agreed to take over responsibility of the Post Road from Magdalen Bridge to Ravenshaugh Burn).

1. *. . . from the Clockmiln Bridge to the Entry to the Fishwives' Causeway where there is a Water Channel only on one side of the Road except for the space of three chains or thereby at the beginning by laying thereon Hard Stones broke as small as Pullets' Eggs six inches thick upon the high side decreasing gradually to three Inches at the Water Channel, The Water Channel to be thoroughly cleared and the water syver at the Smith's house to be raised and enlarged.*
2. *From the Entry to the Fishwives' Causeway to the Freegate Burn which will admitt of a Water Channel on each side of the Road, the said Water Channels to be thoroughly made and cleared, the Road to be made by laying thereon hard stones broke as small as Pullets Eggs fifteen feet broad, six inches thick in the middle, decreasing gradually to three inches thick at the sides and two new water syvers to be made at the places necessary.*
3. *From the Freegate Bridge to Portobello Bridge the Road to be formed as above, but 18 feet broad, 12 inches thick in the middle and four inches thick at the sides.*
4. *From Portobello Bridge to Duddingston New Salt Pans, in a similar manner to (1) and (2) above.*
5. *From Duddingston Pans to Magdalen Bridge, 18 feet broad, 14 inches thick in the middle and 4 inches at the sides, and in case upon trial the finishing of this last part of the Road with Gravel in manner before-mentioned shall not stand good and give satisfaction to the Trustees – Thomson and MacDowall to re-lay this part of the Road.*

Further, a Covering of small gravel to the whole Road upon which hard materials are to be put agreeable to this construction and the Trustees.

Interesting features of this tack are that it was over a period of 15 years and that it was let initially to merchants, and not road builders. The introduction of detailed road specifications, albeit in a rather quaint way, was yet another interesting demonstration of how the Committee dealt with the road problems. The well-known advertising slogan, "to go to work on an egg" takes on yet another meaning.

Another significant development was the taking over, by the Magistrates of Musselburgh, of the responsibility of their section of the Post Road. This was the "beginning of the end" of the Post Road District Committee, although the end actually took a long time to come.

The entry to the Fishwives' Causeway is the present one on Portobello Road, and not the original one at Jock's Lodge. The Smith's house was, approximately, in a position which would now be in the middle of the road in front of the Abercorn Inn. The section between the entry to the Fishwives' Causeway and the Figgate Bridge was via the High road, and not the Causeway.

The dimensions of the road structures in the different road sections vary significantly:

1. Jock's Lodge to Fishwives' Causeway - from 3″ to 6″ thick.
2. To Figgate Bridge - 15′ wide and 3″ to 6″ thick.
3. To Portobello Bridge - 18′ wide and 4″ to 12″ thick.
4. To Magdalene Bridge - 18′ wide and 4″ to 14″ thick.

This obviously reflects the problems already seen regarding the state of the roads, i.e. the sections east of the Figgate Burn were heavily used and, at the Magdalene Bridge end, had not been "made". The actual position of Portobello Bridge is not shown on any maps (there were no other sizeable burns), but it is likely to have been between Hope Lane and Bath Street, otherwise that part of the road would not have been (a) big enough to have been a separate section and (b) called the Portobello Bridge. (An arched tunnel covering a ditch was often referred to as a "bridge" at that time). In Chapter 1, in the boundary definition of the lands of Figgate, a "lech", or ditch, was mentioned. It is likely that Portobello Bridge was an arched tunnel over this ditch.

The Petty Customs included - sixth of a penny for a loaded horse and a half-penny for Carts, Waggons, Sledges, laden or unladen.

Sledges were used to circumvent the original toll regulations, which only referred to loads on wheels. But the law caught up eventually. There were two and a half old pennies in one of our new ones; and yet, the toll for a loaded horse was one sixth of an old penny.

There were no meetings between April 1785 and October 1789.

1789-90: NEW TOLL BARS AND TOLL HOUSES

An Act of Parliament introduced 5 new Toll bars, including 2 at Jock's Lodge on the Great and Cross Road there. The two toll houses have been erected at Jock's Lodge. The cost of the 5 bars was:

	£ s d
John Douglas, wright, erecting 5 Tollbars	*38 07 08*
Wright work to the Toll House at Jock's Lodge	*32 18 00*
Robert Nisbet, mason, building Tollhouse at Jock's Lodge	*50 00 00*
Alex Laidlaw, Tinplate worker, for a lamp to the JL Toll	*00 15 00*

One of the toll houses at Jock's Lodge attended to the traffic on the Post Road, the other one charged the traffic on the "Willowbrae" road.

Advertisements put in newspapers concerning upkeeping the Post Road (same sections) and for making a new Turnpike Road from Leith to Seafield till it joins the Post Road at the west end of the Long Sands. George Welsh was approved and the road was to be 35 feet wide.

Obviously, the people who took the Post Road tacks did not retain them for the full term of 15 years. This is the making of the Seafield Road as it is now known. It replaced a footroad which came from the west end of the Promenade (Long Sands).

FIRST BORROWING

Robert Nisbet, mason, built the Jock's Lodge Toll Houses. The Trustees agreed to borrow £2,000, by now permitted by law, upon an assignment to the Tolls within the Post Road District. Sir Arch. Hope was the lender; he was also the Chairman or the Convener of the Post Road District.

The act of borrowing money was yet another stage in the development of the Post Road District's evolution. Incidentally, the name of this gentleman's son can still be seen on a stone plaque on the south side of the Abercorn Bridge (Baileyfield Road); it commemorates the building of that bridge, by the Trustees, in 1826. Sir John Hope was the Convener at that time.

NEW TACK FOR THE POST ROAD

Welsh also got contract to repair and upkeep the Post Road from the Watering Stone to Magdalen Bridge:
42 feet broad - widen and form where authorised
level that part east of Fire Engine
straight that part near the salt pans
hard mettle 30 feet wide, 12 inches thick in middle, 9 at sides
water channels and drains
Road from Post Road to Sands - 300 yards side of Hillcoats property
10 year upkeep
Cost = £1,561 00s 01d stg
+ covered drains at 2s per foot
+ road repair at £35 per mile
+ footroad repair at £2 per mile yearly (pavement)
+ Sands road repair £2 03s 02d yearly

Another contractor was appointed for the Post Road. Note that the road is now to be 42 feet wide almost all the way along and that part, at and east of the salt pans, had to be levelled and straightened. The hard metalling is now much deeper than before and the difference in width allows for walkers. The road to the Sands later became King's Road and Hillcoat's property was on the site of the (much) later Power Station (on the Craigentinny lands).

As a further encouragement to George Welsh, application shall be made for liberty to him to take materials from the east end of the King's Park by a gate

Plate 47 *Jock's Lodge toll house*

The triple marks on the wall of the toll house indicate the position of one of the toll-gate posts. The road to the left is the road to Edinburgh and that to the right goes, via what became known as "Smokey Brae", to Restalrig and Leith.

to be made near the Watering Stone – Trustees' expense . . . and can have what broken stones in the King's Park now belong to the Trustees and their tools. Nisbet built a dyke round the new quarry in the east part of the King's Park.

The gate was possibly the first to be made in the dyke at this place. Although the Duke's Walk was there at that time, it is not known whether or not there was previously a full entrance to the Park but there was a stile.

Estimate from Welsh re repairing Cross Road from Duddingston Mill Bridge to Leith. Mill Bridge to Jock's Lodge = 235 roods 5 yards, at 18/- per rood. Foot Road from Magdalen Bridge to join that at Coal Engine = 241 roods 2 yards to be covered with Pan ashes at 2/6d per rood.

A cross-road was the name given to a bye road; it was nothing to do with a four-directional junction. (One linear rood was about seven yards.)

The distance from the Watering Stone to Magdalen Bridge = 3 miles 88 roods.

This section of the Post Road ran from today's entrance to the Park, near Meadowbank, to the Maitland Bridge, near Eastfield.

Welsh's contract (7th October 1790) includes:
Keep the roads always free of Rutts, Tracks, or Checks as also of mud or Slush and shall shovel or rake the mettle part once between 1st November and 1st March yearly at least. May use good gravel from the seaside on the Post Road, with permission.

Restrictions in the taking of materials from the seaside were now necessary. One wonders how much material was actually removed from here over the years.

Advertisements in the Mercury *and* Courant *on 10th July 1789. Allowed Tacksman of the Tolls Room Rent to Tollgather at Jock's Lodge 10 weeks before Tollhouse was ready.*

Paid Notary and expenses taking a Protest against Mr Cauvin for building at Jock's Lodge - 31st December 1789.

Mr Louis Cauvin, Jnr taught Robert Burns French for a period of three months when the poet came to Edinburgh. Cauvin, who is said to have been impressed by Burns's ability to learn the French language, leased ground at Jock's Lodge, and near Duddingston Mill, from Abercorn. He was a somewhat colourful character and more of him is yet to be mentioned.

Making of Duddingston Mill to Jock's Lodge Road delayed (May 1791); Welsh agreed.

1791

Walter Scott, for Abercorn, rejected compensation rate of £100 per acre at Jock's Lodge (road widening). Justices of the Peace approved £200 in total.

This was Sir Walter Scott's father, who was the factor for Abercorn.

Paid Welsh £84 15s 00d for repairing Jock's Lodge to Duddingston Mill Road.

This was a lot less than the estimate.

Extra Toll bar erected at the corner of the houses near to St Margaret's Well - to stop toll evasion; same at Clockmill.

1792: USING STONES FROM SALISBURY CRAGS

Welsh proposed to use blue stones from Sallisbury Hill at £120 per mile and to increase his charge as that quarry is a mile further off. Agreed.

Salisbury Crags have been much used for road making; this explains the "bites" out of the cliff face.

Where road is so narrow as not to admitt any kind of summer road, 2 feet in breadth of the mettle should be taken from each side of the road and laid upon the centre to raise it and allow water to run off. If a summer road - take 2 feet from the other side.

A summer road was simply a part of the road used for walking.

The blue whin from Sallisbury Rocks are of a better quality.

August, 1792, agreed to widen road at Jock's Lodge. £200 per acre is the compensation rate.

Plate 48 *Abercorn Bridge and Baileyfield Road*

It is thought that the old Fishwives' Causeway crossed the Figgate Burn at about this point.

Plate 49 *The King's Road junction*

A "powerful passing place" – horse, electricity and steam. King's Road was, prior to King George IV's visit of 1822, known as "the road to the sands".

There had been a series of road widening exercises at Jock's Lodge over the years. The old houses which once stood here were positioned well into the middle of today's road (between Willowbrae Road and Abercorn Inn).

The Town Council of Edinburgh, other societies and individuals, kept up the Post Road. Hill, MacDowall and Scott had immediate charge of it.

The Trustees appear to have delegated their responsibility for a period. The first two gentlemen were previous tacksmen of the tolls and the third was Andrew Scott of Northfield.

1793

Tollgatherer's house at Jock's Lodge was built on Mr Simpson's land - free of charge.

This is Mr Simpson of Parson's Green (Parson's Knowe). Parson's Green House, situated on the hill above Meadowbank, was demolished in the early 1970s. That estate bordered Duddingston on the north side and included the land next to Jock's Lodge, on the west side of the road. It was part of the lands of Restalrig.

1796: LAND SURVEYOR ATTACKED BY BURNS'S FRENCH TEACHER

John Lawrie assaulted and attacked by Mr Cauvin, french teacher in Edinburgh, between Jock's Lodge and Duddingston Miln, violently cutt and bruised in several parts of the body.

John Lawrie was a surveyor, whose maps of the area are still readily available in the archives today. What Lawrie did, if anything, to provoke such an attack, or what happened to Cauvin for doing it, is not known.

2nd November 1796 - agreed to pay Welsh 1/6d per rood for foot road from Duddingston Miln to Jock's Lodge. 221 roods = £16 11s 06d.

This is the first pavement on what became Willowbrae Road. The only houses on this road were at the "Milne Toun", on the mill side of the road, and a small house stood on "Willowbrae" at the foot of Paisley Drive.

1799

Paid John Lawrie for Bullwark opposite Abercorn Saltpans.

This reflects the fact that salt pans were also on the south side of the road. John Lawrie seemed to do all the building, so he was possibly a mason as well as a surveyor.

NEW DUDDINGSTON MILL BRIDGE

Contract between Trustees of Dalkeith District and John Young, mason, Duddingston, dated 17th July 1798 - to build new Duddingston Bridge. Dalkeith are now claiming half of cost and interest. Paid them £114 13s 02d. Robert Martin, mason, for rebuilding Magdalen Bridge in August, 1800; cost was £938 03s 06d and Musselburgh Magistrates to pay £200.

The series of problems with the old bridge was at last to come to an end. Or was it?

1801: COAL MINE COLLAPSES UNDER POST ROAD

A large sitt of an edge seam of an old wrought coal the property of the Marquis of Abercorn fell in on the side of the road near the 3rd milestone and runs across the road at no great depth from the surface. Thomas Scott to be told to sort.

A sitt was a collapsed coal mine and the third milestone (within Post Road District, but four miles from Edinburgh) was just east of the salt pans. Mr Thomas Scott was the estate factor. See Plate 29 for the "shape" of the Post Road in 1801.

1802

Toll bars now at Jock's Lodge, St Magdalen's Well and Restalrig. Still none actually in the main part of Duddingston Estate.

To building a Bullwark at the salt pans to defend the road from encroachments from the sea and parapet wall - £748 14s 11d.

A watering stone to be erected at the road-side on the side of the brae north of Duddingston Mill.

St Magdalen's Well was situated on the site now occupied by Meadowbank Sports Centre. It is marked by a stone near the railway, but the stone structure which stood over the well now stands over a spring in Holyrood Park, near the Palace of Holyroodhouse.

The watering stone was situated half way up Willowbrae Road, where the water from Dunsapie Loch runs, before it flows down to the foot of Paisley Drive, under Willowbrae Road and Northfield Broadway, before making its way to the Figgate Burn near the footbridge below Duddingston Primary School! The water is now in pipes, but about two years ago, a pipe burst causing water to flood a house in Ulster Gardens. Slight subsidence problems may have been experienced on some properties on that part of Willowbrae Road (original address for which was Meadowfield Terrace) and it is thought that the houses were built quite close to the original "ditch" in the 1930s. Until about 1960, a water trough still stood at the site of the "watering stone", for the purpose of providing horses with a drink - at that time, the horses using it belonged to the "Co-operative Society".

The old Magdalen Bridge and road section to be sold.

This old bridge, still in existence, has been recently re-pointed, but does not lead anywhere, as a large, stone wall stands at the west end of it.

Duddingston Mill bridge to be attended to (1802). Foundations secured in 1803.

The quality of the new bridge was suspect.

1804: NEW ROAD TO EDINBURGH

Committee to consider proposed line of new road from Leith Walk to Jock's Lodge.

This is the first reference, in the minutes, to the building of today's road from the Meadowbank Stadium area to Leith Walk, via Abbeyhill. No road was there previously. Incidentally, Princes Street was completely built by 1805.

1806

Intimation by Louis Cauvin re his intention to build upon a piece of ground situated on the west side of the high road.

His father, also called Louis, had rented a house and ground at Jock's Lodge, where he died in 1778. The son also rented ground at Jock's Lodge, as well as a farm (Earl's Farm) on the site of "The Woodlands" (now Woodlands Grove). The house mentioned in this passage was called "Louisfield" and stood in its own grounds on the corner formed by Willowbrae Road and Duddingston Road West. After his death, in 1825 (aged 71), a trust fund set up under his will provided for the house to be altered (large pillars and facing stones added) and to become a "hospital", or school, for the sons of teachers and farmers, whom failing the sons of respectable master printers or booksellers, and the sons of respectable servants in the agricultural line. The boys were maintained in the school for six years, and were taught ordinary branches of education and Latin, Greek, French, German and mathematics. This building is now the main one of a superb Sheltered Housing Complex. His brother, Joseph, who was a sub-tenant at Earl's Farm (Woodlands) for a time, died in 1815, aged 62. The Cauvin family is buried in Restalrig churchyard.

1806

Welsh's contract ended by agreement - he could not keep up with costs and 24 person coaches ruining the road.

This passage has a modern application also.

Plate 50 *Louis Cauvin and David Scott*

Cauvin, the founder of Cauvin's Hospital (now Willowbrae Sheltered Housing Complex) and Scott, of the fourth successive generation of his family to farm in Duddingston.

THE NEW ROAD FROM PORTOBELLO TO DUDDINGSTON KIRK

In 1825, the road from Duddingston Mill to Portobello (Duddingston Road) was made - or at least part of it. The minutes record, " . . . not hitherto been able to obtain a convenient entrance into Portobello for the new line at present making from Duddingston Mill . . . propose to open up that part of the projected road from the junction of the Seafield and Post Roads to Niddry Mill as far as the new line from Duddingston Mill whereby an access though not direct would in the meantime be had into Portobello."

Mr Baxter, architect and builder of Brighton Crescent and Place, refused the Trustees permission through his land, and the road to Portobello therefore had to turn left at Southfield to the Fishwives' Causeway, then right to the High Road and right again, into Portobello.

In this residential area, new social considerations were now finding their way into developmental regulations. For example, when the houses in Sandford Gardens (originally Sandford Street) were built, the residents could not "deposit dung or rubbish etc. for sale; use houses as shops, taverns or tap room; no brewing, distilling, tanning leather, making soap, candles, glue, cudbear (dye) or vitriol (acid); could not erect glass works, foundries of brass, iron or other metals, engines, manufactories of soot or blood, or kilns for burning lime or brick or other businesses or manufactories which may be hurtful or disagreeable to the neighbourhood". They could, however, put down pan or kiln ashes on the road and lanes to keep them in repair - no doubt some of the ashes from the salt pans were used there - and they had to pay for half the expense of keeping up Sandford Street; half the expense of the covered drain running along the street and quarter of the expense of the drain at the chapel. The present church, St John's Roman Catholic Church, was not built until 1908. Incidentally, such restrictions in the New Town of Portobello were not new; in the 1802 deeds of the Flint Mill (later a white lead mill), near Adelphi Place, read a clause which may have been regarded by some as rather vague, if not sinister; the purchasers could take down the mills if required, but "could not erect or carry on any manufactory that is not allowed to be carried on in towns in England".

So, to protect such a haven from the intrusion of a main road, Mr Baxter forced the Road Trustees, who had already planned what were to become Baileyfield Road and Duddingston Road South, to expedite the first section, from Southfield Place to the Fishwives' Causeway. They would initially, pay for this part of the road, and a bridge over the Figgate Burn (Abercorn Bridge), and the remainder of the road to Niddrie Mill would be made later. This proposal was accepted.

Thus two new bridges over the Figgate Burn were built - Duddingston Road (near the mill) in 1825 and the Abercorn Bridge (Baileyfield Road) in 1826.

Incidentally, it was in 1825 that Robert Louis Stevenson's father was again asked to report, this time on mills on the Figgate at Portobello. The problem surrounded the level of the damhead of Mr Smith's White Lead Mills (where Adelphi Place now is), which had allegedly been raised by about 27 inches. Mr Stevenson suggested that the problem could be removed if the tenants were encouraged to keep the burn free from rubbish. Mr Smith's upper mill had an undershot wheel originally, which was replaced by a breast wheel, 18 feet in diameter.

In a sketch of the turnpike roads and gates, dated 1841 (RHP 10231), the following roads are shown:

1. Jock's Lodge to Portobello
2. Portobello to Musselburgh
3. Jock's Lodge to Duddingston Mill

Plate 51 *Woodlands*

This fine house was demolished in 1960 to make way for Woodlands Grove, and stood on the site of Duddingston Hut, or Earl's Farm.

4. Duddingston Mill to Southfield (Baileyfield Road/Duddingston Road)
5. Duddingston Mill to Cairntows (Craigmillar/Duddingston Road West)

The only toll bars in the Barony at that time were Jock's Lodge and Southfield. In a County Road Map of 1850 (RHP 10230), there were toll bars at Jock's Lodge, Southfield (Place) and on the coast road, where Easter Duddingston Farm was, at Eastfield.

When did Duddingston Road finally break into Brighton Place? Twenty-one years after the road from the mill to Southfield toll bar was started - i.e. in 1846.

Although the following descriptive lines are taken from an old north-east ballad, they illustrate adequately the reality of making the old turnpike roads and are therefore shown to sum up this section:

The hielan' and the lowlan' chiels	(young men)
Cut doon the knowes wi' spads and sheels,	(spades and shovels)
And bored the stanes wi' jumpin' dreels,	(drills)
To get the road in order.	

The Meerisons, the Wichts and Giels,	
Were swack and willin' workin' chiels,	(quick)
Sae weel's they banged the barrow steels	
To gar the road gae forder.	
The road's as smooth's a harrowed rig,	
Wi' stankies on ilk side fu' trig,	(drains, each, tidy)
And ilk bit burn has noo a brig,	
Where ance we had to ford 'er.	
The turnpike it will be a boon,	
To a' the quintra roon and roon,	(country)
And lat folk gae and come frae toon	
Wi' easedom and wi' order.	

On fit ye're owre it free to stray,
But if a beast ye chance tae hae
At ilka sax miles ye maun pay
For gaun a bittie forder.

CHAPTER 8
TURNING BACK THE MILL WHEELS

THE MILL TOWN

If the map of the Barony of Duddingston is shaped like a boot, with the toe at Eastfield and Portobello forming the laces, then roughly where the ankle, or pivot of the foot, would be is the "pivot of life" in the Barony of Duddingston - the Mill Town.

It has been seen that this place sits on an ancient route from Leith to the south and on an even more ancient route also - a water course which has taken water off the Pentland Hills since time immemorial; it is "callit the Figget fra it cum fra Craigmillar". As will be seen, however, there is some doubt about the exact course the burn has taken over the centuries.

To see the Mill Town in perspective, one must recall the layout of the Barony of Duddingston. During the last few hundred years, almost all of the people who lived in Duddingston lived in the two "touns" - Easter and Wester Duddingston. All the farming tenants rented rigs, or strips, of land in fields spread throughout the Barony and this arrangement was a good way of distributing the tenants' access to the richer, as well as poorer, soils.

The landowner, who thus obtained rents for the use of the land, also obtained income from the use of the mills. One of the conditions of tenancy was a requirement that all grain had to be milled at the landowner's mills; this system was called thirlage and multure duties were paid in order to have the work done. The Barony of Duddingston, like all similar arrangements, was big business - for the owner.

Why then, did Duddingston Mill, as we knew it, come to be on its present site and how long has it been there? Obvious geographical reasons can explain why mills were built at that place; water could be easily captured by a dam before losing height, allowing some of the water to be channelled off to feed mill wheels, before being allowed to run back to the Figgate Burn.

As far as the second question is concerned, mills have been on or near this site for hundreds of years. Baird quotes passages from several Kelso Abbey charters, dating back to about 1300 (for Wester Duddingston and 1221-36 for Easter Duddingston). A typical section in old charters like these is, ". . . shall hold the foresaid land of us and our successors in meadows and pastures, in mills and waters . . .". The Laing Charters, that is the collection of old charters bequeathed to the University of Edinburgh by David Laing, Librarian to the Signet Library and resident of Portobello where he died in 1878, open their Duddingston story in November 1534. Again, mills are a central part of the title deeds, as they were an important means of income and control. The Court of Session case of 1559-64, previously mentioned, is the earliest recorded evidence of mills having been on, or near, the present site, but it is reasonable to assume that this situation had prevailed at least since the time of the earlier charters, mentioned above. It is quite possible that mills have been operating on the Braid/Figgate Burn within

Duddingston for at least a thousand years. (That part of the burn south of Duddingston crossroads, which is now called the Braid Burn, was then called the Figgate Burn.)

Ownership of Duddingston was, in the earlier centuries, shared. For example, in the Court of Session case cited above and described in an article by H. M. Paton in Volume 23 of *The Old Edinburgh Club*:

> *Andrew Murray, of Balvarde had the half lands of Wester Duddingston with the half mill thereof, with pertinents lying in the regality of Kelso and sherrifdom of Edinburgh, holding feu of the abbot and convent of Kelso and Thomas Thomsoun (ypothegar of Duddingston and burges of Edinburgh) had that part of the lands of Easter and Wester Duddingston which pertained sometime to Robert Bertoun, with the other half of the said mill, also holding in feu of the said abbot of Kelso and his convent as part of the patrimony of the Abbey.*

Further examples of shared ownership, together with general ownership details, can be seen in Appendix III.

EXAMINING THE OLD WATER SYSTEMS

The Court of Session process of 1564, which took place only about 50 years after the first book was ever printed in Scotland, says they (Murray and Thomson) have been in possession, " . . . of ane dam maid of stane athort the burn callit the Figgat burn abone and besowth thair said miln with ane clowse (sluice) thairintill quhairthrow thair discendit fra the said principall burn ane small watter quhilk ran thairfra be ane small leid and wattergang wrocht and maid be mennis handis throw the saidis landis of Dudingstoun onto the said miln and servit the same of wattir", and they have been in continual possession "be ane vaill (valley) litill bewest the said burn of the said dam clowse leid and wattergang passing to the said miln be maner and passing foirsaid and of that parte of the saidis landis quhairthrow the said leid and wattergang passit".

This passage is very important to the understanding of the development of the topography of the Bingham/Duddingston crossroads/Mill area, because it indicates that the course of the Figgate Burn, between Duddingston Golf course and the Figgate Park, has been altered significantly since 1564, viz:

1. The dam was on the Figgate and was above and south of the mill.
2. A man-made lade ran from the dam and sluice *through the lands* of Duddingston to the mill.
3. The valley was *a little west of the burn* (this "valley" is the ravine which lies between Duddingston Golf Course and the Figgate Park, and which now carries the Figgate Burn).

That is, the Figgate Burn apparently did not run from its present course from Duddingston Golf Course, through the "valley" towards the Figgate Park; it ran further east. In an earlier chapter, it was mentioned that there used to be a public road from Wester Duddingston to Niddrie, which crossed the Burn near what is now Bingham Way. This is where the dam and sluice appear to have been in 1564. The burn did not turn to its left as it does now, through the remainder of Duddingston Golf Course, but came a little to the east, (crossing, at the one point, the roads to Niddrie from both Wester Duddingston and Leith) before turning north - thereby passing somewhere a little to the east of the present site of Southfield Farm and the "valley".

This view fits in with No. 3 above and explains the italicised phrase in No. 2, i.e. if the lade referred to was the length of the "present" one (about 300 yards), the process would hardly use this particular wording.

The records of Duddingston Kirk assist here also, as there is an entry in the Accounts, dated 12th October, 1693: "To Expence (*sic*) on building ye Crannes Bridge - £11 8s.6d". The chapter on field names relates the variations Cranvas, Cranies, Crannes and Cranny to an area near Bingham Way and the chapter on the old roads illustrates the old road from Wester Duddingston to Niddrie crossing the burn about this point in 1752. This entry in the Accounts (a) confirms the existence of the road crossing a burn in this area and (b) gives credibility to the idea that the mill dam was once here, if one accepts the interpretation of Crannes and so on as being related to a sluice.

EXAMINING THE MILL SITES

From the sketch drawing, dated 11th March, 1564, which accompanied the relevant Session Papers, it would seem that the mill, owned by Murray and Thomson, was further down the Figgate Burn than the present mill site. One has to interpret this sketch with caution, however, as the features are out of proportion to each other and, taken on its own, exact positions of items, relative to today's layout, are difficult to determine. It would also seem that their mill lade left the burn at the same sluice mentioned above, ran northwards, just to the east of the line of the present burn as it runs towards the dam, within the Golf Course, and that it was this *lade* that ran down the "valley", on the present Figgate Burn route, to serve the mills. It is interesting to note that there is, within the Golf Course grounds, a ditch running towards the dam in this position; could this have been a retained feature when the Earl of Abercorn laid out his Policies, or was it a hidden walled ditch feature (a "Ha-Ha") of Robinson's new Policy garden layout?

The idea that mills used to be further down the burn from the present site has to be taken seriously, as later estate plans clearly show that, prior to about 1830, when the present shape of the Duddingston Mill area was formed, there were several mills on or near the present site, including ones further down the burn, near the present footbridge over the burn (next to Duddingston School grounds).

Returning to the 1564 Court Case, the reason the case arose at all is important to this study. In 1558, a Robert Lawson of Humby, together with his servants, built another mill, cut another water lead to it and thereby starved Murray's and Thomson's mill of water and, it was alleged, did all this without any right to the ownership of the land. Lawson and his men also cut through the two high roads when making their new lead; the road from Wester Duddingston to Niddrie at the "Bingham corner" of the burn and the road from Leith to Niddrie, probably quite close to where Duddingston crossroads is today. As can be seen in Appendix III, Robert Lawson was the Tacksman to John Bertoun in 1538.

According to the process, Lawson had four charges to answer:

1. *Taking the water* which previously served the existing mill.

> *. . . has biggit and alterit the said dam and closit the said clowse thereof, stoppit the watter to discend thairthrow to the said leid and wattergang as it usit to do of befoir, and hes biggit ane new clowse upoun thair said dam and hes thairthrow drawin the said watter of the said burn quhilk servit the saidis Andro and Thomas miln foirsaid be the said ald leid and wattergang quhilk the said Robert hes causit mak throw and langws the commoun passage lyand fra the sowth to thair said miln be quhilk all personis resortand thairto fra besowth the same usit to pass with their laidis (loads), swa that the said ald leid and wattergang is thairthrow in onder the said ald clowse becum dry or at the leist thair discendis nocht nor rynnis thairthrow samekill watter as is abill to serve the saidis Andro and Thomas miln and gar the same gang as it did of befoir.*

2. *Damaging and stopping the use of the High Road.*

> *. . . maisterfullie and violentlie brak the common gait and passage quhilk passis fra the said Westir toun of Dudingstoun to the eistir toun thairof and hes drawin the said watter throw the same.*

3. *Building a mill without any right to do so.*

> *. . . hes wrangowslie violentlie and maisterfullie biggit ane miln within the ground of the saidis landis of Duddingston ane litill abone the said Thomas miln.*

4. *Building wooden bridges which were too narrow for carts*

> *. . . and biggit ane brig of tre* (wood) *quhair the gait is cuttit. The gate, or road, is "mikle war* (worse) *of the bigging of the briggis nor it wes of befoir, and carts and wains* (waggons) *that went easily before will not go now"*. (Two bridges were actually made by Lawson.)

Lawson's new mill lade therefore appears to have been running more or less on the present line of the burn from the "Bingham corner" to somewhere near the present dam area (but possibly a little further west), and possibly to the vicinity of Duddingston crossroads. From there, where it cut through the High Road, it curved down to his unwelcome mill, which would have been on or about the present mill site ("ane litill abone the said Thomas miln").

His mill lade then crossed the original one, before meeting the Figgate Burn. The original lead met the Figgate Burn at a lower point.

From this, it can be reasonably assumed that Lawson's "rogue" mill therefore became the first one to occupy the present mill site. It is marked on the old sketch as "Linsone Myle", and both mills have a round building, marked as a "hut", near them.

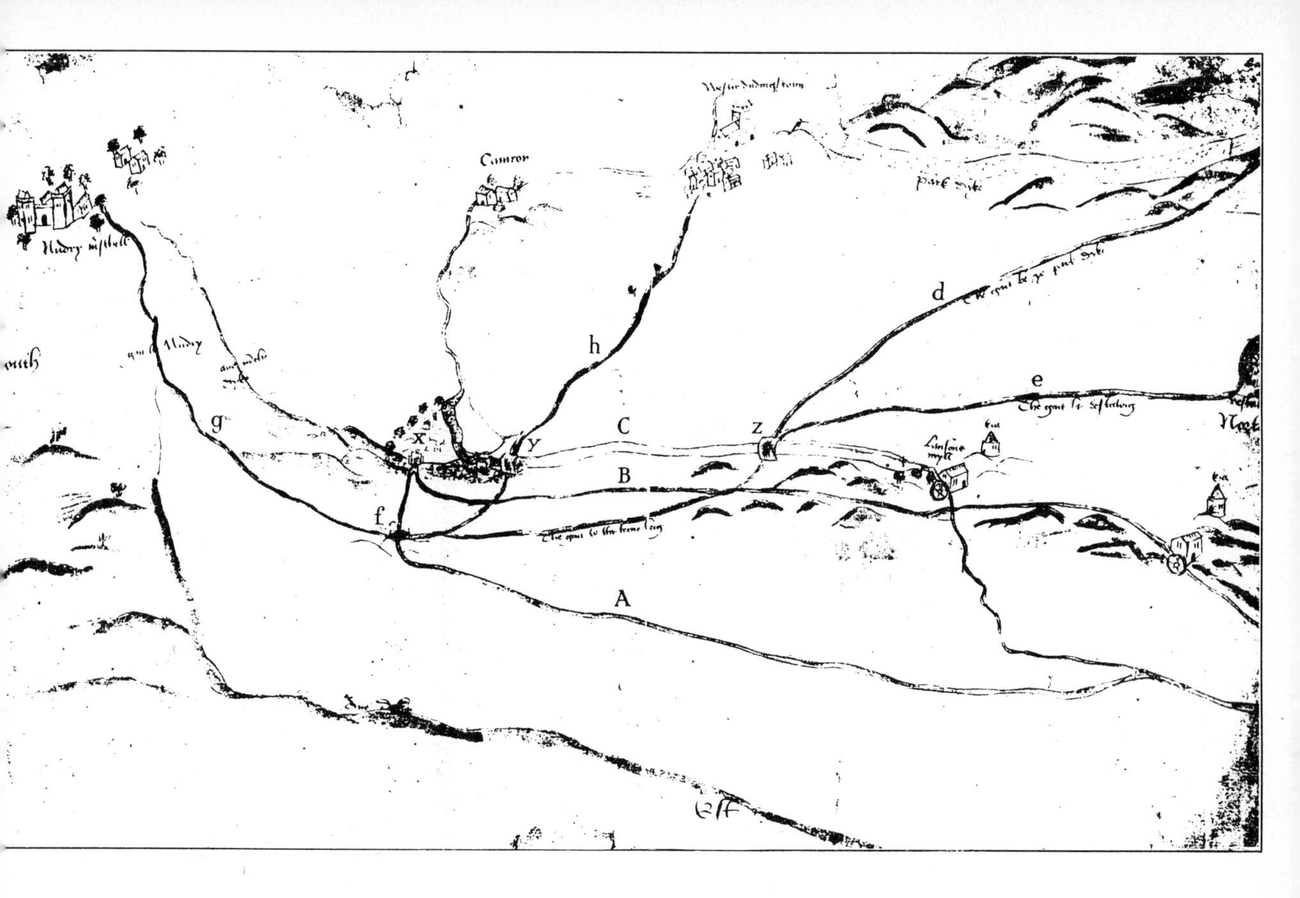

Plate 52 *Sketch plan of water supplies to Duddingston Mills – 1564* (Reproduced with permission of the Keeper of the Records of Scotland)

Roads and water

A = *Figgate Burn*
B = *"original" mill lade to "original" mill*
C = *"new" mill lade to "new" mill*
d = *road to Edinburgh from approximately Duddingston crossroads*
e = *road to Edinburgh, Restalrig and Leith*
f = *where Niddry Road crossed the Figgate Burn*
g = *road to Niddrie*
h = *old road from Wester Duddingston to Niddrie*
X = *"original" mill dam*
Y = *"new" bridge over "new" lade*
Z = *another "new" bridge over "new" lade*

Buildings *(from left to right)*

Niddrie Marischall (demolished this century)
Camron (as in Cameron Toll; an old Cameron House still survives)
Wester Duddingston Toun
"new" mill (Linsone Mill)
"old" mill
St Anthony's Chapel (at top)
Restalrig (below)

The assumptions made above, from the data in the Session Papers, can only be regarded as "reasonable ideas" at this stage, as they need to be supported by other evidence. None the less, they help to put the jigsaw together in an interesting way.

Both parties to the case brought forward witnesses and some of the statements made by these witnesses throw more interesting fragments of light on the layout of the land and ways of life here over 400 years ago.

Robert Henderson, barber, 40, married, " . . . knew the old mill, but did not know who possessed the whole mill, except that the deceased James Lawson (Robert's father) had the Abbots part thereof before John Bertoun got it in feu and as to the vaill he understandis betuix the auld wattergang of the burn and bray on the north west side thairof fra the auld dam to the auld mylne wes unlaborit and kepit in gerse (grass) as it is yit". He used to "play at the rowbowlis (bowls) thairupoun the hard hie gait (road)". Henderson's statement regarding the "vaill" supports the idea that where the Figgate Burn now flows between Duddingston Golf Course and the Figgate Park was previously the route taken by the "original" mill lade. Bowls were popular at this time, as Edinburgh Town Council petitioned to make more ground available for the activity in 1552; in 1581, however, Sunday bowling was made illegal.

Robert Scaithwy, burgess of Canongate, aged 56, married, knew the old mill and dam for the past 40 years "be inspectioun of his awin ene (own eyes)".

Thomas Cheslie, reader in Duddingston, aged 56, born in Duddingston and has lived there ever since, deponed that a piece of common ground, "ever held commoun to the toun", extended for 100 feet between the tilled land and the old dam. This is the gentleman who said the burn "is callit the Figget fra it cum fra Craigmillar".

In the end, Lawson was able to prove that he did, in fact, have a charter (probably via his father, as deponed by Henderson) showing his right to land on both sides of the burn where the new mill and lade were built. Mr Paton, in his article in *The Old Edinburgh Club* 1940 edition, reasonably assumed that Lawson could therefore keep his mill and lade; but he had to restore the water to Murray's lade, and repair the High Gait. Just how he managed to do that, and keep his own mill in production, is not too clear. The picture has been "smudged" somewhat, by the apparent altering of the direction of the Figgate Burn since that time, and the conversion of the old muirs and runrig fields into that part of Duddingston Policies – now Duddingston Golf Course.

It is of interest to note that this case occurred only ten years after a sluice was first installed at the east end of the Nor' Loch, below Edinburgh Castle, to regulate the level of the water in that loch.

Some threads of information on the Duddingston water systems, to be seen on both Roy's map (1753) and the 1801 map, are possibly relevant. The stone-lined lade, carrying water from the burn, near the "Bingham Corner", to Easter Duddingston, may have something to do with the original course of the burn, as far as that part of it which ran from the Golf Course towards "Milton Road" is concerned. In addition, Roy's map shows the whole course

Plate 53 *Line of Mill Lade through garden of Mill House – 1930s*

The mother-in-law of Mr David Bell, the mill foreman, sits on the grassy bank of the lade which carries the water to the overshot wheel. The wheel is in the shadowy corner to the rear of the main mill building.

of the Figgate Burn, from the Mill Town to the Figgate Whins, as being significantly different from the present one. Is this a map-making error, or is it part of the above problem? The 1801 map shows a water course, appearing from "nowhere" (on the site of Portobello High School), running towards the Figgate as it approaches the sea. Mention was made, in an earlier chapter, of sheep milkers going to Portobello via "the burns".

Were there therefore two "streams" running to the Figgate Whins; or the burn plus a spring; or was the line of the burn altered?

MORE ON OLD ROADS

There are two further comments to make on the contents of the 1564 sketch; first, the road from point Z, indicates the existence of a road from "Duddingston Crossroads" to Edinburgh, via what became Meadowfield Farm and Parson's Green Estate. Second, no other "tenants'" roads are shown. Although the legal process itself mentions the road to Easter Duddingston, it is not, for some unknown reason, on the sketch. It is not known whether the "Musselscape Road", from Wester Duddingston to Edinburgh, via what is now the Park Entrance near Meadowbank, or the road from Wester Duddingston to Leith, via the "Willowhead Road" (by-passing the Mill Town), were actually there in 1564. It seems reasonable to assume, therefore, that some "main" roads only were shown.

EARLY 19TH CENTURY

The pattern of two or three separate mill sites, mentioned above, seems to have continued up to about 1830, but prior to that time each site seems to have housed at least one mill, as different types of grain mills were developed.

On 8th January, 1807 (ten years before the first publication of *The Scotsman*), the following advert appeared in the *Edinburgh Courant*:

MILLS TO LET
day of Roup fixed

To be let for 21 years from Candlemas next, the Mill and Mill Lands of Duddingston, lying within two miles of Edinburgh and Leith: there are two Flour Mills, a Corn Mill, Barley Mill, Kiln, large Granaries and every convenience for servants, besides a Dwelling House for the Tacksman. The Mill Lands are sufficient to give ample accommodation to a tenant - Entry at Candlemas next. The Roup will take place at Duddingston Mills on Saturday the Tenth of January 1807, at One o'clock afternoon.

The Articles of Roup are in hands of Thomas Scott, WS who will give every necessary information. Edinburgh Dec. 17, 1806.

The lease, which gives valuable information about the mills and water supplies, mentions:

> *... two flour Mills, Oat Mill, Barley Mill, Large Granary, Kiln and whole furniture and Machinery ... Mill Lands lying upon the Braes and in the Bog contiguous to the said Mills ... dwelling House, Barn, Stable, Stackyard, garden and Cottage Houses all lying contiguous upon the east side of the high road leading from Duddingston to Jock's Lodge ... House and Smithy ... House and Garden ... Cottages ...*
>
> *... shall be exposed to Public Roup at the time and place foresaid during the running of an half hour sand glass, and shall be set up at the sum of One Hundred and Fifty Pounds Sterling of yearly rent, one bode or offer being reserved for the Marquis of Abercorn and the highest Offerer at the outrunning of the said Glass and three several calls of the Auctioneer ...*
>
> *... a certain quantity of the water which is contained in the Pond of Duddingston is carried off to the village of Easter Duddingston and the quantity so carried off is measured by a cast metal trough containing a circular hole in the end thereof, capable of discharging 120 pints in a Minute and which quantity must at all times flow in that direction ... in no case be entitled to abstruct the said run of water or to shut up the hole through which the same flows nor to interfere in any shape with the said trough or Sluices therewith connected ...*

This is how the water was taken from the "Bingham" corner of the Braid Burn, to serve Easter Duddingston. Presumably, the cast metal trough was simply a means of getting the water to the stone cast mentioned in an earlier chapter. This is the area where the "original" mill dam seems to have been in the sixteenth century. It has already been said that the initial course of the stone cast may have followed the original line of the Braid Burn, before the burn turned north.

> *... that part of the Aqueduct which lies under Ground and which was to be maintained and upheld in good order by the Earl of Abercorn ...*

This aqueduct was the mill lade section between today's Golf Course and the mills and the section in this clause was that from today's Duddingston crossroads, via the mills, to the point where it emerges in the Figgate Park.

The lease also provided for the tenant taking water from Duddingston Loch to supplement the Figgate Burn, by a covered "cast" through what is now the site of Holyrood School and part of Duddingston Golf Course. It had been agreed with the proprietor of Prestonfield in order to keep the level of the Loch down, thereby draining certain parts of the lands of Prestonfield. The tenant would, of course, have to pay for it.

The wording is:

> *... not altering any of the present leads of Duddingston Ponds without leave on writing obtained for that purpose, and making the Cast for bringing in the Water a covered aqueduct and sowing the top of the same with grass seeds, so that the Beauty or profit of the ground shall be no way injured and paying also surface damage for breaking the ground which conditions being observed and a*

perpetual grant of the water being obtained in favour of the Marquis of Abercorn, the Marquis shall become bound and Obliged at the expiry of the tack to keep the Water of Duddingston Loch at all seasons two feet beneath its present level, and all tacks granted to future tenants shall contain a clause to that purpose, the preferred Offerer binding himself during the currency of his tack to reduce the Water of Duddingston Loch as aforesaid . . .

It is not known if the "preferred Offerer" actually carried out this expensive operation. There was, however, a perpetual problem in maintaining sufficient water levels in the Figgate Burn in order to drive the mill wheels; carrying off the water to Easter Duddingston at the rate of 15 gallons a minute did not help the cause of the tenant. The "preferred (and only) Offerer" was David Scott, farmer at Northfield.

The tenant "shall be bound and Obliged to flit and remove himself and his family servants and dependents and haill goods at the expiry of the said tack Viz from the Mill Lands at the separation of Crop 1827 from the ground, from the Mills Granaries and the Millars houses at Candlemas 1828 but his subtenants in any of the Cot houses shall have the liberty to remain therein till Whitsunday 1828, they being bound to pay their rent for that three months possession to the Marquis of Abercorn or his incoming tenant, And from the Threshing Barns at Whitsunday 1828 . . . "

This clause obviously allowed for the timings of the various agricultural processes. The years 1827–8, being at the end of the tenants' leases, were to be the years in which activity would take place to reorganise some of the farms and rebuild the mills.

REORGANISATION OF THE FARMS

In preparation of the expiry of the farm and mill leases, a survey report of 1822 recommended the reorganisation of the various farms with a view to maximising returns from the produce of the land. The following proposals were made:

1. . . . the situation of Southfield Steading is extremely inconvenient and considerable alteration and additions being indispensable, it becomes a matter of consideration, whether an entire new steading ought not to be erected in a situation more centrical and better suited. If the proposed new Road from Portobello takes place, as it certainly ought, the new steading would be in the field Mid Langlands. This will make the finest on the Estate.

This report rang the death knell for the old Southfield Farm, which stood on the site of today's Lismore School playing fields. The proposed new road from Portobello was built in 1825 and is now called Duddingston Road. The new Southfield Farm steading which was built about 1827, was demolished about 20 years ago, but the House is still standing and is in fine condition. Of all the old farm buildings in the Barony, it, together with the House of Duddingston Mains (in Hope Lane and built in the 1820s also), are now the only buildings which still stand.

Northfield and Meadowfield, built in 1761 and around 1770 respectively, were retained following the report, but were both demolished within the last 30 years.

2. *Baws Inch field lies most convenient for Sir Robert Dick. At all events, it ought to be laid out into pasture grass, by an arrangement with Mr Cauvin the Tenant. The same applies to the field of Northfield called Dixon's Park, the fields of Meadowfield called Barnyard South and North Parks; all of which from their contiguity to the Post Road and to Edinburgh will yield more Rent in pasture, and also have a better chance of being feued if in that state; and of course ought not to be let in Lease, but annually.*

Strictly speaking, Baws Inch really belonged to the Dicks of Prestonfield (see Chapter 5). It is quite clear that a change was taking place in the area as far as revenue was concerned. It was now more profitable to let certain fields for grazing, rather than grow crops. The fields mentioned can be seen on the 1801 map; the Northfield and Meadowfield fields mentioned are all at Jock's Lodge, next to the Post Road.

3. *The lands of Hardyflatt (54 acres) as possessed by Mr Scott would make a valuable addition to the adjoining Farm of Easter Duddingston; the Steading of that Farm being sufficiently adequate for both. The brewery houses are ruinous and certainly ought to be removed. The Farm House and offices attached with the garden, and probably a small park adjoining might be let separately at a good rent.*

Mr Scott was David Scott, son of Andrew, grandson of Peter (builder of Portobello House and the Figgate Bridge) and was the "Preferred Offerer" at the Mill roup. The farm of Easter Duddingston, on the coast road, later became known as Eastfield, which name is still used. Baird mentions, as an appendix, an interesting account of the tenancy of Easter Duddingston Farm in the period 1788-1808.

4. *Duddingston Hall (tenant - Miss Black) - This small Farm is not subdivided. The Steading of Houses is ruinous and inadequate, but it is proposed to join the lands to another farm; any repair upon it may be deemed to be unnecessary.*

This explains what Duddingston Hall was, and why it disappeared from the maps. It was built in the 1760s and is shown as West Mains on Armstrong's map of 1773 and last appears on Thomson's Atlas of 1821; this is in keeping with the report.

5. *Eastmains - The same remarks as to Houses apply to this as to Duddingston Hall.*

This Eastmains, or Eastfield, was the farm near Brunstane Burn, across the burn from where Asda is now. On Roy's map of 1753, it is shown as South Mains and it, together with North Mains (later called Duddingston Cottage) were the only farm steadings in the Barony at that time. The farm steading was removed in the 1820s, in accordance with the report.

> 6. *The reporter considers it a matter of great importance to several of the Farms, and to the Estate in general, to open such a Road as is proposed, between Portobello and the Parish Church, and the Valuation which has been made, has been upon the supposition that this improvement is to take place. To three of the Farms, in particular, this communication will be of essential advantage, by allowing a ready market for their green crops in that thriving and populous village, as well as affording a facility of procuring manure.*

The three farms benefiting from the building of Duddingston Road were, the new Southfield Farm, Northfield Farm and Meadowfield Farm. The unexpected reference to manure relates to the street dung of Portobello. The use of such manure was by now common and was "pioneered" by one of the Dicks of Prestonfield, when he used such material from the Old Town.

Returning to the Mill Town, all these developments affected the ability of Duddingston Mills to cope with the workload and, in the late 1820s, the phased rebuilding of the mills and all the surrounding buildings and mill access road, began.

REBUILDING THE MILLS

When the mill lease expired in 1828, Guthrie Wright, the Factor and Commissioner for the Estate, realised that the condition of the buildings, comprising the mills, was too dilapidated for profitable leasing. He arranged for an architect from Uphall, Mr Thomas Brown, to survey the site and draw up plans for a new mill complex, which would include new houses for the millers and labourers. He also negotiated with two millers, James and Archibald King, who were interested in taking over the lease.

In his dealing with the Earl of Aberdeen, curator for the Marquis of Abercorn, Mr Wright pointed out that the Messrs. King were willing to pay £6 per annum for each of the six acres attached to the mill, £14 for the use of the water and 7.5 per cent per annum of the cost of building the new mill and that this deal was better than the alternative of demolishing the mills and using the ground for agricultural purposes; and £90 per annum more than the previous rental. The millers were thought very highly of and their suggestion that Mr Brown's estimate of £3,970 was about £1,000 more than what it would cost to satisfy their requirements, together with the interest rate offered, were factors the financial managers found impossible to ignore.

Mr Brown's report on the condition of the old buildings stated:

> *That the whole of these buildings may be said to be in a ruinous state, the roofing in the last stage of decay, all of it really dilapidated, and in some places dangerous; and that the machinery of all three Mills, with the exception of a few articles, may be said to be in the very worst condition. This being the case, it is my decided opinion that it would not be advisable for the proprietor to be at any expense in making repair on the Mills as they now stand.*

His following comments on the proposed new mills describe the birth of the mill buildings which have only recently been demolished:

In regard to the erection of new Mills, it is considered preferable to have two instead of three, as at present, and these two mills to be all under one roof . . . two pairs of stones on one wheel and one pair of stones on another, with Boulting Machine (sieve). One pair of these stones to be for oats, and the others for wheat.

There were three previous sites – the present one, one in the Figgate Park, near Duddingston Primary School and one near Duddingston crossroads. The new mills had an upper and an under wheel, and the most "obvious" one, the upper wheel, was at the rear of the main building, facing Duddingston Road. It was inside a stone housing and the under wheel was within the structure of the building, further down the complex. The upper wheel was a high breast bucket wheel, with a cast-iron axle and rings, wooden spokes and sole, and sheet iron buckets. And size? It was . . . "24 feet in diameter and four feet broad on the inside, has ten wooden arms eight inches by five inches, and makes about six and a half revolutions per minute", according to the notebook of Alexander Kedslie, an Edinburgh corn merchant who emigrated to Poland in 1829, the year in which the new Duddingston Mill became operational.

It was an "overshot" wheel, which meant that the water fell on to it, and turned it, from above; this was the most efficient type of waterwheel, as the weight of the water falling vertically onto the wheel gave more power per unit of water than that provided by breast or undershot wheels.

The Scottish Country Miller, by Enid Gauldie, illustrates well the main features of mill stones and associated machinery . . .

Each stone is grooved on its grinding side with deeply scored lines which are divided into ten harps *each with four* furrows, *the flat surfaces in between being called* roads *or* channels. *The purpose of these grooves is to allow the meal, once ground, to sift away from the grinding surface to prevent the space between the stones becoming clogged. The edges of the stones must be kept sharp and deep enough to ensure that the meal is kept moving and distributed towards the periphery of the stones.*

The introduction of more complicated systems of gearing allowed the use of two pairs of stones and the mechanisation of the fanning and sieving processes. One pair of stones without grooving was then maintained as a suitable set for shelling. A chute from there carried the mixture of husks and oats into the shieling *and* fanning *boxes where the husks were removed to fall out of a small door in the fanner into waiting sacks. The oats were then carried by an* elevator *to the second pair of stones. Elevators consist of a series of tiny buckets, or cups, fixed to a continuous leather or webbing belt working inside a wooden casing, which carry the oats upwards and return for refilling in a circular motion.*

The second pair of (grooved) stones ground the oats into meal which was then fed by a chute into the meal sieve. *This was of course, another operation previously performed by hand, and old mills often have hand sieves of woven cane or wire hanging still on their walls. The mechanised meal sieve is a hanging box, containing, as a chest of drawers contains its drawers, a series of rectangular wire sieves of increasing fineness. The sieve is swung and shaken backwards and forwards over the perforated wire. The first sieve drawer catches the whole oats, of which a few always escape the stones and must be returned for regrinding. Imperfectly set or worn stones will let through quantities of oats and large particles of grain to be caught at this stage. The second sieve will catch the* groats *(shelled oats) and send only meal through to the third. The third may be the last, holding the meal and rejecting only dust, or there may be a fourth so that two grades of oatmeal, fine or course, are provided for customers with different tastes.*

The following statistics were taken from Alexander Kedslie's notebooks. The new technology installed at Duddingston Mill was important enough to be so noted by a man who had a great interest in such things. It is thought that Kedslie did not have any direct involvement in Duddingston Mill, but simply noted the mill's statistics, as an enthusiast might note the features of a new type of car today.

DUDDINGSTON WATER MILL

FLOUR MILL

Flour stones are 4′ 6″ in diameter and make 100 rpm.
Sheeling stones make 160 rpm.
Dressing engine 200 rpm and angle of inclination is 18 degrees.

CORN MILL

Meal stones are 4′ 9″ in diameter and make 100 rpm.
Sheeling stones are 4′ 9″ in diameter and make 130 rpm.
The pulley on the sheeling mill stone spindle is 16″ in diameter, on the spindle of the shaker 12″ in diameter, the crank for the oatmeal sieves has a one and a half inch throw.

BARLEY MILL

Stone mills are 4′ 2″ in diameter and make 250 rpm.
Cases are 4′ 6″ in diameter and make about 6 rpm.

The architect of the new Duddingston Mills, Mr Brown, drew up a plan which included details of mill machinery designed by an Edinburgh mill wright, a Mr Moodie.

In the plan, accommodation can be got for erecting a Steam Engine should it be wanted, and as there is generally a scarcity of water during the heat of Summer, it would likely be considered by a Tacksman of great advantage the having a Steam Engine, thereby insuring to his Customers a steady and regular service the whole year through. The part where I propose the apparatus and Boiler of the Steam Engine to be placed is in the sunk part of the under Mill opposite the water wheel. This Steam Engine to be made to work only one of the Mills, which is considered quite sufficient for the purpose intended. From the arrangement however presently in contemplation for the purpose of increasing

THE OLD DUDDINGSTON FLOUR MILL

Plate 54 *The Old Duddingston "Flour" Mill - 1951*

Taken a year after the mill had stopped operating. The mills and granary were housed in the building on the right, the stables were on the left and in the centre were the "new" granary and cart-sheds (archways blocked). The latter granary, which is the only part of the complex to survive, has recently been renovated and now houses several families.

> *and husbanding the supply of water, it is likely that an Engine will not ultimately be required, but as a place can be prepared for it in the building, with very little additional expense, it may as well be done, and either employed or not as may afterwards be found convenient. A Kiln and Granary will also be required, and these can either be built to join the Mills, or a little apart as may be considered to answer best.*

The steam engine seems to have been added at some stage, however, as the *Statistical Account* of 1865 says, "Duddingston flour and barley mills . . . contain machinery of the very best and most improved kind and are driven by steam and water". The under mill and boiler were near the lower, right-hand corner of the "U" shaped complex, near the new road that now curves round the remaining part of the old building. The kiln and granary were attached to the mill building and all these buildings represented both the first phase of the new complex and the right-hand side of the later "U" shaped layout. The new dam and lade are mentioned.

> *The Kiln to be 18 feet square within, to have iron ribs, wire cloth top, and otherwise fitted up in the most approved manner. The Granary to be sixty feet long, by 22 feet wide, to have three floors. Besides these buildings, it will be necessary to have a dwelling house for the Tacksman, and at least three houses for servants, a Cart shed, a stable for 4 Horses and a small barn for holding either victual or Straw.*
>
> *The buildings should be done with substantial rubble work in walls, Hewn work in doors, windows, corners; strong ashlar about the water wheels and neatly worked strong hewn work about the stone troughs. The tail race built arched; the timbers to be all foreign, and all roofs covered with best slate.*

The dwelling house was to become known as Mill House, the cart-shed and stable, it is thought, were in a separate building between the mill and the burn. The tail race was, and probably still is, underground; it certainly can still be seen emerging further down the burnside, towards the footbridge, in the Figgate Park.

ARCHITECT'S ESTIMATE OF COSTS

	£ s d
Building and finishing the Mills, including cutting out foundations and excavating the sunk parts of the Mills, arks, tail course and building and arching the same, putting up Kiln.....	*1,300 00 00*
The Mill wright work for Machinery of Mills	*800 00 00*
Building and finishing granary 60 feet long, 22 feet wide within, with three wooden floors, all done substantially...........	*500 00 00*
A dwelling House, consisting of Kitchen and three rooms of moderate size on the first floor, with two garret rooms above will be sufficient accommodation..	*400 00 00*
(This is Mill House, which still survives)	
The three cothouses to fit them up any way decently, and covered with slate cannot cost less than £70 each........................	*210 00 00*
(Five terraced cottages were actually built - and were recently tastefully renovated)	
A stable for 4 horses, cart shed for 4 Carts having two posts, a small barn...	*230 00 00*
(This building would appear to have been that shown on maps and plans as being between the mill and the burn)	
If a Steam Engine is required, it is considered that one of twelve horse power will be sufficient to work two pairs of stones and an Engine of that power will cost	*480 00 00*
The vent will require to be heightened should an Engine be put up...	*50 00 00*
TOTAL AMOUNT SHOULD AN ENGINE BE ERECTED...........	*3,970 00 00*

Plate 55 *The Old Mill building, c 1915*

This scene is a symbol of the link between the land and the ever growing numbers of people who had to be fed. The carts advertise "James Aitken and Son" (Robert) and the two horses per cart were necessary to carry the heavy loads up the lane and Willowbrae. The structure which carries the water to the wheel is in the shadows on the right and the oriel window with the simple dignity belongs to the mill office, whose staff (left to right – Miss Hannah (married name Wylie, who died in 1988, aged 92, Mr Whitelaw, the Cashier and Mr Andrew Gillespie, Senior) are standing on the loading bay. The man on the left on the upper loading bay is Mr David Bell, the mill foreman. The six-sided structure was also used as an office at some stage. The mill complex, as can be ascertained from this picture, was built in phases (c 1830), but was altered following a fire about the turn of the century; it was re-roofed and a tall chimney was removed.

WHAT THE MILLERS WANTED

The Kings, however, adjusted Mr Brown's ideas:

> *We have seen the Plans made out by Mr Thomas Brown but it appears to us that some alterations may be made on them, which would have the effect of rendering the Mills more suitable to our purposes, and at the same time lessening the expense of the operations; and if these alterations shall be adopted, that is to say, if a Flour Mill and Corn Mill, with proper Granaries and Kiln, and also a dwelling house for the Tacksman with houses for the Mill Servants and a Stable shall be erected, we agree . . . . to pay the sum of £50 stg per annum for the land and the privilege of the water, together with interest at the rate of 7.5 per centum per*

annum, on the sum to be expended by the Proprietor in the erection of the Mills, houses, Machinery; including the making of water courses or Mill lead, and every other expense connected with the premises.

They did not initially require a steam engine and obviously played a part in the final layout of the buildings. The last part refers to the substantial alterations which, from what can be seen from old maps, were carried out on the water courses, or leads. The formation of the slopes of the "braes" probably altered too, with the building of the road bridge over the Figgate Burn (on Duddingston Road).

A new stone-lined lade, or lead, brought the water to the mill wheels from the mill pond (the dam for which still survives) next to Duddingston Golf Course. The section of the lade between the south side of Milton Road West and the garden of Mill House was, and still is, hidden under Milton Road West, Duddingston Road, Mr Robertson's joiner's yard and the old school garden. It no longer exists between the school (now an Adult Training Centre) and the area containing the surviving granary, but probably still survives between this area and the surviving outlet in the Figgate Park. This was the "arrangement in contemplation for the purpose of increasing and husbanding the supply of water", mentioned by Mr Brown, the architect, in 1828.

In 1958, Mill House became the property of the late Mr and Mrs Andrew Melrose Morrison (Mr Morrison was a great-grandson of Andrew Melrose, founder of the Melrose Tea firm) who, when landscaping their garden, converted the line of the lade, which ran through the garden, into a path. They also converted what had been formerly the old Mill Office, into a three-car garage and later owners used it as an Art Gallery. Early this century, that building replaced the original mill office, which was in the granary building next to the garden of Mill House. It was too dusty in that office and the summer house standing in the garden of Mill House was converted into a new office.

The Kings continued:

As it would be of importance to us to keep the mills going and the customers together, we propose that the upper Mill should not be taken down till the new ones are erected, and that we should have possession of it as well as the land of the ensuing Season . . . but it is understood that none of the houses, which have hitherto been let along with the Mills, nor the ground and gardens thereto belonging and which are at present occupied by the tacksman of the Mills, their servants and others shall be included in the Lease - and also that the road to the Mills shall be changed, so as to enter from the Niddry Road and be carried on the line of the north boundary of the ground belonging to the Schoolhouse, which road shall be the boundary of the field to be let to us.

The Kings thus brought about the present road from Willowbrae Road to Duddingston Mill. It replaced an older road which served the mills and which ran from Duddingston crossroads to the three mill sites.

All this "planning" took place between December 1827 and February, 1828 and, incredibly, in October 1828, Mr Wright reported to the Earl of Aberdeen:

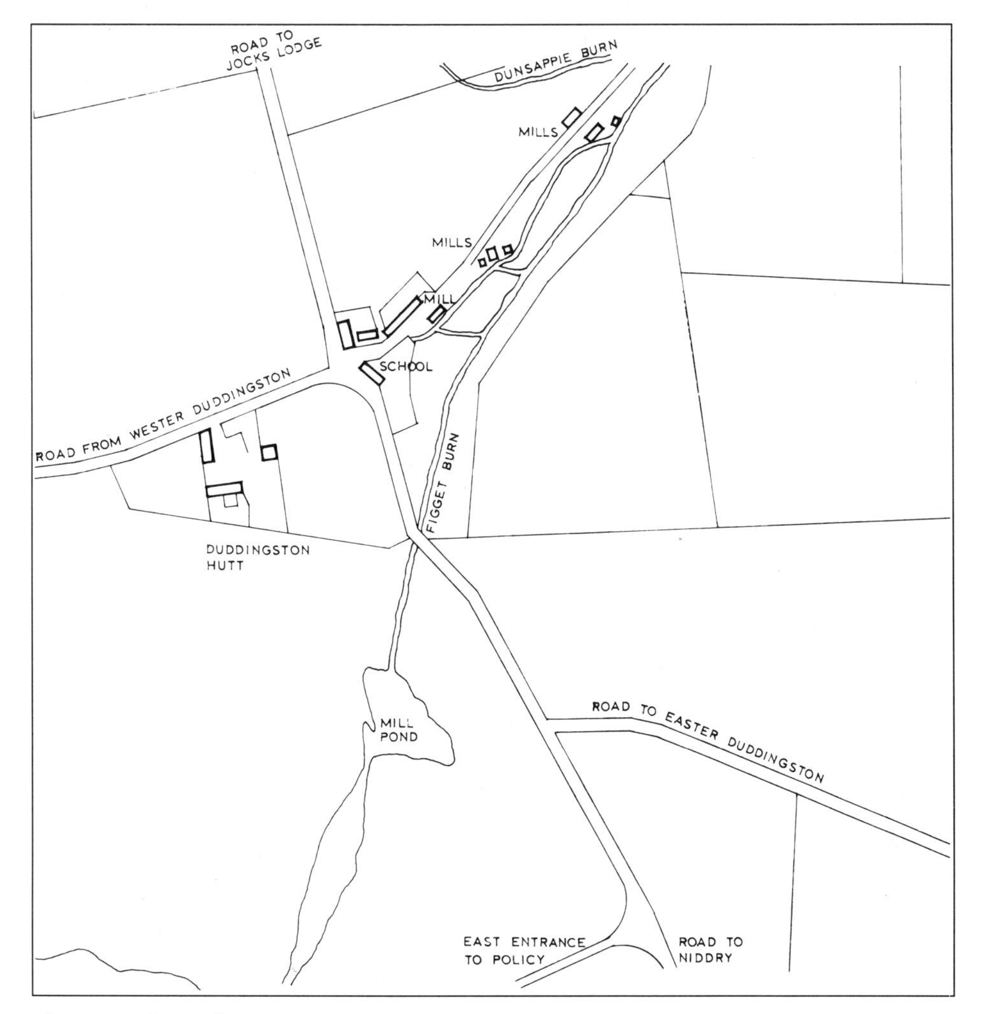

Plate 56 *The Mill Town area in 1801*

> *The new Mills and houses at Duddingston are now nearly completed, and will be ready for occupation at the ensuing term of Martinmas and I am happy to say that the whole work has been finished in a style of excellence which must give the highest satisfaction.*

The "whole work" was the right-hand section of the "U" shaped mill complex, mill house and the five cottages.

THE NEW MILL TOWN

Bearing in mind that Duddingston Road, and its bridge over the Figgate Burn, had just been built three years earlier and that the old school had just reorganisation that occurred here at that time. It is evident that, after the new school was built, the old road to the mills, from what is now the corner of Willowbrae Road and Duddingston Road, was still used and that the upper of the three mill sites was still being used. That old mill, as has been noted earlier, was next to the lade, just inside what became the school playground.

The old road to the mills was closed and its space taken up by part of a cottage (at the crossroads), the school garden, Mill House and part of its garden, part of the new mill complex and part of the Figgate Park. The new, shorter, access road became known as Duddingston Mill Lane, then Duddingston Mills Cottages before being changed to Duddingston Mills. It therefore appears that it was the Kings who brought about, not three "cothouses", but the five terraced cottages. They were rather unusual in that their windows were of the horizontal sliding type. Mill House was the tacksman's house and the description given in Mr Brown's report obviously portrays it before the "garret" windows were replaced by the present, larger, dormer windows.

The surviving tenement just up the lane from the school was probably built at, or not long after, this time; the older cottages which stood on Willowbrae Road until their removal in 1917, and the smiddy that stood behind them, would have been built around this time also. The row of grand, stone houses across the road - from the corner of Duddingston Road West to Paisley Drive - had been there for some 20 years, although Cauvin's Hospital ("Louisfield") was still in the form of the original house; without its polished stone front and pillars.

EXTENDING THE MILLS

In August 1831, James King approached Mr Wright again, this time to request permission to extend the mills. Again, Mr Brown drew up plans and a report:

> *Owing to the increase in business at the Mills, Mr King finds that the accommodation he already possesses in Granaries is not sufficient for his purposes . . . additional Granary be built for him of three floors, having under them a Cart Shed sufficiently large to hold six carts, a thing that he greatly wants. He further says that the Barley Mill, being at present in the same room with the oat Meal Mill, is an inconvenience and a very considerable hindrance to his operations, and he therefore proposes that the walls of the Shed of the water wheel of that mill be raised so as to have two lofts formed over the wheel, in one of which the Barley Mill would be placed, and the other would serve for forming benches on, for the same purpose.*
>
> *. . . Cart Shed and Granary, consisting of a building 35 feet long and 22 feet wide inside measure, formed into Cart Sheds below and three floors above."*
>
> *Costs . . . new granary and cart shed £330*
> *. . . alteration to Oatmeal mill, heightening wheel shed, forming two floors over it for Barley Mill, and finishing everything £45*

The rate of interest, agreed at 5 per cent, "Is as much as I am able to give considering the high percentage I now pay for the other buildings already built."

Plate 57 *Nairne Lodge (formerly Caroline Cottage) c 1945*

The house was built in 1805 and the Nairne's only son was born here in 1808. It now operates as The Lady Nairne Hotel.

That building is the right-hand (south) section of the only remaining part of the whole complex and was built shortly after September 1831. The building that remains, resplendent again in its cleaned and dressed stone and slated roof, and vibrating with life since its proud flat-owners have moved in, represents both the phase of building just mentioned and a later one. The three arches on the right are smaller than those on the left and a "join" can be clearly seen up the wall to the left of the smaller arches.

Mr Brown, the architect, surely had a premonition when he said, " . . . the Cart Shed and granaries would be a most useful and permanent improvement to the Mills . . .".

The new stables were yet to be built; evidence of where they once were can be seen on the west gable-end of the surviving building.

A SENSE OF RELIEF

In 1843, the Marquis of Abercorn effected a Private Act of Parliament, to "recoup a portion (three-fourths) of the monies laid out on the improvement of the estate, and to enlarge the power of feuing of same". The Act referred to a previous Act "passed in the Tenth Year of the Reign of His Majesty King George the Third, intituled 'An Act to encourage the Improvement of Lands, Tenements, and Hereditaments in that part of Great Britain called Scotland held under Settlement of strict Entail'".

The sums stated to have been spent were as follows:

DUDDINGSTON (& BRUNSTANE) IMPROVEMENT EXPENDITURE

	(1)			(2)		
	£	s	d	£	s	d
A. 27/1/1818 to 18/1/1825	13,084	05	05	2,818	13	06
B. 18/1/1825 to 18/1/1832**	7,641	08	10	1,344	18	05
C. 18/1/1832 to 31/12/1841	6,139	17	05	2,262	09	00

A = Period of administration of the Earl of Aberdeen as Tutor Dative of the Marquis
B = Curatorial Management Period
C = Period since the Marquis attained Majority
1 = Building and repairing farmhouses, offices, mills and so on as well as repairing mansion house of Duddingston.
2 = In fencing, draining, trenching, planting, etc.

** = Period in which the reorganisation of the Mill Town took place.

The map sketches show the changes in the layout of the Mill Town and cover the dates 1801 and 1853. The main features are:

THE 1801 LAYOUT

The Figgate Burn is in the "valley". There is no road to Portobello and therefore no "crossroads". There are three mill sites, one on the "present" site, one further up, and one farther down, the burnside.

Although the lade is not shown on its way from the dam area, it seems to be on the route of the one that was on-site until a few years ago; the lower end is open (between the two "lower" mills), whereas it was latterly covered; the "upper" sluice is still to be seen, but the "lower" one either disappeared with the rebuilding in the 1820s or was covered over.

The "middle" mills are not the buildings comprising the recent mill

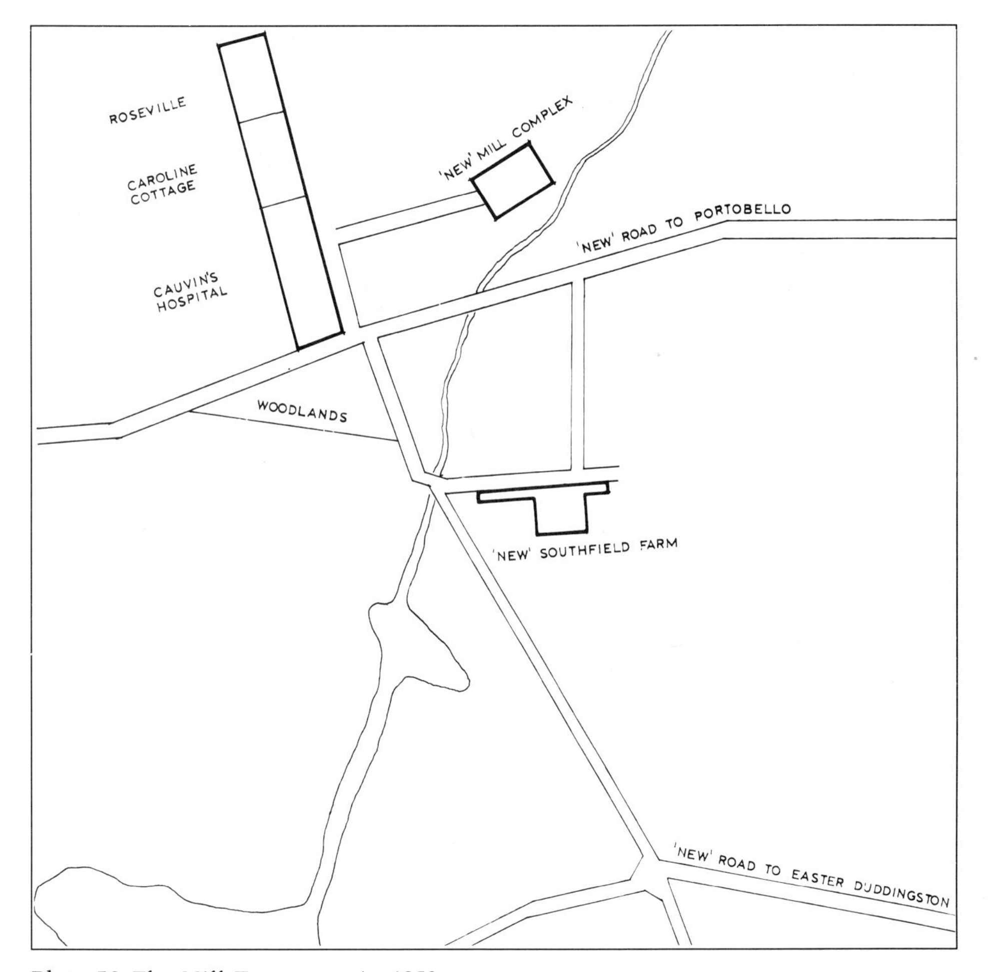

Plate 58 *The Mill Town area in 1853*

Sketch showing the main changes since 1801 (*see* Plate 56).

complex and the cluster of buildings near the future crossroads have all been swept away in the changes of the 1820s.

The building which straddles the future access to Portobello was an old school building. That line of fine old houses (Cauvin's Hospital, Nairne Lodge, Roseville and Bellfield Villa) was not built until 1805–6. The "Hut" was "Earls Farm" and preceded the "Woodlands". A "hut", in this context, was a "smaller second house built in the grounds of a larger mansion and occupied as a town or suburban house by wealthy families". Southfield Farm was still standing on "Duddingston Row" (Lismore School playing field site).

The access road to the mills ran at an angle from the present corner of Willowbrae Road/Duddingston Road, past all three "sets" of mills, to a point below the "lower" mills. The "middle" mills were on the site of Lawson's mill, and Murray's/Thomson's was on the site of the "lower" mills on this sketch. From the 1801 map, it appears that one of the mills stood beside the lade, at a point which is now just inside the "playground" of the Adult Education Centre (old Duddingston School) and it may be that the boundary wall of that "playground" is either the base of the old mill wall, or that its stones came from the old mill building.

The roads were probably less than half the width of the present ones and the curve in the road from the Mill Town to the section leading to Duddingston Mill Bridge is a marked one.

A Leith baker, Wm. Laing, leased all the mill premises from 1786 to 1805, from which date James Law, dentist in Edinburgh, and Robert Duthie acquired right to them. Yet another Court case arose, because Laing did not leave the premises in good order, in accordance with his lease, and he also removed mill stones. The repairs due were assessed by cabinet-makers, engineers, wrights and by David Scott, farmer at Northfield.

Laing had previously put in "two large and expensive (£40) blue, German millstones, replacing the ordinary French ones, to grind flour for the purpose of making sea-biscuit; a purpose for which the original stones could not be employed". He then leased mills at Gorgie, where he had, prior to leaving Duddingston, fitted the German stones.

THE 1853 LAYOUT

Duddingston Road has by now been in existence for 28 years. The new Southfield Farm has been standing for about 20 years. The Mill Town had now been entirely rebuilt for about 20 years.

The new mill complex, built in phases during the late 1820s and 1830s, is complete and all the old ones have been removed. Mill House was built at the same time as the new mill, and was the mill tacksman' s house. The new school is to be seen on the site on which the Adult Training Centre now stands, but, sadly, the last of the stone buildings of the school were removed within the last ten years. On the 1853 sketch, part of the previous school building (in the "middle of Duddingston Road") has apparently been spared by the Duddingston Road builders, but its subsequent use is not now known. Incidentally, according to an estate plan of 1827 (RHP 10575), there was an "old school house" opposite the Kirk Gate in Duddingston Village - the first building on the right on the way towards the Sheep Heid Inn. Another plan (RHP 10581) of 1833 shows the older formation of mill buildings, even although the new buildings had by then been erected, thus demonstrating the care that is necessary when studying maps.

Returning to the Mill Town, the buildings along the main road, from the new "Crossroads" to Mill Lane, are new also, as is the one a little way down the lane, on the right; it still survives, but all those on the main road were removed in about 1917 for the widening of Willowbrae Road.

Duddingston Hut has been replaced by "Woodlands" and Cauvin's Hospital, originally built as the house of Louis Cauvin, Senior; Nairne Lodge, home of Lord and Lady Nairne and previously called Caroline Cottage (the present "Caroline Cottage" was the Nairnes' coach-house); Roseville and Bellfield Villa can all be seen, in their spacious gardens.

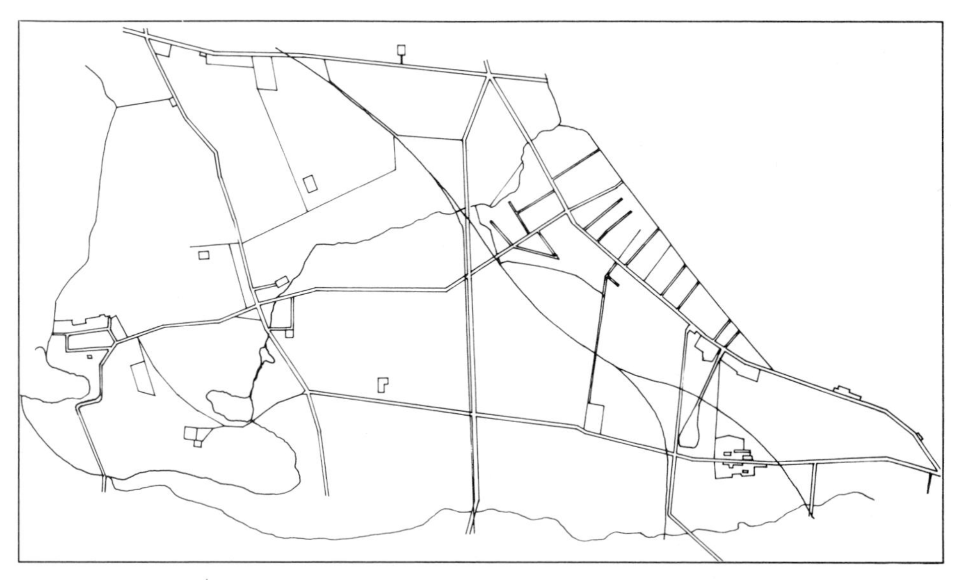

Plate 59 *The Barony of Duddingston in 1853*

Portobello has absorbed Joppa, the railway has been in operation for seven years and Joppa Quarry is a conspicuous feature. The Mill Town has been renewed and the long awaited access road to the Kirk, Duddingston Road, has been in place for 28 years. Agriculture is still the dominant feature.

The Mill Town had now become a grand place; perhaps not the sort of place where one would expect to see a man playing "rowboulis" in the middle of the road.

When the first Ordnance Survey map was compiled for the area the surveyor's report, dated November 1849, described Duddingston Mills as ". . . a little hamlet on the Estate of Abercorn about half a mile north east of Wester Duddingstone, consisting of well built villas, and comfortable dwellings, for mechanics and a few agricultural labourers, the Parish School, Cauvin's Hospital and a large flour Mill, which is said to have been here in the reign of James VI". From what we have seen, mills were certainly here in James VI's reign (1567–1603 - Scotland and 1603–25 - Great Britain), but the buildings were not the same ones which were shown on any Ordnance Survey maps.

MORE WATER PROBLEMS

Mention has been made of problems concerning the sufficiency of water supplies to drive the mill wheels. In 1799, the Marquis of Abercorn and William Laing (the Leith baker and maker of sea-biscuits) raised an action against the Magistrates and Council of Edinburgh, as Duddingston Mills suffered a loss of water due to the Edinburgh Water Supply drawing water from the burn which fed the Figgate Burn. The Council was fined £400 stg. In 1564, water was said to have been "illegally" diverted for the benefit of one man, but this time, it was for the population of the Auld Toun of Edinburgh.

In The Edinburgh Water Company Act of 1856, provision was made for compensation to be made to owners and occupiers of lands, mills and other properties on the Bonaly and Dean Burns or the streams into which they flow in their course to the sea "... and more particularly to the mills on the estate of Duddingston belonging to the Most Noble the Marquis of Abercorn", if the Water Company did not maintain the discharge of a certain volume of water from the Bonaly and Torduff reservoirs.

The requirement was ". . . to discharge out of the said reservoirs, and deliver into the Bonaly Burn, just below the present junction of the Torduff and Dean Burns, a quantity of water amounting at least to sixty cubic feet per minute; and in order to ensure such delivery of the said quantity of water, the Company shall place and maintain on the Bonaly Burn, at a point not exceeding one hundred and fifty yards below the east end of the offices attached to the House of Bonaly, a proper water guage, which shall readily show and determine the amount of water so sent down the said burn . . . ". Any interested party could refer to the Sheriff upon a summary application and in the event of the Company failing to comply with the Act, a penalty of five pounds per day was payable. Such was the importance of getting the water through.

LATER CHANGES TO THE MILL TOWN

The only changes to the Mill Town between the first Ordnance Survey map, in 1853, and the one in 1896, were (a) Roseville was now called Braefoot (now the site of Braefoot Service Station) and (b) the miller, Mr James Aitken (who succeeded Mr James King), had moved out of Mill House and into his new villa on Duddingston Road, called Milford. It is so called because he had to ford the Figgate Burn to get to his work at the mill. His house is now a Private Nursing Home, and is still called Milford. Mill House was, from then until the end of the mill's working life, the abode of the mill manager or foreman.

The changes to the area surrounding the mill, as depicted by the 1896 and 1931 Ordnance Survey maps, were relatively significant. As already indicated, Willowbrae Road was widened in about 1917, at the cost of all the houses between the mill lane and the crossroads. A cottage which used to be at the top of the lane, and a row of cottages running to the corner of Duddingston Road, were taken down and the buildings in their place stand about ten yards further back. The smithy, which used to be behind the row of demolished cottages was now re-sited on the main road and the present old-fashioned "tenement", with the crow-stepped gables, at the top of the lane was joined to the older tenement, thereby closing the entrance to the old smithy.

The old lodge house to the Woodlands used to stand on what is now the Edinburgh-bound lane of Milton Road, at the traffic lights at Duddingston crossroads, but this was rebuilt inside the drive of the Woodlands. Milton Road was widened in about 1906, and the bridge over the Figgate Burn was extended on the east side. Further widening operations were in vogue at the crossroads about six years ago, when still more road space was gained at the same place where the old "Woodlands" lodge house used to be.

On the 1931 map, Cairn Lodge appears on Duddingston Road West and Northfield Broadway breaks off Willowbrae Road. "Regiments" of houses were "marching" along from Jock's Lodge on either side of Willowbrae Road (Ulster, Paisley and Northfield) and Milford House was still managing to hold off the "attack" from bungalows "coming up" Duddingston Road.

In the Sheltered Housing Complex ("Cauvin's Hospital"), across the road from the smiddy, there lived the late Mrs Christine Egan, who died in 1989 aged 86, whose father was "one of the blacksmith's sons of the master blacksmith, Dickson Weir Horsburgh". Mrs Egan, who lived in a thatched cottage in the middle of what is now Northfield Broadway, opposite what used to be the chemical works and what is now glassworks, used to walk, when aged about eight, past Northfield Farm to the school in Mill Lane. She recalls paddling in the mill lade at lunchtime and visiting her father in the smiddy, "and sharing my father's girdle scones with bacon and egg and tea from a syrup tin with a wire, which had been held over the forge fire. There were three fires in the (old) smiddy and I used to love to go in and smell the hooves burning when they were shoeing the great big horses which nearly touched the roof. There was a huge stone ring on which the cart rings were shaped after being resurfaced to give them hold on the roads".

GRINDING TO A HALT

Messrs James Aitken and Son (Robert) worked the mills of Duddingston for over 60 years. "It was always claimed, perhaps justifiably, that the flour from Duddingston Mill was the finest in Scotland", said an *Evening News* article in 1951. "There is an art in milling and the good qualities of the mill's products resulted from three things over and above the quality of the grain - expert millers, the fact that stones were used for the grinding, and the choice of the type of millstone best suited for the job.

"In its hey-day, Duddingston Mill supplied flour and oatmeal to bakers and grocers all over the Lothians, and even to places as far afield as Coatbridge, Glasgow and the Orkneys and Shetlands. Half a dozen horse-drawn lorries, the vehicles and their drivers white with flour dust, did their daily local rounds to customers over a wide area".

Mr Robert Aitken recalled when "The young Mr J. Mackie, of J. W. Mackie and Sons, Edinburgh, used to bring grain to the mill to be ground". In its latter years no flour was produced, only wheatmeal and oatmeal.

Mr Aitken recalled that children would often dam up the burn with stones and earth, resulting in the manager having to go up past the dam to give them a "flighting" and break up their dam.

"It's all over now, though," said the *News* article. "In August 1950, the mill wheels turned for the last time. Whether the cause is that no one cares whether oats are stones-ground or roller-ground, or whether no one cares for oats whichever way they are ground, it is hard to say. But the mill's day is over. Like an animal weary of life that creeps into a corner to die, the old mill awaits the end. And the trim cottages, the cottagers and the shades of

Plate 60 *Duddingston School in 1923*

Just below the low, stone wall, to the rear of this group, runs the lade. The children are; Back row – *Annie Ramage of Abbeyhill; William MacLeod of Duddingston Village (DV); James Wilson of Abbeyhill; Alfred Revel of DV; John Stevenson of DV; Innes Will of Mill Lane (tenement).* Middle row – *Mary Robertson of Southfield Farm; (?) Shaw of DV; Hettie Bell of Mill House (daughter of the mill foreman); William Bruce of*

Southfield Farm; Jackie Brown of DV; (?) Houston of Meadowfield Farm; Agnes Boyd of Mill Lane (middle cottage). Front row – *Nellie Hunter of DV; Lizzie Anderson of East Lodge (was at east entrance to Duddingston Policy); not known; (?) Shaw of DV; Edna Rae of DV; Beatrice Short of DV; Chrissie Hold of DV; last two (twins) not known, but lived at Meadowfield Farm. The teacher is Miss Reith.*

Plate 61 *The Mill Town c 1915*

This was the scene since about 1830 and before Willowbrae Road had been widened in 1917. Mill Lane drops down to the left and access to Milton Road requires two sharp turns. All these houses were swept away when the road was widened and the present

buildings replaced them. The lodge at the entrance to the Woodlands was replaced by one which stood within the drive. Today's Duddingston Forge is now on the main road, whereas the "original" one was behind the row of cottages in this photograph.

Plate 62 *The Mill Town in 1988*

This is the scene (see Plate 61*) today – the wall of "Cauvin's Hospital" (Sheltered Housing Complex) is the only recognisable feature.*

Plate 63 *A gardening lesson at the Old Duddingston School, c 1910*

The children are well dressed and attentive, but smiling for the camera is still, apparently, forbidden. This is a fine view of the schoolmaster's house (demolished a few years ago), with the school buildings behind it. The old tenement (second from the top of the lane today) is on the left and, on its left, is a space where the entrance to the old smiddy was. Classroom "huts", which are the only part of the school now remaining,

have not yet appeared and the top of a mill shed can be seen in the background. Under the surface of the garden, roughly where the camera is standing, runs the mill lade, secretly carrying water to the wheel – about 100 yards to the right of the garden. A newly appointed schoolteacher requested permission to keep his cow in this garden, but the School Board refused.

yesteryear's owners and workers will mourn its passing. Only the pylons and the prefabs flaunt a youthful indifference."

When fire broke out on Thursday, 7th January, 1954, the "end" had apparently come. The fire, which was first noticed at 9.30 p.m., was brought under control within an hour, but firemen from the surrounding districts continued working until the early hours of the next day. The buildings had by now been empty for three and a half years, and the part most affected by the fire was the actual mill section, which was nearest to Duddingston Road.

At the time, the complex was owned by a car dealer and used as a caravan site and scrap yard. The Water Board were asked, by Edinburgh Corporation, to take over the property, but they declined, and a local builder, Andrew Swain, bought the mill and lands round it in 1954 (after the fire) for £1,500 and, in 1963, obtained permission to reconstruct the semi-derelict mill buildings by removing the upper storey, infilling the old window and door openings with stone to match the existing stonework. Viz:

Old Mill section of complex (side nearest to Duddingston Road)

1. South section - converted for use as large garage.
2. Central (east) section - open storage bays for builders' materials.
3. North section - stores on ground floor and workshops on first floor. The flat roofs were covered with mineralised felt.

Central and north sections of complex (part of which remains)

1. Builders' stores, toilets and five offices.

North-west section of complex

1. Lock-up garages for letting.

Duddingston Mill, which had been managed by members of only two families from 1828 to 1950, was thus a builder's and joiner's premises for about 20 years. In 1981, Mr Swain sold the property to Balfour Properties for £215,000 and, in 1983, they sold most of it to Morrison Homes, for £270,000.

The surviving building of this past era may not now be involved in the production of food from the old farmtouns but it is to be hoped that it, together with all the old buildings in the Barony, will be permitted to continue to produce a sense of quiet contentment.

Plate 64 *The mill foreman and his dog*

The building behind Mr David Bell and his clever dog, is the "new" mill office, converted from an earlier summer house to replace the orginal office (see Plate 55*). The "Dutch-barn" style of the mill building is clearly seen, unlike the elusive mill lade to its right.*

CHAPTER 9
CONCLUSION

From the time of the earliest surviving records to comparatively recently, the lands of Duddingston were, largely, lying in a wild state; partly tree-covered, partly well drained due to the sand, and partly boggy due to the underlying rock and clay.

Man had made a tenuous start to shaping the land his way, by digging drains, toiling with animals to cultivate the best ground, building mills to grind the corn, making roads to communicate with other parts of the Barony and elsewhere.

This slow, but sure, progress came about by virtue of the feudal system, some aspects of which existed until as late as this century. Landowners controlled the activities on the land by thirlage and multures, and terms of leases, with the result that the land became more and more useful for farming, but the majority of the population were encouraged to live in relatively small areas.

In the 16th century, the main roads were that from Edinburgh, via Restalrig, to Niddrie, i.e. Willowbrae Road, and that from Wester Duddingston to Niddrie. The old Roman road, the Fishwives' Causeway, ran from Restalrig, through the Figgate Whins, to Musselburgh. Other roads were "footroads" and were those from Wester Duddingston to Easter Duddingston and to Duddingston Mills, and from Duddingston Mills to Edinburgh via the Parson's Knowe, or what became the lands of Parson's Green. A footroad from Leith to Musselburgh included the line of the present promenade. Other "footroads" may have existed at that time.

The only houses which stood in the area then, as far as one can now tell, were in Easter and Wester Duddingston. The lands were a combination of myres, common grazing areas and fields used for agricultural purposes. The Figgate was, of course, a desolate place covered with whins and sand-dunes and a rough, coarse grass.

In the 17th century, the only significant new development was the building of the salt pans on the coast, in an area which, about 150 years later, became known as Joppa. It is probable that this activity also introduced, or at least increased, coal-mining at that time, and that the first road from the coast to Brunstane was made - the Black Road. The Figgate Whins were still just that and the runrig farming system still operated.

The 18th century was the time when real changes began to take place in the Barony of Duddingston and the lands of Figgate. Agricultural areas expanded as drainage methods improved; the Figgate Whins were burned, fields extended and the birth of the new Village of Figgate took place. Industries grew on additional uses of the indigenous clay, such as brickmaking, tile-making and earthenware manufacturing and people were attracted to this new place near the sea, where they could escape from the crowded confines of Edinburgh.

Some of the old roads were altered and others disappeared altogether.

The road from Jock's Lodge to Niddrie remained a principal route but was improved; that from Jock's Lodge to Portobello and Maitland Bridge was created and replaced the old Fishwives' Causeway as a main thoroughfare. Roads such as that from Wester Duddingston to Easter Duddingston; from Wester Duddingston to Duddingston Mills; from Wester Duddingston to Craigmillar and from the coal works, on the coast road, to Brunstane all remained "estate" roads in the 18th century. The much-reduced Fishwives' Causeway remained a public road.

Another major change occurred when the Earl of Abercorn purchased the Barony of Duddingston in 1745 and began to enclose, drain and generally improve it during the 1750s. Duddingston House and its Policies replaced several old fields and common grazing areas. The runrig system was replaced by new large farms - Northfield, Meadowfield, Southfield, Midfield, Eastfield, Duddingston Hall and Easter Town Mains. The roads from Wester Duddingston to Edinburgh, via the Parson's Knowe; from Wester Duddingston to Niddrie, and from Wester Duddingston to Jock's Lodge, via the lands of Meadowfield, were closed.

Coal operations increased, using steam engines instead of water or horse-powered machines, for raising water and coal.

The layout of Wester Duddingston altered significantly and it was reduced in size by about five acres, due to the creation of Duddingston Policies. The path from the village to Edinburgh, via the King's Park, was altered from a single track through the rocks to a proper path six feet wide. The population of Wester Duddingston was 438 in 1703, 444 in 1794 and is about 200 at present.

The new name, Joppa, appeared at the end of the century, and was apparently attached to new brickworks which had been built outwith Portobello, near the salt pans.

Early in the 19th century, the small farm of Rabbit Hall, which was built towards the end of the 18th century, just to the east of the village of Figgate, was gradually swallowed up by the expanding village, by now known as Portobello. The development of the grounds of Rabbit Hall is interesting, as it marked a significant change in the use of land; from agricultural rent income to feu income. The units of houses and attached ground could not exceed one eighth of an acre in area, according to the title deeds of the Barony of Duddingston, and the first entry in the Sasine Register is in 1802, when five "Lotts" were feued for development purposes. Tradesmen, probably made prosperous from the huge building programmes in Edinburgh, began to buy property and plumbers, masons, wrights and slaters were among the first to do so at Rabbit Hall. "Over the wall", in the old Village of Figgate, by now called Portobello, the profession of the owners included "surgeons and Writers in Edinburgh".

The section of the Rabbit Hall grounds which contained the farm, was between the rear garden wall on the east side of today's Marlborough Street (the eastern border of the old village of Figgate) and Pitteville Street Lane, and between Abercorn Terrace and the seashore. The farm itself stood to the west of Pittville Street Lane, not far from Abercorn Terrace.

The promenade followed the line of an old footroad and the village was extended eastwards towards Joppa.

Plate 65 *Rabbit Hall*

Its location can be seen on the 1801 map.

The old Southfield Farm; Duddingston Hall, Eastfield and Easter Town Mains disappeared, but a new Duddingston Mains and Southfield Farm were built. Duddingston Hut gave way to the Woodlands and land here was beginning to be feued for building houses instead of being used for agriculture (as in Portobello), for example, Cauvin's Hospital, Lady Nairne's House, and other houses, in Willowbrae Road.

Duddingston Road, Baileyfield Road and the North British Railway line were all built in the first half of the century. A branch line from Leith to Niddrie travelled beside what is now Baileyfield Road and is still evidenced by the raised bank, now tree-covered, on the west side of the road, between the Figgate Park and Durham Place Lane. The Innocent Railway, built in July 1831 at the southern edge of the Barony, was one of the first railways in the world. The Mill Town was rebuilt and new mills, school and houses were constructed in the period 1825–30.

By the end of the century, Portobello had forced its way to Joppa on the east and to the "new" eastern end of the Fishwives' Causeway and King's Road on the west. Jock's Lodge, in addition to houses, had a nursery and cemetery (1887) and Willowbrae House (then Willow Bank) had been erected at what is now Willowbrae Avenue. Easter Duddingston was attended by Joppa Quarry and Portobello Cemetery was, like that at Jock's Lodge, accompanied by a nursery.

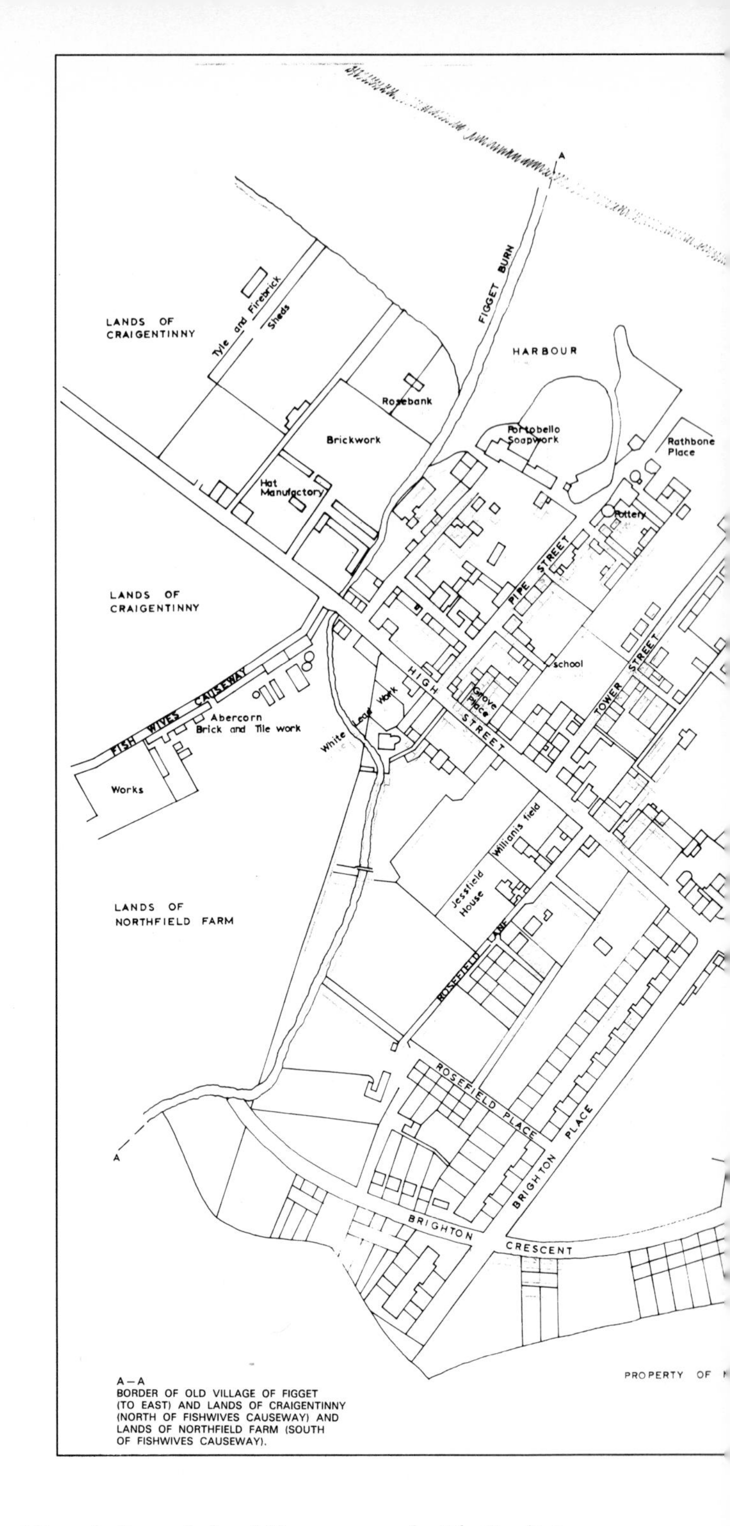

Plate 66 *Portobello 1824*

This is a sketch from Wood's Plan of Portobello and should be compared with Ainslie's Plan of the Village of Figgate in 1787. These are the only surviving (detailed) maps of Portobello prior to the 1850s.

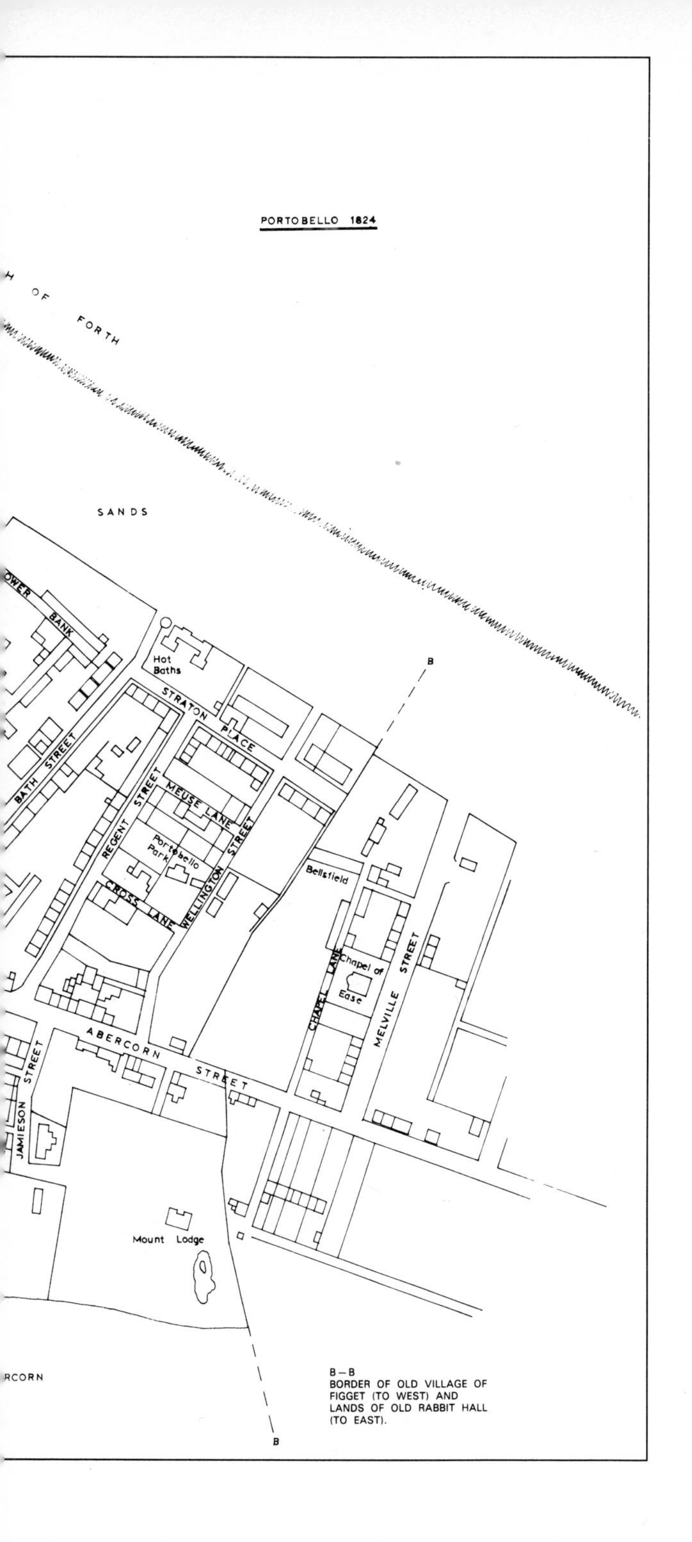
PORTOBELLO 1824
OF FORTH
SANDS
BANK
Hot Baths
STRATON PLACE
BATH STREET
REGENT STREET
MEUSE LANE
Portobello Park
WELLINGTON STREET
CROSS LANE
Bellsfield
CHAPEL LANE
Chapel of Ease
MELVILLE STREET
ABERCORN STREET
JAMIESON STREET
Mount Lodge
B
B
B — B
BORDER OF OLD VILLAGE OF FIGGET (TO WEST) AND LANDS OF OLD RABBIT HALL (TO EAST).

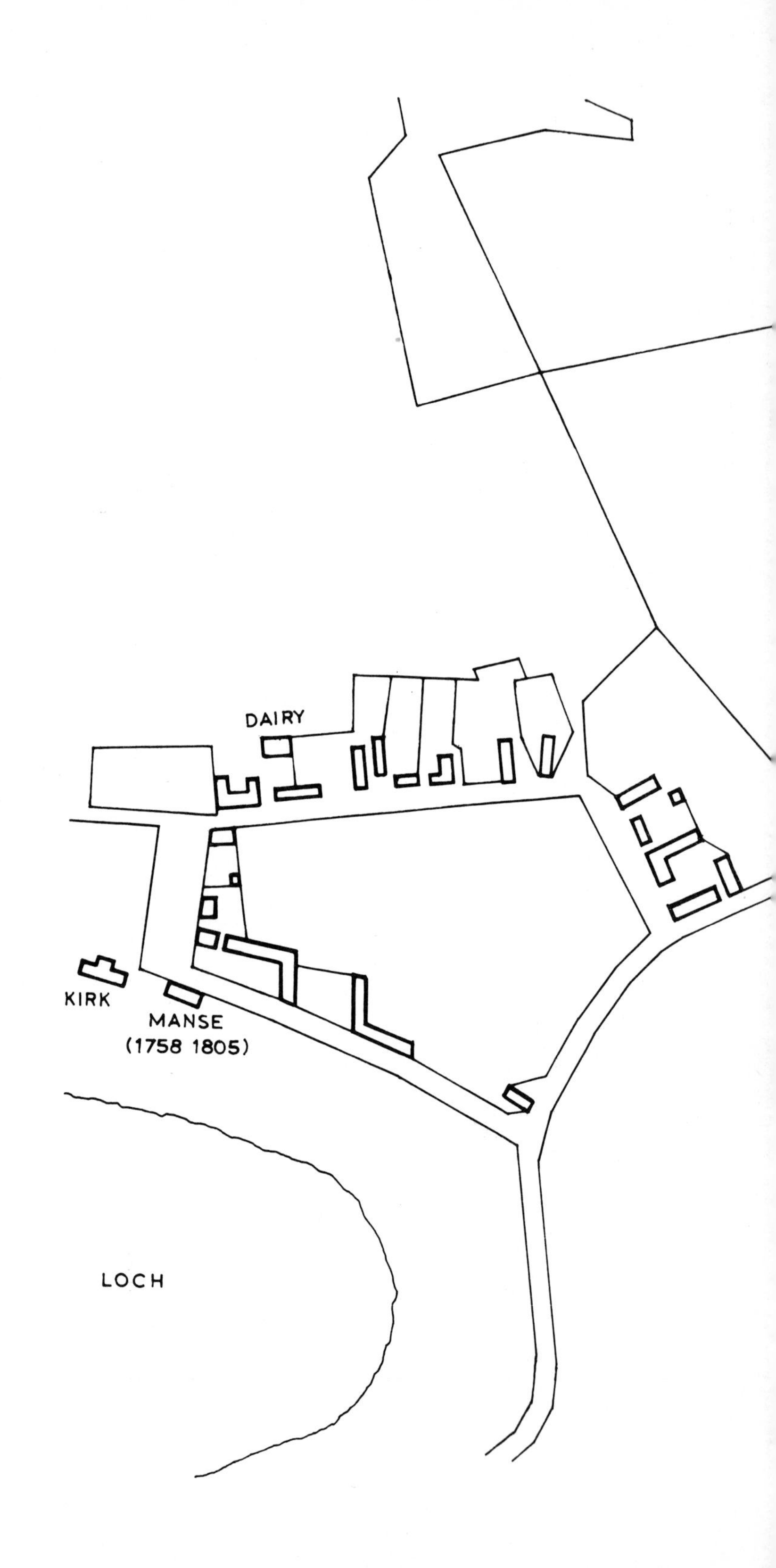
DAIRY
KIRK
MANSE
(1758 1805)
LOCH

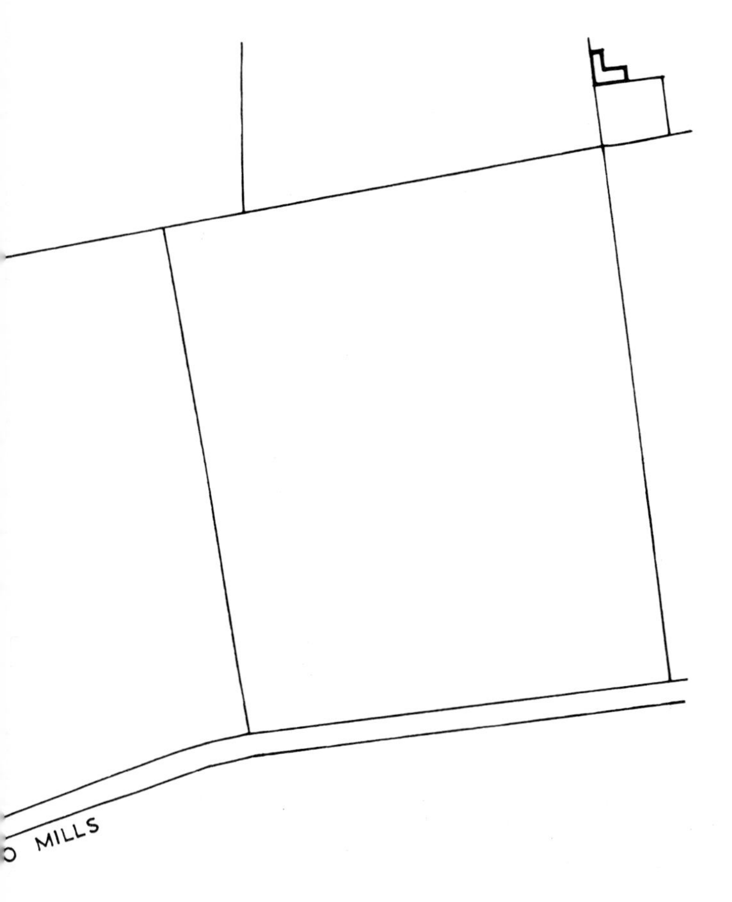

Plate 67 *Wester Duddingston Toun in 1801*

The eastern section of the future Old Church Lane, from Duddingston Road West to the church, was built around 1805 but the western section, from the church to the park, was laid c 1860, to link up with the "new road through the King's Park". The layout in this sketch was, historically, an interim one, with the road passing by the site of the present manse.

The village of Wester Duddingston had assumed its current shape, having discarded an earlier "interim" arrangement whereby the road from the Kirk, instead of going down Old Church Lane, went towards the east end of the Loch, past the present manse. The old manse stood next to the church gate and this arrangement was altered when, around 1805, the new manse and some of the present houses in the village, were built. Old Church Lane was made, from Duddingston Road West to the church, around 1805, and was extended to the Park around 1860, about 20 years after the Queen's Drive was constructed.

Duddingston Policy grounds were, by 1896, used for Cavalry Training and as a Golf Course. That row of fine, stone houses, the "Twelve Apostles", had been built in Duddingston Crescent. A Fever Hospital stood next to the road (Duddingston Road South) at the Brunstane Burn, where industrial units stand today, and the new Portobello School stood in Duddingston Park. This building, the first part of which was built in 1876, ended its life as a school in May 1989, after serving latterly as an annexe to the "new" Portobello High School (completed in 1963) in Duddingston Road.

The remainder of the lands were still under the plough, as indeed they were until well into this century. In 1951, for example, most of the land between the houses in Duddingston Road West and Ulster Crescent still produced grain, and field layouts, seen on the 1801 map, could still be identified.

The Scott family, members of which have played such a significant part in Duddingston life for almost 300 years (farms, mills, coal, roads, bridges and church activities), surely deserves to be adequately commemorated and perhaps a future development in the Barony of Duddingston (or Brunstane) may yet contain a "Scott" address.

The present world of Duddingston is extremely remote from that of Old Duddingston. Today's needs, tools, occupations, transport, clothes, houses, colour schemes, food, attitudes, beliefs, values, customs, interests and even speech are vastly different from those of generations of people who lived or toiled in the very space in which today's population watches television, drives cars or programmes various electronic gadgets. Leisure time is a truly modern phenomenon.

History is many things to many people, but at the very least, it offers a sober perspective and provides a potential basis for future changes. In any event, the Lands of Duddingston and Portobello will always be enhanced by the presence of Arthur's Seat and the Firth of Forth; what happens in between is, of course, future history!

APPENDIX I

RECORDS AND EXPENSES OF THE BUILDING OF THE PARK DYKE (From the Records of the Burgh of Edinburgh 1528–57)

(m)=1000; (c)=100; (l)=50; (li)=pounds (less than 50); (s)=shillings; (d)=scots penny; j=1 (e.g. j(c)=100 and viij=8)
[The monetary amounts were shown using a mixture of Roman characters and Pound/Shillings/Pence format (Pounds Scots)]
Some words (in the order they appear in the text) are explained at the end of this Appendix.

THE COMMENCEMENT OF THE BUILDING OF THE PARK DYKE

9th July, 1541 – The qhilk day, the prouest baillies and counsale sittand in jugment oblissis thame and thair successouris to content and pay to our Souerane Lord or ony vtheris to quhome his Grace pleissis gyf command, the sowme of j(m) merkis betuix this and Witsounday nixt tocum for the sowme of j(m) merkis now borrowit fra his Grace be thame, and reauit fra his Grace's thesaurer for expedatioun of the bigging of the park.

EXPENSES IN 1544

The prouest ballies counsale dekynnis of craftis with ane grete part of vther honest men of the burgh, at the requeist of Mare, Drowiar and Regent of this realm, moder to our Sourane Lady the Quenis grace, comperand be my lord of Dunfermeling and Sir Johnne Campbell of Lauder knycht hir gracis maister houshald, consentit to big on thair expens the haill sloppis in the park dike circulit about Arthour Sett, Salisborie and Dudingstoun Craggis, vnder protestatioun that the samin preiugit nocht thame anent the calsay stanis quhilk thai wer in vs to gett furth of the saidis cragis quhen thai had ado thairwith.

1st March, 1554 – The baillies and ane pairt of the counsale ordanis the thesaurar Maister Johne Prestoun to caus big the yettis of the park dyk.

1554 – The expenses maid in the up-biging of the haill sloppis of the Park Dike, biggit be command of the provest, baillies and counsale:

> Item, in primis, the compter is to be dischargit of the sowme of ane hundreth x(li) x(s) quhilk he payit and debursit to James Wond, Andro Slesche, David Ramsay, and Thomas Wod, masonis, quha compleatit and biggit xvij ruds of wark quhilk the said sloppis contenit, ilk rude sett for vj(li) x(s) in warkmanschip and all necessars, quhilks xvij ruds wer mett be David Grahame, Michael

Brussat, and Sir William M'Dougall, master of work, to that nomber; summa
j(c) x(li) x(s)
(£110 10s 00d)

The expensis of three stane yeittis made in the said park dike:

Item, to Thomas Craufurd, quareor, for the wynnyng of xxviij pece hewin work, ilk pece v(d);
summa xj(s) viij(d)
(11s 8d)

Item, to Denne morisoun for wynnyng of thre lintellis to the saids yeittis, xxj fute lang, price of ilk fute vj(d);
summa x(s) vj(d)
(10s 6d)

Item, to Adam Harlaw, carter, for careing of xij pece hewin wark to Dudingstoun and xij pece to Sanct Leonards, with thair twa lintallis, quhilks wer aucht draucht, price of ilk draucht ij(s);
summa xvj(s)
(16s)

Item, to Peter Hill, massoun, and his twa servands, for hewing of xxviij rebettis and twa lang lintellis, to Duddingstoun and Sanct Leonard's yettis, and setting of the greit stane yet at the Abbay;
summa lviij(s)
(58s)

Item, to ane barroman with the said Peter, foure dayis;
summa v(s) iiij(d)
(5s 4d)

Item, for vij pund leid;
summa iij(s) vj(d)
(3s 6d)

Item, for aucht dallis and thre rauchteris to the greit tymmer yet at the Abbay, and mending of barrowis;
summa xxviij(s) viij(d)
(28s 8d)

Item, for beirring of this yet to the Abbay;
summa viij(d)
(8d)

Item, for ane greit stoke loke to this yet;
summa vij(s)
(7s)

Item, to Adam Purves, wrycht, for the making of this yet;
summa xvj(s)
(16s)

Item, for ij(c) plauchoure nallis thairto;
summa v(s)
(5s)

Item, Johne Ahannay, smyth, for vj irne crukkis and vj irne bands with slott and stapillis, weyand vj stane xiiij(li) wecht, price of the stane wecht maid wark xj(s);
summa iij(li) xv(s) iij(d)
(£3 15s 3d)

Item, to him for ij(c) plauchoure nallis and half ane hundreith garroun nallis;
summa viij(s)
(8s)

Summa of the haill park dike j(c) xxij(li) xv(s) vij(d)

(£122 15s 7d)

THE BUILDING OF THE DYKE AT THE LOCH – 1555

Item, twa masonis, twa oulks, to big the park dyke at the loch side of Duddingston and foiranent it agane on Priestfield syde, ilk man in the oulk xv(s);
summa iij(li)
(£3)

Item, of twa barromen to serve them in mortor, wynning of stanis and bering of stanis to thame, ilk man ouklie viij(s);
summa xxxij(s)
(32s)

Item, for ane lang tre to put in the wall that lyis far in the loch for outganging of wyld beistis;
summa vj(s)
(6s)

(This section of wall is still a very distinctive feature.)

Item, for twa laids of Cousland lyme;
summa iij(s)
(3s)

(Cousland Lime Works were, until recently, in operation.)

MEANING OF THE MORE "OBSCURE WORDS"

prouest = provost

vtheris = others

thesaurer = treasurer

bigging = building

moder = mother

samin = same

yet, yeittis = gate, gates

aucht draucht = eight loads

rebettis = cut stones for the gateway

leid, leding = lead (metal)

dallis, daillis, dale = planks

rauchteris = rafters

greit tymmer yet = great timber gateway (with a roof)

stoke loke = lock with a key

plauchoure nallis = flooring nails

irne crukkis = iron hooks, on which the gate was hung

slott, or sloit, and stapillis = bolt and fastenings

weyand = weighing

garroun nallis = large spiked nails

oulks = weeks

tre = wooden beam

APPENDIX II
TODAY'S STREET NAMES AND DERIVATIONS

(The dates refer to the years in which names were applied, if known.)

Abercorn
from Marquis - superior of the ground.

Abercorn Drive, Grove (1932)
See Abercorn.

Abercorn Gardens, Avenue, Crescent, Cowt, Terrace
See Abercorn.

Adelphi Place, Grove
Possibly after the fashion set by Adelphi Terrace in London.

Argyle Crescent
From previous owners of Duddingston.

Baileyfield Road, Crescent
After William Bailey, first Provost of Portobello (after his house which stood next to his bottle-works).

Baillie Terrace, Place, Grove, Path
As in Baileyfield.

Baronscourt Terrace, Road
After the Irish seat of the Abercorn Family, in County Tyrone.

Bath Street, Place
After the first public bathing premises in Portobello.

Beach Lane (1967)
Formerly Ramsay Lane - renamed because of duplication.

Bedford Terrace
In 1832, 1st Duke of Abercorn married the daughter of 6th Duke of Bedford.

Bellfield Street, Lane, Terrace
After Bellsfield (Wood's map dated 1824) and probably refers to the church bells - Chapel of Ease.

Bingham Broadway, Avenue, Circle, Crescent, Crossway, Drive, Place, Street, Road (see Duddingston Row) (1946). In 1894, 3rd Duke of Abercorn married Lady Rosaline Bingham, daughter of 4th Earl of Lucan.

Bingham Medway, Way (1966)
See Bingham Broadway, etc.

Brand Drive, Gardens
After a Provost of Portobello.

Brickfield (1978)
On site of William Jamieson's brickfield of 1765.

Bridge Street, Bridge Street Lane (1978)
Existing street was extended. Derives from nearby bridge over the Figgate Burn.

Brighton Place, East and West Brighton Crescent (1820)
Compliment paid by the "other Brighton" to the older English sister - built about 1820.

Brunstane Bank, Crescent, Drive, Road (1935)
From House and Barony of Brunstane; after the old coal road from Duddingston pit to Brunstane House. Used to be called the Black Road and is thought to have been on a different "line" originally.

Brunstane Road South and Brunstane Road North (1967)
See Brunstane Bank, etc.

Brunstane Gardens, Mews(1974)
See Brunstane Bank, etc.

Causeway, The
Original main street in "Wester Duddingston" which led from Duddingston to both Edinburgh and Niddrie.

Christian Crescent, Path, Grove
After a Provost of Portobello.

Coillesdene Avenue, Grove, Drive, Crescent, Gardens, Terrace, Loan
See Coillesdene Court.

Coillesdene Court
From a former mansion on same site. Also on the site of old salt pans and said (by Baird) to be on the site of an old coal pit.

Dalkeith Street
The Duke of Argyle's daughter married the Earl of Dalkeith, later Duke of Buccleuch.

Duddingston
Two theories - Gaelic, "sunny side of the hill", or after 12th-century person named Dodin; the latter being the more likely.

Duddingston Avenue and Gardens North (1933)
See Duddingston.

Duddingston Gardens South (1954)
See Duddingston.

Duddingston Grove, East and West (1937)
See Duddingston.

Duddingston Loan (1966)
See Duddingston.

Duddingston Mills
Formerly Duddingston Mill Lane and Duddingston Mills Cottages - this access road to the mills was created in 1829 when the new mill complex was built.

Duddingston Park
Formerly Niddrie Road - see Duddingston.

Duddingston Park South (1976)
New name for Niddrie Road from Milton Road to Niddrie Mains Road, following petition from residents.

Duddingston Rise (1974)
See Duddingston.

Duddingston Road (1825)
Gave people of Portobello a direct route to Duddingston Kirk. See Duddingston.

Duddingston Road West (1958)
Old road line from Wester Duddingston to the Mill Town and from Wester Duddingston to Cairntows and Craigmillar. See Duddingston.

Duddingston Row
Formerly Bingham Road. Part of the street used to be known as this; altered following a petition from residents. The old road to Niddrie formerly ran between Duddingston Row and the Golf Course.

Duddingston Square East and West (1933)
See Duddingston.

Duddingston View (1974)
See Duddingston.

Duddingston Yards (1983)
Group of light industrial units on the north bank of Niddrie Burn. Site of former school and before that a fever hospital.

Durham Drive, Gardens (North and South), Grove (1932)
See Durham Road.

Durham Place West, Road South, Square (1932)
See Durham Road.

Durham Place Lane (1939)
See Durham Road.

Durham Road and Road South (1890)
1st Duke of Abercorn's daughter married the Earl of Durham.

Eastfield, Place, Gardens
After Easter Duddingston Mains. The original Eastfield Farm was just north of the Brunstane Burn, near Asda. May be after the east field of coal, which was in this area.

Eastway, The
Steep path from Northfield Broadway to Northfield Crescent, opposite Northfield Square.

Elcho Terrace
Family connection - Binghams with Earl of Wemyss (Lord Elcho).

Esplanade Terrace
Descriptive.

Figgate Bank, Street (1965)
Formerly Tower Bank and Street, renamed due to duplication. Variations of the name Figgate are Figget, Figgat, Fichet, Freegate, Feggot, Fichet and Friggatt.

Figgate Street, Lane, Place (1981)
New street on site of section of Figgate Street.

Fishwives' Causeway (Causey)
Road followed by fishwives from Musselburgh to Edinburgh. The old road was torn up by the North British Railway Co. in 1845. The original line of road is thought to be of Roman origin, and stretched from Jock's Lodge to Abercorn Terrace.

Hamilton (1935)
See Hamilton Terrace.

Hamilton Drive, Park, Drive West, Gardens, Grove.
See Hamilton Terrace.

Hamilton Terrace (1901)
After Marquis of Abercorn - the superior of the ground.

Harbour Place (1978)
Near the site of a harbour built by William Jamieson in the 1760s. At low tide, the base of part of the walls can be seen.

Highway, The
Steep footpath between Broadway and Crescent extending to Northfield Circus. See Northfield Broadway etc.

Hope Lane (1825)
After Mr Hope, tenant farmer at Duddingston Mains. The road and farm were made about this time, but the northern end was an old road called the "Easter Duddingston Common Loan".

Innocent Railway (1983)
Walkway on route of early railway opened in 1831 for horse-drawn traffic from Dalkeith to St Leonards.

James Street and James Street Lane (1824)
After John James Hamilton, Marquis of Abercorn, superior. His own naming.

Jock's Lodge
Said to be from a beggar who built a hut there. First appears in 1650 as "Jokis Lodge" (Nicholl's diary).

John Street and John Street Lane
See James Street.

Joppa Terrace, Gardens, Grove, Road, Park
Biblical name, applied to brickworks complex, and its field, west of Salt Pans. First appears *c* 1770.

Lady Nairne Drive, Crescent, Loan, Grove, Place (1956)
After Caroline, Baroness and song-writer. The Nairnes owned what is now a Berni Inn. The original building was built in 1805 and the Nairnes lived there from 1805 to 1818.

Laing Terrace
After David Laing, historian and Librarian to the Signet Library, who lived in this area.

Law Place (1978)
Near site of Bleak Law, a small but prominent hill in the Figgate Whins (Ainslie's map of 1787 shows this feature).

Lee Crescent
Ground feued by J. B. W. Lee, SSC, Edinburgh. Self-named crescent.

Lower Joppa
The part of Joppa which is nearest to the sea. See Joppa. This is where the name first appeared in this area.

Magdalene Avenue, Drive, Gardens, Lane, Medway, Court, Place
From ancient Chapel at Newhailes, which land belonged to the family of Maitland (of Lauderdale).

Marlborough Street (1967)
Formerly Wellington Street. Renamed due to duplication. From Marlborough Mansions, after the Duke of Marlborough.

Maryfield (1804)
From wife of Mr Wilson of Wilson's Park.

Meadowfield Avenue (1936)
After Meadowfield Farm. This farm was off Paisley Drive, where Meadowfield Court (Abercorn Court) now stands.

Meadowfield Court (and Abercorn Court) (1982)
Cul-de-sac on the site of Meadowfield Farm, off Paisley Drive. The farm was built about 1770.

Meadowfield Drive, Gardens (1956)
See Meadowfield Avenue.

Meadowfield Terrace (1954)
Original Terrace was on the west side of Willowbrae Road, north of Paisley Drive - 1938. See Meadowfield Avenue.

Mentone Avenue
A gracious reference to an even more famous watering place.

Milton Crescent, Gardens North and South (1932)
After Andrew Fletcher, Lord Milton, who lived at Brunstane House.

Milton Drive (1934)
See Milton Crescent etc.

Milton Grove (1967)
See Milton Crescent etc.

Milton Road East and West
See Milton Crescent etc.

Milton Terrace (1931)
See Milton Crescent etc.

Morton Street
Possibly after Dowager Countess of Morton, who leased Duddingston house in mid 19th century.

Mount Lodge Place
After house and gardens of same name.

Mountcastle Bank (1969)
See Mountcastle Drive etc.

Mountcastle Drive, North and South, Terrace (1932)
In 1603, the Earl of Abercorn's other title was Lord Mountcastle. The Abercorns did not own Duddingston until 1745.

Mountcastle Gardens and Grove (1934)
See Mountcastle Drive etc.

Mountcastle Green and Place (1971)
See Mountcastle Drive etc.

Mountcastle Loan (1947)
See Mountcastle Drive etc.

Mountcastle Park (1964)
See Mountcastle Drive etc.

Musselburgh Road
The line of the Post Road to the south.

New Bellfield
Flats and court on part of the grounds of old "Bellfield Villa" (Willowbrae Hotel).

New Tower Place (1981)
Renewed reference to the adjoining Tower and to the former Tower Street – renamed Figgate Street in 1965.

Northfield Broadway, Avenue, Circus (1921)
After Northfield Farm which was built in 1761, where Northfield Park is now. The original tenant farmers here were members of the Scott family.

Northfield Crescent, Gardens, Road, Terrace (1921)
See Northfield Broadway etc.

Northfield Drive, Grove (1947)
See Northfield Broadway etc.

Northfield Farm Avenue (1929)
A farm road since the farm was built in 1761, and a field access before that. See Northfield Broadway etc.

Northfield Farm Road
On line of old farm road to Portobello Road. See Northfield Broadway etc.

Northfield Park (1963)
Site of Northfield Farm, which was built in 1761. See Northfield Broadway etc.

Northfield Park Grove (1973)
See Northfield Broadway etc.

Northfield Square (1921)
See Northfield Broadway etc.

Northway, The (1921)
Footpath between Northfield Road and Crescent. See Northfield Broadway etc.

Old Church Lane
Formerly Church Lane (1870s O/S map); South Street on feuing plan dated 1827. Made about 1805.

Ormelie Terrace
After house and garden previously on the site.

Paisley Avenue, Drive (1929)
See Paisley Crescent.

Paisley Crescent (1927)
After town of same name, which area was also owned by the Abercorn Family.

Paisley Gardens, Terrace (1934)
See Paisley Crescent.

Paisley Grove (1960)
See Paisley Crescent.

Park Avenue
Adjacent to Public Park (Golf Course).

Parson's Green
"Personis Knowis", or "the Parson's Knowes" - church land, belonging to the parson of Restalrig.

Piersfield Terrace
See Piershill

Piershill Terrace, Place, Lane
First recorded in 1580 in the form Peirieshill - possibly from the word persche, i.e. osier or willow.

Pipe Street, Lane (1978)
From water pipe from the Figgate Burn to trough at Pipe Street/Bridge Street (then Tobago Street). On line of original Pipe Street.

Pitt Street (1805)
From William Pitt, Prime Minister in 1783. He died in 1805.

Pittville Street and Pittville Street Lane
After house of same name (after William Pitt).

Portobello
From house named after a naval victory at Puerto Bello (Panama) in 1739. The house, which stood between the High Street and Lee Crescent, was built about 1753 by tenant farmer, Andrew Scott, for his shepherd and as a place to "retail ale".

Portobello High Street
Formerly High Street. See Portobello.

Pottery, The (1978)
Site of the earliest of the Portobello potteries founded by William Jamieson.

Promenade
Self-explanatory. Prior to the development of Portobello, this route was used as a "footroad" from Musselburgh to Leith.

Queen's Bay Crescent
Fanciful - after Queen Victoria.

Ramsay Place
After General Ramsay L'amy, a West Indian Veteran who resided in this part of Portobello.

Rathbone Place (1981)
From name of street on Wood's map of 1824. After Thomas Rathbone, distinguished Portobello potter.

Regent Street and Regent Street Lane
After the Prince Regent, who ultimately became George IV.

Rosebank Lane, Cottage
From terraced gardens there, where roses were cultivated.

Rosefield Avenue, Avenue Lane, Street, Place, Lane
After William Jamieson's House and Garden.

Sandford Gardens
From Bishop Sandford of Edinburgh, who inducted the Revd Drummond as first minister in St Marks (site of St John's Church). Formerly called Sandford Street.

Seaview Terrace, Crescent
Descriptive.

Shrub Mount (1981)
Site of garden of property of that name, where Hugh Miller lived until his death in 1856.

South Morton Street
Possibly after Dowager Countess of Morton who leased Duddingston House.

Southfield Bank (1960)
See Southfield Gardens etc.

Southfield Farm Grove (1954)
Old access road to Southfield Farm. See Southfield Gardens etc.

Southfield Gardens East and West (1933)
After Southfield Farm. The farmhouse, which still exists, was built about 1830.

Southfield Loan (1958)
See Southfield Gardens etc.

Southfield Road East and West, Terrace (1935)
See Southfield Gardens etc.

Southfield Square (1938)
See Southfield Gardens etc.

Spa Place (1981)
A physic well on this site was a popular watering place in the early 19th century.

St Mark's Place, Lane
From St Marks Episcopal Church, opened in May 1825.

St Mary Place
c 1880s - evidently suggested by the name of St Mark's Place, since a Mary was the mother of Mark.

Stanley Street
Probably from Henry Stanley, Journalist/African explorer, who found Livingstone in Africa in 1820.

Station Brae (1981)
Formal adoption of a traditional name of road up to Portobello Railway Station, which road is now a private area.

Straiton Place
Origin not known, but it is shown on Wood's map of 1824 as Straton.

Ulster Crescent (1934)
Abercorn's connections with Ulster date from the Plantations there in 1634. See Ulster Drive etc.

Ulster Drive, Gardens, Grove, Terrace (1929)
Abercorn's main family residence is in Co. Tyrone, in part of Ulster. These streets were altered from their original proposed name of Kilpatrick Drive etc.

West Brighton Crescent
See Brighton Place etc.

Whins Place (1981)
After Figgate Whins, which was the earlier name of the lands of the Portobello area.

William Jamieson Place (1978)
After the "father" of Portobello, who developed the brick clays in the 1760s.

Williamfield Square (1960)
After William Jamieson. Stands on the site of old cottages.

Willowbrae Road, Avenue, Gardens
From the Willow enclosures (called the "saughs") which used to stand near Northfield Farm and, probably, near "Willowhead" Road.

Wilson's Park
After the owner of grounds here (sub-feuar of William Jamieson). His wife's name was given to Maryfield.

Windsor Place
Originally Nicholson Street from the maiden name of William Jamieson's wife. On Wood's map of 1824, it was called Jamieson Street. The name was changed after 1824, in commemoration of the visit of George IV to Portobello in 1822 and the southern end was called Windsor Terrace).

Woodlands Grove (1959)
After the name of the house which previously stood here. Previous to that, the property was called the Earl's Farm, or Duddingston Hut.

Woodside Terrace
Sounds descriptive, but no immediate significant woodlands were present when the street was developed. Possibly from its field name - Wardlands.

APPENDIX III
HISTORIC LANDOWNERS OF DUDDINGSTON, FIGGATE AND BRUNSTANE
(Brief Details of Land Ownership According to Baird and Old Charters)

LANDS OF FIGGATE

Early 12th century	Abbots of Kelso
1466	Cuthbert Knightson, Burgess of Edinburgh
1560	Crown (Reformation)
1630	John Lawson of Humbie (from grandfather, James) (half of Figgate and some lands in Duddingston)
1670	John Logan (son of George) of Burncastle
1691	George Logan (son of John) of Burncastle
	Baird lost track of the ownership trail concerning the Figgate "for about 50 years", but the Fletcher of Saltoun Papers (MS 17488) are most revealing in respect of the period 1691 to 1763.
1704	Sir James Dick of Prestonfield was infefted, i.e. invested with legal possession, in 1707. Under a contract of the same date (1704), however, between Elizabeth, Duchess of Argyll and Sir James Dick, the disposition was made in the name of Dick for his further security of a principal sum of 4,600 Marks. Upon payment of this sum (and rents and expenses) the right of the said lands belonged to the Duchess of Argyll. The reason for this arrangement is not clear.
1720	Sir James Dick disponed to Dame Janet Dick, his daughter, the principal sum, rents and expenses upon payment of which the said lands and teinds were redeemable by the Duchess of Argyll.
1731	Dame Janet Dick obtained a precept of Clare Constat from George Logan of Burncastle (superior of the land) for infefting her as heir to her father (infefted 1731).
1732	Dame Janet Dick sold and disponed to Anthony Murray, Merchant in Edinburgh, the lands and teinds of Figgate for security of the principal sum of 4,600 Marks. When he died, his rights passed to his nephew, Sir Patrick Murray of Blackcastle.
1747	Sir Patrick Murray disponed to Thomas Belches, Deputy Sheriff Clerk of Edinburgh.
1753	Belches sold and disponed to Andrew Fletcher, Lord Milton for security of the principal sum etc. Robert Johnstoun's

Report of 1752 (Chapter 3) states that the Figgate "... belongs to the Duchess of Argyll". Although the "original" Duchess of Argyll died in 1735, her heirs still had rights to the lands of Figgate, stemming from the contract of 1704 with Sir James Dick. (Johnstoun quotes the area of the lands of Figgate as being 67 acres, 1 Rood and 20 Falls.)

In 1758, enquiries were made as to how Lord Milton could bring about a reversion of the rights which still belonged to the heirs of the Duchess of Argyll and, at last, in 1763, he paid the long outstanding principal sum, plus interest, totalling £252 11s 9d (and two-thirds of a penny) to the Countess of Dalkeith and "the other Heirs Portioners of John Duke of Argyll". (Lord Milton was Argyll's chief agent in Scotland, as well as a personal friend.)

1763 — Lord Milton sold Figgate to Baron William Mure of Caldwell, Glasgow.

1765 — William Jamieson feued about 40 of the 70 acres:
three in 1765, next to burn on north side of high road
ten in 1766, apparently incorporating the three acres
eight in 1771, south of high road at west end of Figgate
7.5 in 1771, south of high road at east end of Figgate
10.5 in 1771, north of high road, centre of Figgate

by 1787 — In addition to Jamieson, other owners of the lands of Figgate were:
Mr Stewart (formerly Mr Skirving's ground)
Mr Hill
Mr Cunningham
(all their properties can be seen on Ainslie's plan of 1787)
- and previous feuars were:
Mr Andrew Guild, Mr James Sherriff and Mr Wm. Rankine

LANDS OF BRUNSTANE

1410 — Wife of de Crichtoune, Gilbertoun
1447 — Thomas, her son
1456 — George Crichton
1461 — John, his brother
1487 — Edward, his son
1507 — John, his son
1530 — Alexander, his son
c 1550 — John, his son
1597 — Lady Thirlestane (Jean Flemying)
1609 — 2nd Lord Maitland of Thirlestane (son of Jean Flemying) He was the founder of the Lauderdale Family.
1616 — 2nd Lord Maitland and wife - Lady Isobel Seton. She died and he married Elizabeth Lauder. In 1634, he was created Earl of Lauderdale. Their eldest son, John, married Lady Anne Home. The father, the Earl of Lauderdale, rebuilt Brunstane House for the young couple and placed the combined arms of his son and daughter-in-law above the
1639 — principal entrance, with the date 1639. The father died in

	1645 and the son became the Duke of Lauderdale in 1672. His wife died in 1671 and he married again in the same year. His wife was Lady Dysart (Countess of Dysart) and widow of Sir Lionel Tollemache. One of the daughters of her first marriage, Elizabeth Tollemache, married Archibald, Marquis of Lorn and became the first Duchess of Argyll.
1678	Duchess of Lauderdale. The Duke died in 1682. They had already acquired Duddingston in 1673. She died in 1696.
1698	Sir Patrick Home of Renton (see below)
1703	Lyonell, son of the Duke and Duchess of Lauderdale, and 3rd Earl of Dysart. Archibald, Lord Lorn and the Duchess of Argyll (Earl of Dysart's sister) lived at Brunstane. They separated and she lived at Brunstane with her two sons. The eldest son, John, became the Duke of Argyll in 1701 and was much involved with the Union in 1707.
1732	Lyonell, 4th Earl of Dysart (son of 3rd Earl)
1736	The Duchess died in 1735 and John, the Duke of Argyll acquired Duddingston and Brunstane from his cousin, the 4th Earl of Dysart, in 1736.
1744	The Duke of Argyll died in 1743 and his brother, Archibald, became the new Duke. He instigated the rebuilding of Inverary Castle and town which, it is thought, influenced his decision to sell Duddingston and Brunstane.
1747	Brunstane, Figgate (and 19 acres 1 rood next to Brunstane Burn and Magdalene Bridge and the area containing Brunstane Mill) sold to Andrew Fletcher (Lord Milton).
1751	A deed regarding the Roup and Sale of Sir John Home of Manderson's lands mentions that Brunstane was regarded as being previously disponed by Home to Andrew Fletcher (Lord Milton) and that Fletcher had to pay (in 1751) the capital and interest from 1732. The relationship of Home's ownership to those above is, unfortunately, not clear, although the Saltoun Papers indicate that Sir Patrick Home of Renton became the owner of Brunstane in 1698.
1767	Brunstane and 19 acres 1 rood and area containing Brunstane Mill (mentioned above) sold by heirs of Lord Milton to Earl of Abercorn.
1875	Brunstane and the "Eastern Division" of Duddingston sold to the Benhar Coal Company.

LANDS OF DUDDINGSTON (See the end of Chapter 5 for other references)

The ownership trail for Duddingston is more complicated, as there were Easter and Wester Duddingston, other parcels of land, some of which were called the Kirk, or vicarage, lands, and others, such as the "Orchyard", and rights to "half the lands" or "half the mills" of Duddingston, to consider.

DUDDINGSTON (EASTER AND WESTER)

c 1090	Village or estate known as Treverlen - held by Uviet the White. It included most of Holyrood Park. Uviet granted part of Arthur's Seat to the canons of Holyrood, retaining the rest. It is likely that, on Uviet's death, his lands were acquired by the King, who then gave Treverlen and its "crag" to the monks of Kelso.
c 1128	Superiority gifted by the Crown to Abbey of Kelso
c 1147	Dodin de Dodinestun
c 1165	Hugo, son of Dodin de Dodinestun
c 1208	Ricardo, son of Hugo de Dodinestun
c 1208	De Boscho Family (Easter Duddingston)
c 1290	William de Dodingstone (Easter Duddingston)
c 1296	Eleyne de Duddingston (Easter Duddingston)
1311	Geoffry de Fressinglaye (On Bruce's side at Bannockburn)
1311	Robert Hastings (conferred by Edward II)
1314	Geoffry de Fressinglaye (restored after Bannockburn)
c 1330	Sir William de Fressinglaye - half lands of Easter Dudd.
1336	King Edward III confiscated
no information	
c 1420	Abbot of Kelso Abbey: [In the Account of the Lord High Treasurer in 1517, there is the entry, "Item, to Schir Johne Symontoun quhilk past twyis to Dudingstone and summond the tennents for the taxt of Kelso --- iij(s) (three shillings)]
Early 16th century	Easter and Wester Duddingston combined into one Barony
1534	Sir David Murray of Balvaird (whose tenants knocked 24 roods off the newly-built Park Dyke). Half lands of Wester Duddingston. His mother was Margaret Barclay.
1538	John Bertoun, son of Robert Bertoun, of Over Berntoun. Easter and Wester Duddingston and half the mill. His wife was Janet Little. Robert Lawson, son of James, was his tacksman; he is the Robert Lawson who built the "rogue" mill and lade in the 1564 Court of Session case.
1548	Robert Bertoun (son of John). Whole lands of Easter and Wester Duddingston and half the mill.
1552	Andrew Murray of Balvaird and Arngask - half lands and town of Wester Duddingston (Principal Keeper of the King's Park).
1552	Thomas Thomson - other half of Easter and Wester Duddingston. He was an "Ypothecar and Burgess of Edinburgh". His wife was Margaret Bertoun, Robert Bertoun's sister. (Murray and Thomson feature in the

	Court of Session case of 1564 concerning the water supply of Duddingston Mills) Thomas Thomson's wife was Margaret Bertoun.
1571	Alexander Thomson, son of Thomas and Margaret. He married Margaret Preston of Craigmillar - half lands of Easter and Wester Duddingston and half the mill.
1572	Andrew Murray, son of Andrew Murray of Arngask, Knight - half the lands of Wester Duddingston and mill.
1594	Alexander Thomson, granted to his future spouse, Margaret Preston, relict of Walter Cant in St Giles Grange, the lands of Wester Duddingston and half the mill, in liferent.
1603	John Thomson
c 1607	Sir Thomas Thomson, Knight, of Duddingston (son of Alexander Thomson and Margaret Preston and brother of John).
1666	Sir Patrick Thomson, son of Sir Thomas Thomson - Easter Duddingston, parts of Wester Duddingston and the whole mill. According to Session Papers in the Signet Library, Sir Patrick Thomson renounced all right to Duddingston Loch in favour of Sir Robert Murray of Prestonfield (Priestfield).
1673	Duke of Lauderdale - he now owned Easter and Wester Duddingston and Brunstane.
1678	Duchess of Lauderdale (Duke died 1682)
1703	Duchess of Lauderdale died in 1696 and Duddingston (and Brunstane) passed to her son, Lyonell, 3rd Earl of Dysart (legally) in 1703.
1732	Lyonell, 4th Earl of Dysart (son of 3rd Earl).
1736	John 2nd Duke of Argyll
1744	Archibald, 3rd Duke of Argyll
1745	8th Earl of Abercorn
1875	"Eastern Division" sold to the Benhar Coal Company (Duddingston lands to the east of Baileyfield Road).
1891	(Landward part of the "Eastern Division") to Sir James Miller of Manderston.

WHAT ABERCORN SOLD TO THE BENHAR COAL CO. IN 1875

1. The "Eastern Division", i.e. land lying to the east of Baileyfield Road and Duddingston Road South, excluding Portobello, and bordered by the Brunstane Burn on the south and the Figgate Burn on the north (more or less the old Easter Duddingston lands).
2. A triangle of land lying towards Northfield Farm and bounded by the Figgate Burn on the south and the Railway on the north.
3. Brunstane Estate.
4. Seven acres of the Braes - north side of Brunstane Burn, of which 4.5 acres related to a contract of Excambion (exchange) between the (later) 3rd Duke of Argyll and Lord Milton, dated 31st July 1734 and 2.5 acres related to a tack between the same parties.
5. Parts of "Grass Braes" and "Grass Enclosures" on the north side of the burn, of old possessed by Peter (Patrick) Scott and Widow Horn, tenants at Easter Duddingston.

6. "Linky ground" (on the east side of the Public Road at Maitland Bridge) sometime owned jointly by Peter Scott and Widow Horn. (Total of Nos. 4, 5 and 6 = 19 acres 1 rood).
7. "Farthing Haugh" - where the "new" mill of Brunstane was built (one acre).

WHAT ABERCORN DID NOT SELL TO THE BENHAR COAL CO. IN 1875

1. Those portions in the care of the Trustees of the Post Road and Dalkeith Districts.
2. Duddingston Lodge and eight acres of land - had just been taken over, in 1874, by Charles Jenner, founder of the Princes Street shop of that name.
3. Forty-five acres taken up by the North British Railway - main line and Hawick branch and station ground at Portobello (parts of which were in the east and west Divisions).
4. Thirty-five acres on north side of railway (near station) and two acres on the south side.
5. The West Division (more or less the old Wester Duddingston lands).

WHAT WAS ASSIGNED TO THE BENHAR COAL CO. IN 1875

Assigned obligations in his favour contained in the leases of the Brick Works and Joppa Quarry.

THE KIRK AND VICARAGE (AND OTHER) LANDS OF DUDDINGSTON

Kirklands - consisting of 12.5 Acres (originally 14 Acres):

11 rigs in the field called the Langlands.
15 rigs (later nine) on the east side of Wester Duddingston between the road to Niddry and the road to Musselburgh.
6 rigs (later four) in the field called the Clays.
(originally) 1.5 acres called "Carnebukis" between the crofts of Wester Duddingston.

Orchyard - Pieces and pertinents of land upon the south side of the Town of Wester Duddingston between the Kirk land and Yard upon the north, the lands called Butts upon the east, the Loch upon the south, the Grass Yard with the Dovecot upon the west parts.

(From 1747, the Orchyard and Kirklands became known as the West Mains of Duddingston.)

c 1518	The Ker family owned whole church lands of the Vicarage Church and Parish of Duddingston. Kers - Janet Ker, who had life rent of two thirds of the Kirklands of Duddingston, married Richard Lawson of Humbie. After he died, she married Gilbert Wauchope (prior to 1515).
1586	Orchyard - John Fentoun, Clerk of the Rolls Granted by Andrew Murray of Balvaird.

1594	Orchyard - James Fentoun, Keeper of the Orchard of Holyrood Palace. His wife was Marion Hunter.
1599	Andrew Ker, and William, his son, of Lintoun conveyed Kirklands of the vicarage of Duddingston:
	John Ker and Elizabeth Weir } 15 rigs nr. Dudd.
	} 11 rigs in Langlands
1684	John Ker of West Nisbet } 6 rigs in Clays
1684	John Ker of Cavers } 1.5 acres in CarnBuks
1691	George Logan of Burncastle 4.5 bovate in Wester Duddingston (described in Chapter 5 as 3 x 1.5 acres)
1722	Sir Patrick Home of Renton
1732	A deed, dated 1751, regarding the Roup and Sale of Sir John Home of Manderson's lands mentions that the Kirklands and Orchyard were regarded as having been disponed by Home to Andrew Fletcher (Lord Milton) and that Fletcher had to pay the capital, and interest from 1732.
1767	8th Earl of Abercorn.

ANNEXATION OF LANDS TO THE CITY OF EDINBURGH

1896	Portobello
1900	Lands at Easter Duddingston
1901	Duddingston House and grounds and land at Willowbrae

APPENDIX IV
SOURCES AND REFERENCES

MAIN HISTORICAL ARCHIVES

1. Deputy Keeper of the Records of Northern Ireland:
   Public Record Office of Northern Ireland: Abercorn Papers, Plates 11, 21; Main References - Robert Johnstoun's Report of 1752 - D/623/D/10/1; Field/Crop details - 1801 (D/623/D/10/9); Report on Farms - 1822 (D/623/D/10/6).
2. Signet Library: Old Court of Session Papers and Plates 2, 45; Abercorn v Jamieson & Others - 1787 (170:11); Abercorn v Dick - 1768 (134:44, 346:20); Abercorn v Laing - 1806 (232:16); Mawer v Campbell - 1798 (392:20, 394:27-8); Dick v Trotter - 1797 (368:13); Abercorn v Hope - 1767–85 (150:25, 596:1); Wauchope v Macdowall & Others - 1770 (155:11).
3. L. H. J. Tollemache : Tollemache Papers.
4. The Keeper of the Records of Scotland:
   Scottish Record Office : Plates 7,15, 52, Road Trustees' Minutes (CO2.5/1); Kirk Records (CH2/125/2), Plan data (various): Sasine Registers - various RS.27 series.
5. The Trustees of the National Library of Scotland:
   National Library of Scotland : Fletcher of Saltoun Papers, Plan and Map Data, Baron Mure's Papers, Stevenson Collection (Plan, Copied in 1820, but containing data which dates it to around 1801 (in addition to other factors it matches exactly the field sizes, names and positions as in 1801 - D/623/D/10/9 above - and was possibly drawn originally by Knox). It is an Estate Plan of Duddingston and Brunstane and is referred to in this book as the "1801" map (MS 5848 - No. 35) Plate 22.
6. Central Library, Edinburgh Room: Plates 19, 46, 51, 54, 57, 61; Edinburgh Water Act, 1856, Extracts from *Courant* and *Evening News*.
7. British Library: Roy's and other map data.

ILLUSTRATIONS

1. Aberdeen University (George Washington Wilson Collection): Plate 18.
2. British Coal, *A Short History of the Scottish Coal-Mining Industry*: Plates 40, 41, 42, 43, 44.
3. Cambridge University: Plate 39.
4. Edinburgh University (Patrick Geddes Project): Plate 23.
5. Mrs C. Egan: Plate 34.
6. A. L. Foley: Plates 4, 8, 13, 16, 26, 49.
7. A. G. Gillespie: Plate 55.
8. W. Grant: Plates 32, 33, 60, front cover.
9. Hunting Aerofilms: 27, rear cover (left).
10. D. B. Morrison: Plate 35.
11. Scottish Development Department: Plates 1, 25, 38.
12. A. Smith: rear cover (bottom right).
13. Mrs H. Stevenson: Plates 53, 64.
14. W. A. B. Stocks: Plate 63.

(Other illustrations from miscellaneous sources, including my own.)

BIBLIOGRAPHY

1. *Accounts of Lords of Council in Public Affairs 1501–54.*
2. The Revd J. Anderson, *Calendar of the Laing Charters*, 1899.
3. William Baird, *Annals of Duddingston and Portobello*, 1900.
4. J. F. Birrell, *An Edinburgh Alphabet*, 1980.
5. G. P. Black, *Arthur's Seat*, 1966.
6. W. G. Cruikshank, *Duddingston Kirk and Village*, *c* 1975.
7. T. C. Day, *Arthur's Seat – A Ruined Volcano*, 1933.
8. W. S. Douglas, *Cromwell's Scotch Campaigns*, *c* 1900.
9. Edinburgh Geological Society, Quotations from *Building Stones of Edinburgh*, 1987.
10. H. & M. Evans, *Kay's Portraits*, 1973.
11. *First Statistical Account* (1794).
12. A. L. Foley, *Portobello in Old Picture Postcards*, 1985.
13. Enid Gauldie, *The Scottish Country Miller – 1700–1900*, 1981.
14. J. Geddie, *The Fringes of Edinburgh*, *c* 1900.
15. James Grant *Old and New Edinburgh*, 1882.
16. G. Henderson, *Lady Nairne and Her Songs*, 1901.
17. I. G. Lindsay and Mary Cosh, *Inverary and the Dukes of Argyll*, 1973.
18. W. A. Maclean, *St Philip's, Joppa* – the Parish and the Church, *c* 1975
19. Hugh Miller, *Edinburgh and its Neighbourhood*; *(The Brick Clays of Portobello)*, 1883.
20. *Old Edinburgh Club* – Various Volumes.
21. *Records of Burgh of Edinburgh 1528–57.*
22. *Records of the Burgh of Edinburgh 1553–4.*
23. L. S. Reeks, *Scottish Coalmining Ancestors*, 1986.
24. D. Robertson, Miss M. Wood and M. Mears, *Edinburgh 1329–1929*, 1929.
25. G. Robertson, *State of Agriculture in Lothians*, *c* 1843.
26. Royal Scottish Geographical Society, *The Early Maps of Scotland*, *c* 1970
27. *Second Statistical Account* (1845).
28. J. Shaw, *Water Power in Scotland – 1550–1870*, 1984.
29. T. Speedy, *Craigmillar and its Environs*, 1892.
30. Messrs Wright, Adams and Scott, *A Guide to Holyrood Park and Arthur's Seat*, 1987.

MISCELLANEOUS

1. British Geological Survey: Map data.
2. A. D. Scott: Genealogical details of the Scott Family of Duddingston.
3. S. Harris, via Edinburgh District Council, re Street Names.
4. Mrs M. K. Tennent McLeod : Extract from Alexander Kedslie's Notebooks.

INDEX